Wellington's Soldiers

CRAYON DRAWING OF WELLINGTON
IN THE YEAR OF SALAMANCA, 1812

Wellington's Soldiers
The Exploits of the Officers & Men
in the Battles of the Peninsular War 1809-1814

Edward Fraser

Wellington's Soldiers
The Exploits of the Officers & Men
in the Battles of the Peninsular War 1809-1814
by Edward Fraser

First published under the titles
The Soldiers Whom Wellington Led

Leonaur is an imprint of Oakpast Ltd

Copyright in this form © 2012 Oakpast Ltd

ISBN: 978-0-85706-830-9 (hardcover)
ISBN: 978-0-85706-831-6 (softcover)

http://www.leonaur.com

Publisher's Notes

The views expressed in this book are not necessarily those of the publisher.

Contents

Preface	7
The Starting-Point of Victory: How Wellington Avenged Sir John Moore	9
At Talavera: "Old Charley, the Last of the Powderers."	26
In the Ranks of the Enemy:—What Facing Wellington's Men Felt Like	44
The Charge of the Light Dragoons at Talavera	47
Fifty Miles in Twenty-Two Hours: the Mid-Summer March of the Light Brigade	57
The Astonishing Adventures of Wellington's Chief Scout	68
Some Daring Exploits of Wellington's Other Famous Scouts	81
Wellington the War Lord in the Field	90
With the Men Who Took the Eagle at Barrosa	106
On the Day of the "Die Hards": Heroic Albuhera	123
"Daddy Hill" on the War-Path: the Daybreak Surprise at Arroyo	151
One of the Very Bravest: Ensign Dyas of the Forlorn-Hope	171
On Badajoz Night: How Picton's Men Stormed the Castle	180

Wellington's Master-Stroke: the Thunderbolt of Salamanca	192
Where Sabre Conquered Bayonet: the Breaking of the Square	221
Among Officers and Men in Camp and Quarters	226
Foemen Worthy of Each Other's Steel! How the Brave on Both Sides Met as Friends Between Their Battles	240
Triumphant Vittoria and the Royal Spoil	267
Where Wellington's Trophies Are Now	287

Preface

"Dost thou remember, soldier old and hoary,
The days we fought and conquered side by side
On fields of battle, famous now in story,
Where Britain triumphed and where Britons died?
Dost thou remember all our old campaigning,
O'er many afield of Portugal and Spain?"
Of our old comrades few are now remaining:
How many sleep beneath the grassy plain!

"Rememberest thou the bloody Albuhera,
The deadly breach in Badajoz's walls,
Vittoria, Salamanca, Talavera,—
Till Roncesvalles echoed to our balls?
Ha! how we drove the Frenchmen all before us,
As foam is driven on the stormy breeze!
We fought right on with conquering banners o'er us
From Torres Vedras to the Pyrenees!"

So run the words of a splendid song of our soldiers of the fighting days of old, which may well serve here for, as it were, our text.

This book, I venture to think, should be particularly timely at the present moment, when we are in the midst of the bi-centenaries of Wellington's victories of the Peninsular War. The events and episodes of England's Great War with Napoleon here set forth are also—I think I am justified in claiming for the greater number of them—in their details not so well known to most of us; although, at the same time, they are in themselves stories of outstanding merit and exceptional brilliancy, and present telling examples of what the British Army at its best, in the prime of its fighting efficiency, achieved under the leadership of ever-victorious Wellington. I would add that for general materials and incidental details I have gone rather deeply below the surface, exploring among contemporary letters, newspapers, and despatches, and the diaries, journals, memoirs, and personal accounts of adventure, of officers and men who were on the spot, on the battlefield in the thick of the fighting; so as to insure, together with description as vivid as may be, narrative faithful to fact.

E. F.

God of battles, God of England,
Be as Thou hast been before;
Guard us as we form and muster,
Lead us as we march to war;
Thus believing, thus achieving,
This our watchword still shall be,
'England's sons are faithful soldiers,
True to England, true to Thee!'
                 From a camp-song of Wellington's Men.

Leonaur Note

The author of this book makes reference to the United Services Institute Museum. This was closed in the 1900s so items he records as being on display there are, of course, now in other collections. His references to 'modern day' regiments are, of course, those that existed on the eve of the First World War. The location of 'battle trophies' cannot now be taken as necessarily accurate for the same reason.

1

The Starting-Point of Victory: How Wellington Avenged Sir John Moore

It was between four and five in the morning, a little after sunrise, on Friday, May 12, 1809. Wellington and his staff-officers were in the act of mounting their horses after their early coffee at a convent near the little Portuguese village of Grijon, a few miles to the south of Oporto on the Douro, when Colonel John Waters, a British officer of the Intelligence Department, doing duty on special service with the Portuguese army, came hurrying up from the front to give Sir Arthur Wellesley—as Wellington then was—news of the utmost importance. He brought with him a swarthy, olive-complexioned, black-haired little man—a barber from Oporto, as the colonel explained, who had been among the enemy.

According to the man, said Colonel Waters, the French had blown up and destroyed the great pontoon bridge over the Douro, to prevent the British crossing to Oporto; and, further, had carried all the river boats across to their side—the opposite bank. The barber had seen hundreds of men at work, between ten at night and two in the morning, unshackling the pontoons, scuttling some, pulling the bridge to pieces, and blowing up the bridge-head. After that the plucky fellow had slipped away quietly, although there were French patrols in every street all over Oporto, and the people of the place had orders to keep indoors, on penalty of being shot at sight or bayoneted if met outside. He made his way to a small wharf, where, in a dark corner, a small rowing-boat that he knew of had been tied up.

Getting quietly into this, he had let himself drift on the flood-stream up the river, keeping close in the shadow of the low cliff-banks of the Douro on that side for nearly two miles. Then, sculling across, he had run the boat ashore on a mud-bank where the rushes grew thickly. Hiding it near the spot, he, after that, struck across country toward the high road for Lisbon, along which the British army was reported to be approaching. So the barber told Colonel Waters, to whom a British cavalry patrol, who had come across him near the road, brought the man.

Wellington—as we may for convenience call him throughout, although he was still Sir Arthur Wellesley—had landed at Lisbon less than three weeks before, and, after learning the positions of the nearest French armies—one, under Marshal Victor, to the eastward, up the Tagus covering Madrid, and a second, under Marshal Soult, to the northward, on the Douro at Oporto—had decided, first of all, to strike a blow at Soult. Success in that quarter would, besides leading to other advantages, open the Douro estuary to British transports with troops and stores, saving valuable time in the sea-passage from England.

Wellington had set off on the previous Sunday, May 9, with a force 18,000 strong—horse, foot, and artillery; detaching at the same time 6,000 Portuguese troops, under another British officer, Major-General Beresford (who had the local rank of a Portuguese field-marshal as commander-in-chief and reorganizer of the Portuguese army), to his right flank, to cross the Douro higher up. Beresford was to cut the French line of communication between Soult and Victor, so that Soult, if defeated at Oporto, would have to fall back by the difficult and dangerous mountain-road to the north. Upwards of 22,000 men were in Soult's command at that moment, but they were widely scattered: some, to the south of the Douro, watching the Lisbon road; others, away on the French left flank, holding the bridge over the Douro near the town of Amarante, at which Beresford was to strike. Confronting Wellington as he advanced directly on Oporto, the Marshal, after calling in the troops on the south side of the river, had in all from 10,000 to 12,000 men available to bar the passage of the river.

The troops who faced Wellington at Oporto were at the same time mostly veterans of many campaigns, men of the same regiments which had defeated the Austrians at Austerlitz, the Prussians at Jena, and the Russians at Friedland; the soldiers of the celebrated Fourth Corps of the Grand Army. Their leader, moreover, was the most *rusé* and cautious of Napoleon's Marshals; the man whom Napoleon himself, on the battlefield of Austerlitz, had publicly hailed, before the Imperial staff, as "the finest tactician in Europe." The Fourth Corps had come direct to Spain, by forced marches from the Vistula across Central Europe, and had formed the main army before which Sir John Moore had had to make his disastrous retreat. After following Moore's army to Corunna, Soult had turned south, and, taking Oporto by assault, was about to make a victorious march on Lisbon when Wellington landed in the Tagus.

Coimbra, a city to the north of Lisbon, some eighty miles from Oporto, was Wellington's starting-point. He covered sixty miles in three days, driving in the French advance-guard troops on the south side of the Douro after a sharp fight. These, after a rough handling, recrossed the Douro on the night of the 11th and rejoined Soult, blowing up and breaking down behind them, as has been said, the permanent bridge of boats over the river, and bringing over to the north bank all the smaller craft in the neighbourhood. Marshal Soult declared himself absolutely secure in his position, while, on the other hand, Wellington was confronted by one of the most difficult of military operations—the task of attempting the passage of a wide and deep river in the face of a powerful antagonist.

Wellington listened to Colonel Waters' story in silence. It was bad news for him about the removal of the shore-boats, and several of the staff-officers looked at one another with doubtful faces. The barber's story explained the meaning of a tremendous explosion that had startled the British camp miles away at two o'clock—the blowing up of the bridge-head works. The British commander, however, refused to believe that every single boat had been found and taken away. There was on the south side of the Douro, facing Oporto, a large suburb called Villa Nova, and some of the boats ordinarily there, Wellington was of opinion, might well have been overlooked. At any rate, a search must be made at once. He ordered Colonel Waters to go to the riverbank and make inquiries without loss of time. The colonel must manage somehow to procure boats. The Douro had to be crossed in any circumstances Wellington was determined; unless the army got over, and that speedily, Beresford's troops in their isolated position would be exposed to destruction.

Colonel Waters galloped away with the barber while Wellington and his staff continued to accompany the troops on the main Oporto road, along which the British advance guard was moving towards the Douro. Not a single boat though, large or small, was to be heard of at or near Villa Nova. Colonel Waters, on that, questioned the barber as to where he had left the little skiff in which he had come over. The

A French Battalion of 1809: on Parade Before a Fight

man did not know exactly. It was "over there" was all he could say, pointing blankly to the right, up the river. He had left it in the dark, some way upstream, he said; thrust in on the mud among some rushes where he landed. Colonel Waters thereupon took the man to look for the place, and they at length, towards eight o'clock, between two and three miles above Villa Nova, came upon the trampled track through the reed-bed, made by the barber in landing.

The boat was found, as it had been left, stuck fast in the mud and stranded by the falling tide. Some peasants from a village near joined the two in their search, but these men refused to assist in getting the boat off, or in going across in her to get hold of three large boats—wine-barges, capable of carrying some thirty men each—which Colonel Waters had made out, hauled up and stranded on the opposite side of the river. They had been carried over by the French on the afternoon before, said the peasants. All this time not a single French sentry or patrol was in sight on the farther bank—a group of dragoons had been seen riding by an hour before, but none since then;—the peasants continued though to stand timidly by, stolidly refusing to stir a finger in any attempt to cross.

Colonel Waters, who spoke Portuguese fluently, tried to talk the peasants over, but in vain. He offered them money, but they shook their heads and still refused to help.

Then it came out from one of them that the Prior of Amarante was in one of the houses of a village nearby. He was quickly fetched. The priest proved to be a brave and patriotic man, and he at once offered to do what he could. By his impassioned exhortations a couple of the peasants were persuaded to lend a hand, and with them and the prior himself, Colonel Waters and the barber crossed over in the barber's skiff. Their weight nearly swamped the little craft in the strong current, but they managed to get safely across; also, apparently unseen by the enemy. Then, quickly taking possession of the three large boats, they roped them together and brought them in tow over to the south bank, dropping down the stream—the tide was on the ebb by then—to a point as near as possible to Villa Nova. A projecting tongue of high ground, or bluff, which jutted out on the south bank, on the east side of Villa Nova, round which the river wound in a sort of elbow, served, as it fortunately happened, to screen the passage across from direct view of anyone in the city. And still not a single French scout was visible.

Wellington, meanwhile, had himself reached the river-bank.

Threading his way through the troops who had already arrived and were crowded in the streets of Villa Nova, standing in columns close-massed under cover of olive groves and gardens and behind the great storehouses of the Oporto Wine Company—the shippers of port wine to England—he and the staff took their way to the top of the bluff, sheltered by which Colonel Waters and his four boats in tow was returning. The tree-covered gardens of the great Convente da Serra, which covered the *plateau* on top of the bluff, formed an excellent lookout post across the river; its trees and bushy shrubberies concealing the red coats of the British officers from any eyes there might have been, looking in that direction from Oporto.

The whole city was in front of them, spread out in an amphitheatre as it were, rising on the opposite bank steeply from the river brink; the closely massed houses of the Lower Town sloping forward in the nearer distance, and beyond them, in tier on tier, the lofty mansions of the Upper Town, with, standing up everywhere, steeples, and towers, and high convent buildings.

This is the scene, as it came before Wellington's eyes at that moment, as described by one of the staff-officers who was close by the chief's side.

> From this elevated spot the whole city was visible, like a panorama, and nothing that passed within it could be hidden from the view of the British general. The French guards and sentries were seen in various parts of the town, but no bustle was evinced, or even apparent curiosity. No groups were noticed looking at us, which was afterwards accounted for by learning that the French were ordered to remain in their quarters ready to turn out, and the Portuguese not allowed to appear beyond the walls of their houses. There were a few sentries on the quays, but none without the limits, or above the town. A line of baggage wagons retiring beyond the town across the distant hills was the sole indication of our threatening neighbourhood.

Others on our side though, besides Colonel Waters, had been looking for a means of crossing at another place. After hearing that the pontoon bridge over the Douro had been destroyed, Wellington had sent off Brigadier John Murray with a battalion of the King's German Legion—soldiers formerly in King George's army in Hanover, who, on the occupation of that kingdom by Napoleon, had escaped across the North Sea to England and been enrolled as an auxiliary corps of the British Army—a squadron of the 14th Light Dragoons and a couple of field-guns, in the direction of the ford of Barca de Avintas, some four miles up the Douro, with instructions to try and find boats there and cross the river so as to outflank Soult's main body in Oporto.

Word was brought to Wellington of Colonel Waters' discovery immediately the boats arrived. Wellington by then had had time to take in the chief features of the enemy's position on the opposite bank. With him were two or three Portuguese notables who had left Oporto secretly a few days before and were able to describe to him the dispositions of the French troops. Examining the ground carefully with his field-glass—a telescope of exceptional power, which he had brought with him specially from England, paying a high price to get the very best glass made—as he gazed across the water, just the place that he wanted for a landing caught his eye.

Almost opposite where Wellington stood, across the river, at a point upstream, about half a mile above the city, another steep bluff rose abruptly, nearly sheer from the water's edge, up which a wide zigzag path led to a large unfinished stone building that stood close to the edge. It was a big house, in process of building for the Bishop of Oporto and to be used as a priests' college. It was known as the *Seminario*, and was surrounded by a wide enclosure, round which on three sides ran a lofty brick wall. The fourth side was open to the river. In the centre of the front wall stood a large iron gate, opening on the high road from Oporto up the Douro towards Vallonga. The Seminary stood isolated, commanding the *prado*, or plain, all round, with between it and the city only a few peasants' cottages among small gardens. As Wellington's eye fell on the building he instinctively realized how to get his army across and surprise the enemy. Colonel Waters had taken a good look at it as he passed near on his way back with the barges, and was able to report that it was unoccupied by the enemy.

> At ten o'clock, the French being tranquil and unsuspicious, the British wondering and expectant, Sir Arthur was told that one boat was ready. 'Well, let the men cross,' was the reply, and a quarter of an hour afterwards an officer and twenty-five British soldiers were silently placed on the other side of the Douro in the midst of the French army. The Seminary was thus gained, all remained quiet, and a second boat passed.
>
> As the third was in midstream the French first discovered what was happening.

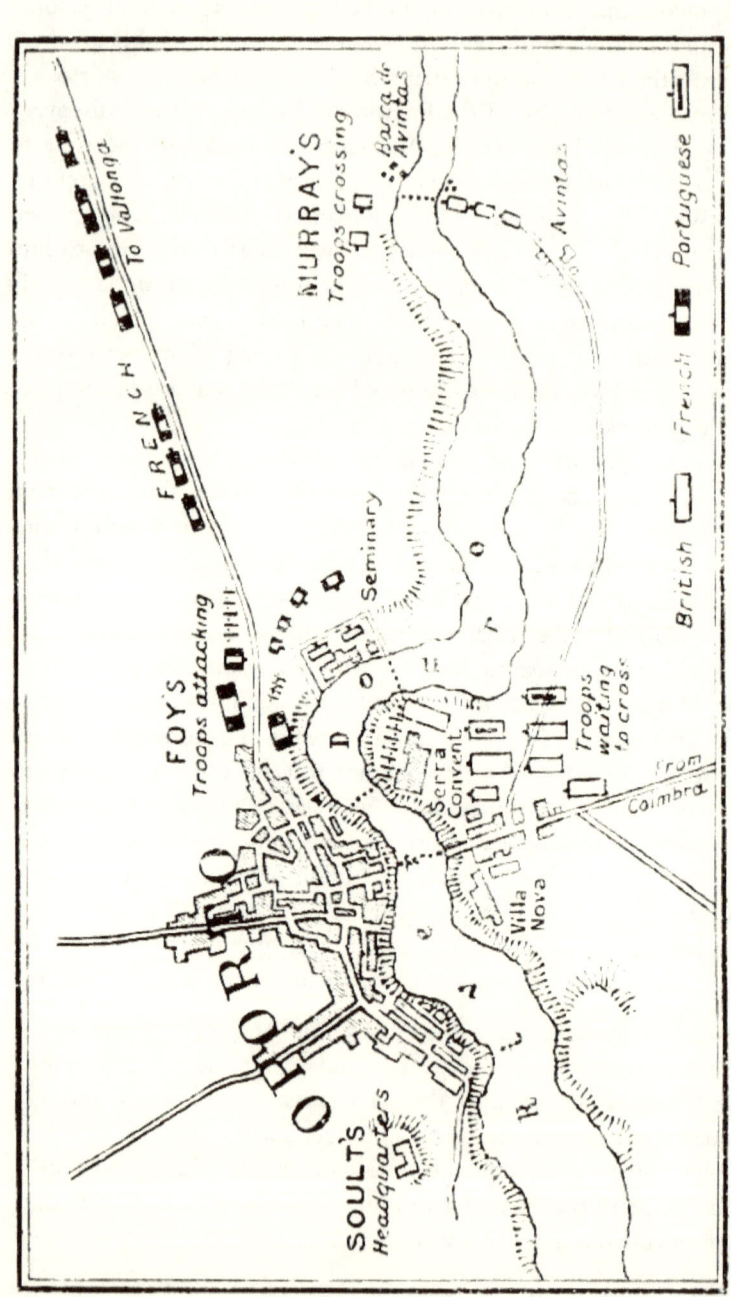

The Passage of the Douro, May 12, 1809

Tumultuous noises rolled through Oporto, the drums beat to arms, shouts arose, the citizens, vehemently gesticulating, made signals from their houses, and confused masses of troops rushing out from the higher streets threw forward swarms of skirmishers, and came furiously down on the Seminary.
(So Napier describes the raising of the alarm.)

An officer and twenty-five men of the Buffs went in the first boat, the light companies of the First Brigade crossed in the second and third boats; men of three regiments—the Buffs, the 48th, and the 66th. The first comers secured the iron gate, and the rest quickly extemporized a *banquette*, or platform, round the walls inside, so that they could fire from behind cover over the wall.

There were no French outposts at all apparently on that side of Oporto, and the first passage over the river, some three hundred yards in width just there, was concealed from view, as has been said, by the bend of the river and steep Serra bluff where Wellington stood.

The daring venture in effect had proved the most complete of surprises.

"Soult," describes our staff-officer near Wellington, in his account of the passage over, "had his quarters on the side of the city near the sea, and having collected all the boats, as he supposed, on the right bank, considered himself in perfect security. He thought if we made any attempt to cross, it would be in conjunction with our ships lying off the bar, and all his attention was devoted to that quarter. He even turned into ridicule the first report of our having crossed, and discredited the fact to the last, until it was incontestably proved by our firing."

The idea of a frontal attack in broad daylight across the river had, in fact, appeared to Soult absolutely impossible.

As a fact, the French marshal was asleep in his quarters, in a suburban villa to the west of Oporto; in bed at the moment of the crossing. He was not well at that time and had been up all night, busy with his dispatches, after a ride round to see the boats brought over and the bridge destroyed. Soult had not been in bed two hours, and his staff-officers were at breakfast in an adjoining room, when the first news arrived. It was brought by Captain Brossard, an *aide-de-camp* of General Foy, one of Soult's brigadiers. The *aide-de-camp* came galloping up, flung himself from his horse, and "raced up the stairs to the breakfast-room four steps at a time," breathlessly declaring that some boat-loads of redcoats had been seen crossing above the city. He was only laughed at by the staff-officers for his flurry and told that he had better sit down and have some coffee.

Immediately afterwards, however, while the officers were still laughing, a sudden burst of musketry was heard, followed by cannon shots. On that all jumped up from table hastily, while Brossard ran into Soult's bedroom to the marshal.

Soult would not believe the attempt was serious, but he got up quickly, and, sending a message by the *aide-de-camp* to "push the English back into the river," ordered his horse to be brought round.

"Foy," one of Napoleon's smartest officers, at that time a colonel and inspector of artillery, and acting as brigadier in Soult's army, "has the credit of being the first to discover our having passed, and instantly ordered the drums of the nearest battalion to beat the *générale*. We heard the drums beat when the whole of the Buffs had crossed, and soon saw symptoms of bustle and confusion in the town, and the French regiments forming on their parades. This was an anxious moment, and just as the whole of the Buffs had landed, a battalion was observed moving down a road towards them. It was their 17th (Light Infantry), brought down by Foy, which was quickly supported by the 70th, and then by other regiments of Mermet's brigade. The first made an attack on the Buffs, who stood their ground, giving a tremendous fire, while our artillery from the opposite side killed and wounded a great number of the enemy." So our staff-officer friend standing close beside Wellington tells the story.

In the third boat went the officer in charge of the right wing of Wellington's army, Lieut.-General Paget, so as to be on the spot at the critical moment. General Paget clambered up at once to the roof of the Bishop's house, where he stood, prominently in the open, directing the defence of the post amid a hail-storm of French bullets, which whizzed all round him, until the gallant general suddenly fell struck down with a serious wound. Fortunately the brigadier commanding Wellington's First Brigade, General Rowland Hill, had crossed at the same time with Paget, and was at hand to take up the command in his stead.

"Hill took his place," describes Napier, "and the musketry, sharp and voluble from the first, augmented as the forces accumulated on each side: yet the French attack was eager and constant, their fire increased more rapidly than that of the English, and their guns were soon opened against the building. The English battery on the Convent rock swept the enclosure on each side and confined the attack to the front; but Murray did not come down the right bank, and the struggle was such that Sir Arthur was only restrained from crossing by the remonstrances of those about him, and the confidence he had in Hill."

Then happened this, told as our staff-officer eye-witness on the Serra rock saw it.

More boats, in the meantime, were brought across, and more troops, the 48th and 66th and a Portuguese battalion landed, and not only defended themselves successfully, but even drove the enemy from the walls, between the town and the Bishop's palace. This success was seen by Sir Arthur and his staff, who cheered our soldiery as they chased the enemy from the various posts. The enemy's troops now came through the town in great numbers, and obliged our troops to confine themselves to the enclosure. The French continued running along the road towards and beyond the iron gate, while our shells and shot were whizzing through the trees and between the houses into the road as they passed. They brought up a gun through the gate to batter the house; but this proved an uncomfortable experiment, as our troops, increasing in number by fresh embarkations, charged and captured it.

To stop the boats a battery of artillery had galloped down to the river-bank at the outset—but only to be overwhelmed by a terrific outburst by the British guns on the Serra rock. At the first round, a shrapnel shell from a 5½-inch howitzer burst just over the leading French gun-team in the act of unlimbering. It dismounted the gun and killed or put *hors de combat* every man and horse of the team.

Another battery of French field-artillery next opened fire from the outskirts of the city, in an attempt to bombard the little garrison out of their stronghold, but their practice was poor: "they were tamely, if not badly, served."

Every effort that the French repeatedly made to attack the Seminary on the flanks was held in check by the Serra battery, and then, a very short while afterwards, all of a sudden, something else happened. The French skirmishers as they fought in front of the Seminary became aware of the approach of Brigadier Murray's detached troops. These had found two damaged ferryboats near Avintas, and patching them hastily, had got across, as planned by Wellington, and were coming on towards Oporto.

We soon descried them making as much show as possible, marching, with their ranks open, towards the Vallonga road; thus threatening the communications of the enemy.

Murray's approach now disclosed an unexpected danger to Marshal Soult.

The discovery decided the fate of the fight for the French. Up to then Soult had hoped to be able to keep the British at bay and hold the city. He now had to change his plans. Orders were given to withdraw the brigade which had been holding the city and retreat as rapidly as possible on the Vallonga road towards Amarante, to rally on the French division there.

Soult's withdrawal offered Wellington the chance for striking a decisive blow at the enemy. The French pickets and sentries on the French quays along the river front were called in; they disappeared to join the regiments of the rearguard mustering in the streets and squares. At once the whole city rose to assist the British over.

On their deserting the quays, the Portuguese jumped into their boats, which soon transported across, amidst the cheers of the people and the waving of pocket-handkerchiefs of women from the windows, the Guards and General Stewart's brigade, who proceeded through the town with the greatest speed.

A *furore* of popular enthusiasm indeed welcomed the Guards on landing. Cheers and shouts of "*Vivan os Ingles!*" "*Viva Gran Britania!*" "*Viva O Gran Wellesley!*" resounded on every side, while casks of wine were brought into the streets, the heads knocked in, and the contents ladled out and handed round among the men as they hastened by.

As the French were falling back and getting clear of the outskirts this smart little affair took place. The Buffs, who had now been joined in the Seminary by the whole of the 48th and 66th, taking advantage of the panic that had so unexpectedly seized the enemy, made a sortie from the Seminary towards Oporto. They "dashed into the city and cut off a battery of artillery in retreat, which, becoming jammed between that regiment and the 29th (now the 1st Worcestershires - as at time of first publication) which had crossed over with the Guards, received the fire of both and was captured." Napier tells in his vivid way the story of what happened. General Hill, with whom the Buffs fought, "was pouring a heavy fire into the disordered masses as they passed his front, when suddenly five guns galloped out of the city on his left, but appalled at the terrible stream of musketry, pulled up; while thus hesitating a volley from behind stretched most of the artillerymen in the dust and the rest, dispersing, left the guns on the road."

The sudden fire came from the 29th, who had been among the foremost of the troops ferried across into the city and had landed on the outskirts on the side towards the Seminary. They crossed in the same barges that had brought the Buffs over.

"Led on by Sir John Sherbrooke," says one of their officers, "we overtook the retreating enemy ere they quitted the town and opened a fire on their rear, in consequence of which several pieces of cannon and ammunition wagons were captured."

"We afterwards," adds the officer, "drove them from a rocky height, and continued pressing them very closely, they running away as hard as they could, cutting off their knapsacks and throwing away their arms and ammunition. Many came out of houses and surrendered themselves prisoners. We were rapidly gaining on the enemy and those we overtook begged for quarter."

At one point they had cornered some of the enemy and were about to charge home on them with the bayonet, when, to their great disappointment, a staff-officer rode up and headed off the regiment. Placing his horse across the road he called out to the colonel: "I order you to halt, to let the cavalry pass to the front!" The staff-officer, of course, had to be obeyed. Then, after the cavalry had cleared past them, just as the 29th were continuing their advance, Wellington himself stopped them. He ordered them to line a wall by the edge of a wood near the road and not to move from there till he sent word. That held the 29th fast until the battle was over, until seven in the evening, and then they were marched back into Oporto.

They had as well the experience of all but firing into a friendly regiment: the 16th Portuguese. It was while they were lining the wall. Sir John Sherbrooke himself was near the 29th at the moment, and he mistook the uniform of the approaching Portuguese for French. He fronted the grenadier company towards the newcomers and gave the word to make ready. Fortunately, the presence of mind of the surgeon of the 29th, Dr. Guthrie, who happened to be riding with the Portuguese, just saved the situation.

"We were too far off to be heard in time," says Surgeon Guthrie telling the story, "yet close enough to be shot, and it was plain they took us for French. I bethought me I had a red round jacket on under my blue undress coat, and, as little time was to be lost, I stood up in my stirrups and opened the blue coat as wide as possible so as none of the red should be lost. The grenadiers at this moment came to the 'Present!' I thought we were gone; when in an instant I saw them irregularly changing to the 'Recover.' They knew me and called out 'the doctor and Portuguese!' I was never so delighted in my life and galloped up to them forthwith. Sir John Sherbrooke saluted me with 'By God, sir, if you hadn't shown that red jacket I would have sent you all in a second more to the devil!' . . . From that day the Portuguese never went into any action that I saw without a white band round the left arm."

The 66th and 48th, at the same time that the Buffs made their sortie, charged a French battery of seven guns while in the act of unlimbering in front of the Seminary, and carried it at the point of the bayonet. The light company of the 66th, indeed, on its own account made prize of three of the guns, spoken of as "fine brass field-pieces." In the charge the gallant leader of the battalion, Major Murray, fell badly wounded. Wellington went to see him after the battle was over, and taking him by the hand said, we are told, with impressive earnestness: "Murray, your men behaved like lions; I shall never forget you!"

The Guards were nearly through the city by this time, pressing hard on the heels of the enemy as they cleared the outskirts of Oporto, the French fugitives streaming in great disorder past in front of the Seminary wall, "while Hill sent his damaging fire into their flank, and the guns from the rocks deeply searched their masses." The news of Brigadier Murray's approach on their flank had spread fast from regiment to regiment of the French, and the retreat speedily became a stampede. It was more than unfortunate that Murray merely demonstrated tamely, hanging back and not venturing to attack. His appearance, however, had sufficed to put the enemy to the run.

The day's fighting closed with a smart cavalry dash.

The squadron of the 14th Light Dragoons with Murray's force was carried off by Wellington's adjutant-general, Sir Charles Stewart, who led it forward and caught up part of the French rearguard column at a narrow part of the road, coming on them round a bend. Met as they came on with lowered bayonets, the gallant Light Dragoons rode into the enemy with fine audacity, their dashing attack scaring the rearguard troops. Trampling their way through the thick of the French bayonets, they sabred right and left and broke the rearguard up.

A French general, Delaborde, was unhorsed in the *mêlée*, and just escaped with his life. Colonel Foy was wounded by a sword-cut across the shoulder, and was all but made prisoner. The dragoons, fiercely slashing their way through the enemy, took upwards of three hundred prisoners, three prisoners to each British trooper engaged. Amongst their wounded were three of the four officers engaged, the gallant officer in command, who led the leading troop, Major Felton Harvey, coming back minus his sword-arm.

One of the officers of the 14th, Peter Hawker, in his diary, gives this vivid description of the fight:

> We formed up in threes, passed all our lines at a full gallop, whilst they greeted us with one continued huzza. After this, going almost at full speed, enveloped in a cloud of dust, for nearly two miles, we cleared our infantry, and that of the French appeared. A strong body was drawn up in close column with bayonets ready to receive us in front. On each flank of the road was a stone wall, bordered outwardly by trees, with other walls projecting in various directions, so as to give every advantage to the operations of the infantry, and to screen those by whom we were annoyed.
>
> On our left in particular numbers were posted in a line, with their pieces rested on the wall which flanked the road, ready to give us a running fire as we passed. This could not but be effectual, as our left men by threes were nearly close to the muzzles of the muskets, and barely out of the reach of a *coup de sabre*. In a few seconds the ground was covered with men and horses; notwithstanding these obstacles we penetrated the battalion opposed to us, the men of which, relying on their bayonets, did not give way until we were nearly close upon it, when they fled in great confusion. For some time this contest was kept up hand to hand, and for the time it lasted was severe.
>
> After many efforts we succeeded in cutting off three hundred, most of whom were seized as prisoners; but our loss was very considerable. Our squadron consisted of scarcely forty file, and the brunt of the action of course fell the heaviest on the troop in front: of the fifty-two men composing it, ten were killed, eleven severely wounded, besides others slightly, and six taken prisoners; of the four officers engaged, three were on the wounded list. For my own part, my horse being shot under me, the moment after a ball had grazed my upper leg, I had to scramble my way on foot amidst the killed and wounded—among whom the enemy from the side walls were continually firing—and

thus effected my escape from this agreeable situation.

On the approach of our infantry the French brigade was compelled to retire. Our few remaining men, coming threes about, brought with them the prisoners in triumph. Our commanding officer and squadron had the satisfaction of receiving thanks from the commander-in-chief. On the merits of the charge, the comment of the French general ought not to be omitted: he sent for some of our men (who had been his prisoners and afterwards escaped) and declared to them that in his opinion 'we must have all been drunk or mad, as the brigade we had attacked was nearly two thousand strong.'

The bold charge of the Light Dragoons practically finished off the day's work: Wellington's brilliant *coup de main* had been accomplished with astonishing success. The news of it, when it reached Napoleon in the midst of his Wagram campaign, gave the Emperor, we are told, a bad night. The much-sneered-at British "Sepoy General," at the outset of his career in Europe, had proved more than a match for the famous Marshal, whom Napoleon himself, as has been said, on the battle-field of Austerlitz had proudly acclaimed as "the finest tactician in Europe!"

At four o'clock that afternoon Wellington entered Soult's quarters of the morning, and sat down to enjoy the excellent dinner that the marshal's *chef* had cooked for his master.

His beaten antagonist learnt at that same moment that his line of retreat to the east had been barred through Wellington's strategy before the battle. The luckless Soult, in consequence, found himself forced, in desperation, to attempt escape by scrambling through the mountain passes to the north—with utterly disastrous results. "Unable to carry with him his guns and ammunition, he destroyed them at Peñafiel, abandoned his baggage, and, guided by a Spanish pedlar, led his shattered forces through the Sierra Catalina to Pombeira. His retreat was one of terrible suffering. A storm of wind and rain began on the 13th and lasted several days; numbers of his stragglers and wounded were murdered by the country people. Six months had not run since he entered Portugal with 25,000 men in pursuit of Sir John Moore; of these not more than 19,500 mustered at Pombeira; of his fifty-eight guns, he had lost or destroyed every one."

It was at Oporto, as a fact, that the fate of Sir John Moore, and the compulsory embarkation of Corunna, six months before, was avenged; and on the very men at whose hands Moore had met his doom. It had been Soult before whose army Sir John had had to retreat; Soult's corps which had so relentlessly pressed the pursuit of the outnumbered British to the last. Now the exultant pursuers had been put to headlong flight; the cannon which had fired down on the British soldiers as they left Corunna Bay were either British spoils of victory, or lying scattered amid the rocks of a Galician ravine as shattered scrap-iron.

"I have just returned," wrote Wellington, on May 22, to the Duke of Richmond, "from the most active and severe service. I have been on the pursuit, or rather chase, of Soult out of Portugal . . . I think the chase out of Portugal is a pendant for the retreat to Corunna."

Wellington took the first of his titles—when King George, after Talavera, a few weeks later, created him a peer—from his exploit at Oporto, as Baron Douro of Wellesley. He was the first British military officer to take a title from the scene of his victory.

The authorities of Oporto, it may be added, as one way of showing their appreciation for the recovery of the city, renamed the street leading from the bridge the Ruo do Wellesley, and also had a *fresco* painting placed on one of the *piazzas* facing the bridge, of Wellington, mounted on a long-tailed flowing-maned charger in mediaeval style, with his knees nearly level with his mouth, brandishing a huge sword and in the act of dealing death among a crowd of unhappy-looking French soldiers!

2

At Talavera: "Old Charley, the Last of the Powderers."

A widely celebrated character in the British Army of that day died a soldier's death on the battlefield at Talavera—Colonel Donellan of the 48th, known far and wide throughout the Service by his regimental *sobriquet* of "Old Charley." He had another name also, "The Last of the Powderers." "He persevered to the last," relates one of his brother-officers, "in maintaining the good old cauliflower head, and would as soon have appeared on parade without sash and sword as have omitted to undergo the operation of having his hair dressed with powder and *pomatum*. From early youth he had accustomed himself to the process, and it formed, in his estimation, a vitally essential part of a soldier's costume.

"Old Charley," continues the narrator, "was most remarkable for his close adherence to the custom, and he was often heard to mourn over the economy which had reduced the number of iron pins employed, and the animal matter used, from two pounds per head *per diem* to three ounces. The 'powdering rooms' with which barracks were formerly provided, for the express purpose of twisting the tails of the battalions into dense knobs, and beautifying the soldiers' heads with a conglomeration of rancid suet, whiteing, and meal, were by him held sacred; and he would never permit those sanctuaries to be denied by their being applied to less honourable purposes. Jackboots and white buckskin breeches were also objects of his adoration, and when grey overalls and short 'Wellingtons' were ordered to be substituted he complied only as far as regarded those under his orders. To the last, in his own person, he adhered to his favourite costume."

Colonel Donellan, all the same, proved himself in many ways an ideal commanding officer.

Among his whims was that of governing his soldiers without flogging; and in this task (which is no very easy one) he succeeded so well that when his regiment, the Second Battalion of the 48th, was reviewed by Sir David Baird on the Curragh of Kildare, that general officer complimented him by saying that it was 'as fine and as well disciplined a corps as he would ever wish to command.'

The First Battalion, however, was Colonel Donellan's favourite, and that with which he had most to do. He was at the head of it in his last battle.

"Old Charley" was not with his old battalion when Wellington landed in Spain. For some time past he had been away from it, in command of the Second Battalion. He was, however, transferred back and arrived at headquarters on the eve of Talavera. He reached the army a day or two before the fighting began, on the morning that Wellington reviewed his whole force in order to show them to his ally, the Spanish General Cuesta. Before taking over his command Colonel Donellan was invited to accompany the staff on their ride along the array of drawn-up troops. His own men had not yet seen him on his return—and it was not yet known among them that "Old Charley" had actually joined the army. This is what happened when the discovery was suddenly made by them, during the ride:

> As the generals rode along the line, which was of immense extent, each soldier stood fixed in his place; each battalion silent and motionless; scarcely the eyelids of the soldiers twinkled as the cavalcade of the chiefs and their staffs rode by. All of a sudden a bustle and murmur took place in one regiment. Its line lost its even appearance, and caps, and heads, and hands, and tongues moved, to the utter dismay of the officer who was in command of it. In vain did he endeavour to check this unseemly conduct in his men, and Lord Wellington was himself astonished and exasperated at the circumstance.
>
> The fact is, the irregular regiment was the First Battalion of the 48th. Colonel Donellan happened to be riding along with the staff, in his stiff buckskins, powdered hair, and square-set cocked hat, and as soon as his men, from whom he had been separated, perceived their beloved commanding officer, every one murmured to his comrade, 'There goes old Charley!'—'God bless

the old boy!'—'Success to him!'—'Does not he look well?' and so on, bustling and smiling, evidently from an impulse they could not resist.

The cause of the commotion explained to Wellington, he laughed and expressed himself satisfied. "Old Charley" at the same time turned to his men and to their great delight uncovered and waved a cordial salute to them with his cocked hat in return for their compliment, "while showers of white powder from his hair filled the air all round and covered his shoulders and coat."

No regiment in Wellington's army rendered better service at Talavera than the First Battalion of the 48th. "The battle," said Wellington himself, "was certainly saved by the advance, position, and steady conduct of the 48th Regiment."

They got three opportunities, indeed, of crossing bayonets with the enemy and showing the French what the Northamptonshire lads were made of; the first encounter taking place in the late evening of the first of the two days over which Talavera lasted—on the evening of July 27, 1809. At that time the 48th were posted on the left of the British position; with the 29th Worcestershires and a composite battalion, made up of various companies of regiments elsewhere at the time, called the Battalion of Detachments; in General Richard Stewart's brigade.

The fight that evening was the outcome of a daring attempt of the enemy at a surprise.

A little after dark a French division—General Ruffin's, numbering 6,000 men, as some prisoners told later—under cover of the night "rushed and carried a spur jutting out to the front from the hill where the 48th were, which formed an important tactical point on the British side of the battlefield. The spur was held by a brigade of Hanoverian infantry of the King's German Legion, who fell the first victims to the French onslaught. Their sentries, it would appear, gave no warning of Ruffin's approach until the first of the French were actually on them. The Germans were first roused by the enemy seizing them as prisoners, or firing into them at *brûle-pourpoint*." Those who escaped fell back fighting.

A captain on Wellington's staff describes the scene, as he saw it from a little way off:

The summit of the height on the left was suddenly covered with fire, and it was evident that the enemy had nearly made a lodgement in our line. The flashes of the retiring fire of the broken and surprised Germans marked the enemy's success and the imminent danger of our army.

Colonel Donellan and his men were at that moment in bivouac on the farther side of the hill, with the rest of the division to which their brigade belonged. They heard the firing and stood to arms, while their leader, the commander of the division, General Rowland Hill, together with a staff-officer, Brigade-Major Fordyce, went forward to see what the commotion was about; and as it befell also, to come within an ace of being shot or taken prisoner.

How that happened is one of the episodes in the story of Talavera.

It could only be an outpost affair, thought Hill, and while his troops were falling in he and the brigade-major started off. The two were cantering up to where the Hanoverian brigade was posted, when, to their surprise, dark figures appeared clustering along the crest above. Then musketry suddenly blazed out, the bullets whizzing past them in the direction of the soldiers behind. The general could not understand it. They could only be some of our own men firing by mistake in the wrong direction. "I thought," explained Hill in a letter, "it was only the old Buffs making some blunder as usual." Spurring up their horses he and Fordyce now galloped forward, shouting to the men above to stop firing. The next moment the two found themselves in the midst of a swarm of French skirmishers who had run forward over the crest towards them. Hill, indeed, first knew that something was wrong when one of the French *tirailleurs* sprang at his bridle and roughly bade him yield himself prisoner.

He shook the man off, just escaping with his life from a bullet that the *tirailleur* fired at him. The bullet flew close past his head. Wheeling his horse round, Hill, with Fordyce at his side, plunged back through the French down the slope and got clear. As the two got past a dozen muskets went off, aimed at them. One of the bullets wounded the general's horse; another shot the brigade-major dead. The Battalion of Detachments was already hastening up the slope. The 29th and 48th were coming on a short way behind them. General Hill, without dismounting from his wounded horse, on reaching the two regiments -turned and led them straight at the enemy, who, however, before Hill could get to the top again, were already in fight with the composite battalion.

As the 48th came up a number of the enemy ran forward, "some of them calling out that they were Germans, others that they were Spaniards." But the men of the 29th and 48th were not deceived. They went on and speedily closed on their adversaries with the bayonet. The Battalion of Detachments was already being forced back when the 29th and 48th reached the spot. They "disputed every inch of ground," according to an officer, "but, outnumbered by their assailants, were gradually giving way, when a loud cheer was heard, followed by a crashing volley, as Rowland Hill at the head of the 29th charged up the height and fell upon the enemy." One of the officers of the 29th, indeed, asserts that the Battalion of Detachments failed through faulty leadership, and fell back grumbling at being badly led. "The soldiers seemed much vexed; we could hear them bravely calling out, 'There is nobody to command us. Only tell us what to do and we're ready to do it!'"

But others were on the ground to restore the fight. The 29th and 48th, side by side, went at the enemy and attacked them man to man. After a fierce and sanguinary fight they forced the French to give back. Then, regaining the spur, they drove the enemy down into the ravine, across the valley, and on to the farther side whence they had come, leaving behind many dead and wounded and many prisoners in our hands. Among these last was the colonel of the French 9th, badly wounded.

The enemy beaten back, the victors retired to their former positions, the soldiers of the 29th and 48th keeping guard on the hilltop they had so gallantly regained. "The troops sat down with their firelocks at hand to wait for the dawn of day."

Never before—and never after—did Donellan's men experience such a night. Nor, indeed, did Wellington himself, or his army. One and all expected a fresh attack under cover of the darkness at any moment. Their Spanish allies on the field were worse than useless, while the French in front, barely a quarter of a mile off, outnumbered them by two to one. To give the alarm promptly pickets and sentries were pushed forward to the very verge of the ravine which ran along the front of the British position; "so close to the enemy that we could hear them challenging their visiting rounds." All along the front during the night shots kept incessantly going off. "Our younger soldiers, shaken by the French surprise attack, and nervous and unsteady, constantly fired off their muskets, and at least once the troops in line fired on our pickets, killing and wounding both officers and men."

On their side, the French, as an officer describes, sent forward patrols who "crept as near as possible here and there and fired volleys in the directions of our troops, disappearing immediately afterwards in the darkness." Then, towards midnight, a sudden panic seized the Spanish regiments on the right of Wellington's position, and they suddenly let off a tremendous discharge of musketry, although, as a fact, none of the enemy were on the move in that quarter. Wellington himself, who with his staff was lying on the ground wrapped in his cloak, showed signs of constant anxiety, we are told, "hardly sleeping and repeatedly inquiring what time it was."

Then this disquieting thing happened. Soon after midnight lights began to flicker on the French side, and long rows of torches could be made out moving on the hill immediately in front of where the 48th were. The rumbling of artillery-wheels and the cracking of whips indicated that fresh batteries were getting into position. Daylight, when it came, disclosed a long-drawn-out line of field-guns ready to open fire, with dark masses of infantry ranged in front and extending for over two miles along the lower hill-slopes on the enemy's side. In front of them, close to the brink of the ravine on the French side, hundreds of skirmishers were seen, lying down for the time, but ready at a word to spring up and dash across. In rear, as the light became stronger, could be made out other dense masses of infantry, more batteries, and long lines of horsemen.

"Old Charley" and his men had now not long to wait for their second fight. The blow was struck quickly, with dramatic abruptness.

Suddenly, a minute or two before five o'clock, a white puff of smoke spurted from one of the guns in front, near the centre of the French batteries. It was the signal for the attack. Before almost the boom of the shot had had time to reach the ears of the British on the hill, an answering blaze of flame flashed from end to end along the French line, and a furious cannonade opened from between fifty and sixty guns. The nearest infantry column surged forward instantly, and the swarming throng of skirmishers in advance leapt to their feet and sprang down into the ravine.

And then nothing more was seen. The light easterly wind blowing directly across from the French side to the British, brought the cannon smoke rolling heavily on to the hill in a dense cloud, "completely enveloping us in a dense fog, which shut out for a time all view of the enemy below. Before the smoke thinned off sufficiently to be seen through, the leading skirmishers and the headmost of the

French columns at their heels were hustling their way up the British hill-slope, the French drums rattling out the frenzied clash of the *pas-de-charge*, amid wild shoutings of '*En avant!*' '*À la baïonnette!*' and '*Vive l'Empereur!*'"

The glimpse of the French skirmishers as they ran forward into the ravine when the signal gun went off was the last thing seen from the British side before the smoke of the cannonade shrouded in all view.

To combat the French guns was impossible. Wellington's weak artillery, half a dozen batteries in all, could make no head against the tremendous tornado of shot and shell hurled across from the enemy's batteries.

The British infantry were hastily drawn back a few paces behind the hill-crest line, and ordered to lie flat on the ground. But only for a brief moment. The French came up the hill so rapidly that our men had to be ordered forward again at once. The enemy were already emerging from the smoke within sixty yards of the hill-top. Quickly now the 29th, with Donellan's 48th and the Battalion of Detachments, lined the crest at one point; the Buffs, the Second Battalion of the 48th, and the 66th—Hill's three regiments that had so finely held the Seminary at Oporto—lined it at another. They all went forward "with their arms ported, ready to rush on the ascending foe as soon as they could discern them through the dense smoke."

The French came on at speed, and "got quite close to the top." They were fired on and charged the instant they showed themselves by the 48th and the other regiments with them, the men darting forward at them in line, bayonets levelled. The dash and impetuosity of "Old Charley's" men in their counter-attack was not to be withstood. "By a desperate volley and charge we overthrew, as they topped the hill, the enemy, who fled with the utmost confusion and consternation, followed by our troops even across the ravine."

This, in detail, is what took place.

That first tremendous volley from the three battalions, drawn up in line, two deep, and overlapping the head of the French foremost column, shattered the enemy at a blow. It smote on them hard and fiercely, crashing into them with terrific effect. "It brought the enemy to a standstill; their whole front had gone down under the deadly fire. They lost the impetus of the advance; they then halted and stood still, keeping up a hot musketry fire." Immediately on that Brigadier Stewart gave the word to charge. As he did so a tremendous volley of British musketry thundered forth on the right as the other troops along the ridge there attacked in flank the next French column. The crashing outburst seemed suddenly to shake the enemy's nerves, and as the gleaming line of the bayonets of the 48th came at them, they flinched, and recoiled, and went back. "On we went," in the words again of a British officer, "a wall of stout hearts and bristling steel. The enemy did not fancy such close quarters, and the moment our rush began went to the right-about. The principal portion of them broke and fled, though some brave fellows occasionally faced round and gave us an irregular fire."

It was the same, at the same moment, on the hill-side farther along; and thereupon the six battalions of the two British brigades swept forward, charging triumphantly down the slope, driving all before them, bayoneting the enemy right and left, and in the end hurling them back across the ravine in headlong rout. Not a few of the eager redcoats, indeed, followed the fugitives up the hill on the French side, almost up to where another French division stood drawn up in reserve.

"Our orders," relates an officer of the 66th, Lieutenant John Clarke, in his diary, describing his personal experiences, "were to lie down behind the ridge until the enemy's column had gained the top; then to rise, deliver a volley, and charge. I was sent to the summit by the commanding officer to let him know where the enemy were, and returned with the intelligence that a strong column was only fifty yards off. 'Ready, men!' was scarcely uttered, when a shell fell at my feet. I threw myself on the ground, and it instantly exploded. The commanding officer was wounded in the arm, my brother-subaltern had his right arm carried off, two men were killed, and several wounded. But there was no time to spare; the volley was delivered, and we rushed on them with the bayonet. At first they appeared as if they would stand the charge, but when we closed they wavered, then turned and ran down the hill in the wildest confusion. The commander-in-chief with his staff was close to me. As the enemy's column advanced, a French officer rushed to the front, fired a pistol into the group, and fell himself, covered with wounds.

> After this affair the enemy retired to their position of the morning, and we sat down amidst the dying and the dead. Those who were so fortunate as to have a crust and a little wine in their calabashes took a little and shared with those around.

> After the beating off of the morning attack the cannonade continued for nearly an hour; then it began to slacken by degrees, until,

between eight and nine o'clock, it died entirely away.

Before, however, the French gunners stopped firing, the 48th and the other regiments, as a staff-officer incidentally mentions, had already begun to bury their dead on the field.

> As the weather was dreadfully hot, and it was impossible to know how long we should occupy this ground, orders were given to bury the men who had fallen the night before and in the morning attack, lying round the hill interspersed with the living, . . . It was curious to see the soldiers burying their fallen comrades with the cannon-shot falling round and in the midst of them, making it probable that an individual might be employed in digging his own grave!

The French artillerymen, indeed, for most of the time kept steadily bombarding the troops on the hill. "They threw shot and shells on it," sometimes, as we are told, "with terrible precision. One shell killed four horses held by a man, who escaped uninjured. Their fuses, however, often burned too quick, exploding the shells in the air, forming little clouds of smoke."

The charge cost the victors between 700 and 800 killed and wounded. General Hill received a bullet-wound on the head that temporarily incapacitated him from duty. On the French side more than 1,300 killed and wounded all told bore witness how the 48th and their comrades had used their bayonets. "The dead of the enemy," describes an officer of the 48th, "lay in vast numbers on the face of the hill. They had been tall, healthy, well-limbed young men, and with good countenances, and as a proof of their courage their bodies lay close to our ranks."

The cannonading ceased, and as it did so, before the eyes of the men of the 48th and of the others on the hill-top, a gorgeously attired cavalcade of plumed and cocked-hatted French officers came prancing out on Cascajal, the hill near the centre of the French line. They halted there, and in a few minutes a second gorgeous group rode cantering up. King Joseph and his two marshals, Jourdan and Victor, were meeting to hold a council of war and survey the field. The conference lasted for just two hours, during which time many of the soldiers of both armies went down to the brook in the ravine, and, tacitly agreeing, as it were, to a sort of armistice, mingled together amicably as they quenched their thirst in the muddy water. Wellington, it is told, used the interval to lie down and get a quiet sleep. His immediate anxiety was past. He had only to hold his ground, and he could trust his men.

The council of war ended about eleven o'clock, and the French leaders rode away. They had decided to make one more attack, this time in full force. "*Si on n'enfonce pas ça, il faudrait renoncer à faire la guerre!*" exclaimed one of the French marshals, Victor, with an impatient gesture, sweeping his arm in the direction of the thin red lines along the opposite slopes. Marshal Victor knew better before dark.

Half an hour afterwards signs of the new movement became apparent to the watchers from the British side. Wellington was on his feet again and alertly observing the enemy.

It was the moving up of General Sebastiani's division before advancing to attack the British centre and bring on the fight in which the 48th made their mark by rescuing the Guards and Hanoverian Legion from threatened destruction with a splendid charge which had its part in deciding the fate of the battle. "Old Charley," led his regiment on—to meet a soldier's death in the middle of the onset.

At a few minutes before noon, as the staff-officer already quoted describes, "immense clouds of dust were seen rising above the woods opposite the centre of the allied army, implying the movement of a large body of troops. It meant the preparing for a general assault, and was occasioned by Sebastiani's corps forming in column of attack. The dust drew near in the woods and a vast column was seen preparing to advance."

There were some 8,000 of the enemy in that quarter, and not far from them another division was drawn up, that of General Lapisse, some 7,000 strong. The two divisions were to combine for a concentrated effort to break through the British centre, where, immediately facing them, stood Wellington's First Division, three brigades led by General Sherbrooke: the Guards' brigade on the right (1st Coldstream and 1st Scots Guards); General Cameron's brigade (the 61st and 83rd) in the centre; Langwerth's Hanoverian brigade (three German Legion battalions) on the left.

Two other French divisions, those of Villatte and Ruffin—the latter being the troops who had been so roughly handled by Hill's men in the earlier fighting—were on the move towards Wellington's left, apparently aiming to work round the British flank on that side.

The French grand attack opened a few minutes before half-past two. The enemy's artillery began it. As in the morning, a furious fire of shot and shell burst out suddenly all along the French front; a fierce

A MARSHAL OF FRANCE WITH HIS STAFF OFFICERS

cannonade from between seventy and eighty guns, against which Wellington's few batteries, although our artillerymen heroically did their best to reply, could do but little.

The incessant hail of shot and shell smote hard and heavily on the British infantry, most savagely of all on Sherbrooke's three brigades, the chief objective of the coming onslaught; but it was faced with heroic steadiness.

No sign of flinching came from our gallant fellows. Although they were in the open all the time, entirely exposed, with not a bush at hand by way of cover, Sherbrooke's men stood up and took their punishment. All could see what was coming. Right before them, in full view, Sebastiani and Lapisse, with fully 15,000 men, were sweeping forward fast in solid masses, moving in two thick lines of closely packed battalion columns.

The first of the French lines came straight at them, with, out ahead, a surging mass of skirmishers, firing their hardest as they ran to the front, drums beating, and with exulting shouts of victory.

They came on until within fifty yards of where the British stood; drawn up in a thin red line, two deep. Our men were standing, as they had been told to do, stock-still, with ordered arms.

A sharp set-to in some vineyards in advance of the left of the British centre began the conflict; the French light troops on that side being beaten back by the 7th Royal Fusiliers, and the 40th, who captured and spiked six of their guns. Immediately afterwards the French skirmishers of the main attack came hustling across the ravine and made a rapid rush towards where Sherbrooke's men awaited them. Close up behind were the foremost of the battalion columns.

But even then not a shot from the three British brigades was fired in rejoinder. Like a red-brick wall all stood there, waiting with ordered arms, though already the bullets of the skirmishers and the shells from the batteries on Cascajal Hill had made great gaps in their ranks. They had been told to wait till the enemy should get quite near.

They did as they were told, and then the word was given. As the enemy got to the appointed limit, to within fifty yards, up went the British muskets all along the line. The next moment a terrific discharge, aimed low, not a bullet of which could well miss its mark, crashed into the front of the nearest French battalions. The concentrated volley struck with smashing effect into the enemy, carrying death and disorder among their crowded ranks. The long British line, drawn up two deep, overlapped the heads of the narrower-fronted French columns on either hand, and its wide-sweeping fire struck down whole files at once. It sheared away, as it were, the entire front face of the columns, and carried devastation widely along the flanks.

The French were staggered. They had to check their advance and try quickly to reform. As they were in the act of attempting it, in an instantaneous counter-charge the line of British bayonets dashed at them. Sherbrooke's three brigades, all together, with a rousing cheer swept down on them. The sight was enough for the enemy. Apparently seized by a sudden panic, the French gave back and bolted off in confusion, not waiting for the British to close.

Our men followed, bayoneting the enemy as they ran, chasing them back across the ravine, and then pressing on after them on the farther side. But they went too far: almost, indeed, into the heart of the enemy's position. The excited pursuers could not be stopped. Not content with breaking up the enemy, heeding nothing of the French lines in support, which had halted to meet them, eager and carried away by the ardour of the charge, the officers and men in two of the brigades lost their heads. They ran forward pell-mell at the heels of the discomfited French battalions. The Guards on the right and the German brigade on the left, got out of hand and hurried forward recklessly, until they found themselves face to face with the French columns of the second line.

The tables now were turned abruptly. The British pursuers were rushing on in two isolated bodies. The centre brigade had halted. Seeing the danger of a rash pursuit, General Cameron, cooler headed than the two other Brigadiers, had halted his men to rally and re-form immediately after recrossing the ravine.

Guardsmen on one side and Germans on the other found themselves suddenly confronted by an unbroken mass of troops, who instantly charged out to meet them, and set on them, scattering them in their disorder; while the French batteries nearby, and now on their flank, turned their guns on the retreating British, slaughtering them at short range with grape and case shot. There was no time nor chance for re-forming ranks. Guardsmen and Hanoverians alike were sent reeling back, broken and flying in wild confusion. The enemy, reinforced by the quickly rallied battalions of their first line, followed close after them in overwhelming numbers, and "so confident of victory that their officers could be heard shouting out: '*Allons, mes enfants, allons! Ils sont tous nos prisonniers!*'"

In their frantic rush to get back the fugitives broke in among and carried along in a struggling mass with them the battalions of Cameron's brigade, swept away again as these were getting into shape. Thus Wellington's entire centre division was borne back headlong—a stricken crowd of fugitives.

One of the officers of the 48th, catching a glimpse through the battle-smoke of what was happening, from the hill where the regiment up to then had stood, describes what he saw. "The Guards, carried onwards by victorious excitement, advanced too far, and found themselves assailed by the French reserve and mowed down by an irresistible fire. They fell back, but, as whole sections were swept away, their ranks became disordered, and nothing but their stubborn gallantry prevented a total *déroute*. Their situation was most critical. Had the French cavalry charged home, nothing could have saved them."

It was at this moment that the 48th were called upon to save the day.

Donellan's 48th had up to then been, as before, on Medellin Hill, keeping up a musketry action with the nearest French in front. "'Old Charley,'" as one of his own officers says, "showed that he knew the use of gunpowder and lead as well as steel." During the two hours that the musketry firing had lasted so far, he had had two horses shot under him.

> The presence of the fine old soldier, like Charles XII. in scarlet, animated his men, and they fought with the energy of true courage. His voice, as he gave the word of command along the line of his battalion, was like a match to a gun—'Steady, officers! Cool, my men! Ready, pr'sent, fire! That's the way, my lads!' Thus 'Old Charley' at a word sent showers of well-directed balls into the blue ranks before him, and in the heat of a well-returned fire was as cool as when on the parade, and as primly caparisoned. He perceived a few of his men fall from a discharge of musketry, at such a distance as made him doubtful of being within range. 'Curse the fellows!' said he, 'those damn'd long guns of theirs can shoot at two miles off'; and immediately advanced his battalion to such a proximity to the foe, that he soon made them shift their ground.

The situation for Wellington was desperately critical. His battle-plan seemed even on the verge of collapsing in a hideous disaster. His centre had been overthrown: a huge gap had been made right across the middle of the British position. Wellington's foresight and calmness, coupled with the splendid discipline and endurance of his men, the magnificent steadiness of the 48th in particular, saved the situation at the supreme moment.

Keenly watching the progress of the fight, Wellington had at once marked the rash pushing forward of the Guards and Germans and their disorderly pursuit. Anticipating the catastrophe that followed before it actually came about, he had already taken measures to save the perilous situation. To fill the gap, another brigade, Mackenzie's, made up of the 24th, 31st, and 45th, was swiftly sent forward from near at hand and swung across on the ground where Sherbrooke's division had been posted. But Mackenzie's men were not sufficient by themselves, and Wellington had no other brigade at hand that he dared move. He rode up to the 48th and personally bade Donellan go forward and do his best.

"Old Charley" and the 48th went racing to the danger-point with keen alacrity. They reached the scene of the disaster quickly, coming up at the double, "Old Charley" cantering forward proudly at their head, and at once threw themselves into their task. Arriving first in rear of the Hanoverians as these were coming back in a confused crowd, pressed hard by the enemy, they halted here, and broke swiftly into column to allow the retreating troops to pass through. Then, re-forming into line, they dealt the nearest column of the oncoming French a stopping blow, meeting them with a concentrated volley full in their faces.

"We came on double quick," describes the officer of the 48th already quoted, "and formed in rear by companies, and through the intervals in our line the broken ranks of the Guards retreated. A close and well-directed volley from us arrested the progress of the victorious French, while with amazing celerity and coolness the Guards rallied and re-formed, and in a few minutes advanced in turn to support us. As the enemy came on, the men gave a loud huzza! An Irish regiment to the right (the 83rd) answered it with a thrilling cheer. It was taken up from regiment to regiment, and passed along the English line; and that wild shout told the advancing enemy that British valour was indomitable. The leading files of the French halted, turned, fell back, and never made another effort."

"The centre of the British," says Napier, in his vivid way, describing the coming up of the 48th and the rescue of the Guards and Hanoverians, "was absolutely broken, and victory inclined towards the French, when suddenly Colonel Donellan was seen advancing with the 48th through the midst of the disordered masses. It seemed as if this regiment must be carried away with the retiring crowds, but wheeling back by companies, it let them pass through the intervals, and then, resuming its proud and beautiful line, struck against the right of the pursuing enemy, plying such a destructive musketry and closing with such a firm countenance that his forward movement was checked."

The brave old colonel received the wound which brought about his death, a bullet in the knee, as the 48th were coming up in the rear of the Hanoverians.

He beckoned to the officer next in command, Major Middlemore, and, although suffering the most excruciating torture from the wound, handed over the command to him with the same coolness as if he had been on the parade of a barrack-yard. His enraged men went on like lions, taking ample revenge upon their enemies—and that too with the cold iron.

"If the 48th," in the words of our great modern historian of the Peninsular War, Professor Oman, "had been carried away in the backward movement the day would have been lost, but the regiment stood firm and allowed Cameron's and Langwerth's men to form up in rear."

The splendid Northamptons, single-handed at that point, held back Lapisse's mass of battalions; and their steadfastness turned the fortunes of the day. "The French, when once brought to a standstill by the First 48th, lost their *élan* and stood heaped together in a disorderly mass, keeping up a rolling fire but gaining no ground."

Then, at all points, the rallied Guards and Germans, and Cameron's men came hastening back, full of fight, to reinforce the firing-line. Most of the Guards for their part had passed through Mackenzie's brigade and re-formed behind it: most of the Hanoverians had re-formed in rear of the 48th. One and all, the gallant Guardsmen in particular, had pulled themselves together smartly.

> They quickly formed in rear and moved up into position, and their spirit and appearance of good humour and determination after having lost in twenty minutes 500 men, was shown by their giving a hurrah, as they took up their ground; and a report soon after that the enemy's cavalry was coming down upon them was answered by a contemptuous laugh along their ranks.

With no less noble devotion and undaunted stubbornness, Mackenzie's three battalions had, meanwhile, on their side held in check Sebastiani's thronging columns.

The rallying immediately after that of Sherbrooke's battalions to support the fighting-line turned the tide of battle against the French. They made a desperate stand at bay for a while, and a furious musketry duel raged at short range. But the British bullets were too many for the French. The narrow-fronted French columns were outmatched in the firing-line by the long extended British ranks, which both faced them and overlapped them on either side. The superiority of the British musketry fire, of the British "weight of metal," so to speak, decided that fight.

Both of the French attacking divisions gave way before the increasing fierceness of the British musketry as the rallied battalions were brought back again into the fight. First Sebastiani's men yielded ground, and then Lapisse's, disheartened at the fall of their general, who was shot down while trying to incite them to a fresh advance. Seeing their comrades in the other division beginning to retire, with cavalry charging into them, and seeing other cavalry coming up as though to take them also in flank, smitten heavily at the same moment by Wellington's guns, which had had their chance at last and been promptly turned in that direction not long after the 48th brought the French to a stand, Lapisse's men lost heart and began to go back. The retreat soon quickened into a run.

The end of the battle came about immediately after that, with a general retirement of the French from the field.

"Old Charley," the gallant leader of the 48th, was borne off the field during the final fighting. "The colonel, with his knee broken in a most dangerous manner, was, without loss of time, carried to the rear by four of his musicians, and placed on a straw bed in the town of Talavera. Had there been surgeons to have amputated the limb on the instant, it is supposed he would have survived; but this not having been the case, mortification took place, and he died on the fourth day after the battle."

He was buried by the French. Colonel Donellan had to be left behind when Wellington retreated from Talavera in consequence of Soult's reorganized army coming into the Tagus Valley and threatening his line of communication with his base. The dying officer was treated with every consideration by the French who had promptly reoccupied the town on Wellington's withdrawal. "Some of them recalled that they had seen him at the head of his battalion, and warmly praised the veteran's gallantry. His soldier-like appearance, too, commanded their regard, and they carried his body in a cloak to the spot where he had led his regiment so bravely. They buried 'Old Charley' with the true honours of a soldier.'"

The 1st Northamptonshires of today, (as at time of first publication), are permitted to display as a special distinction the battle-honour "Talavera," inscribed not only on their regimental colour, but also on their helmets and their waist-plates.

It was of Talavera, to conclude, that a very distinguished general of Napoleon's army once said:

> This battle at once restored the reputation of the British Army, which during a century had declined. It was now made plain that the English infantry could dispute the palm with the best in Europe.

3

In the Ranks of the Enemy:—What Facing Wellington's Men Felt Like

This is a glance at things on the enemy's side, among the men whom our soldiers fought, under fire, on the battlefield. It is in point here, and also of interest incidentally as a study of temperament.

"Nothing," says one of Wellington's officers, describing the way in which the enemy made their onset in battle, "can be more spirited or impetuous than the first attack of the French troops. They come on for a while, slowly, and in silence; till, having reached within a hundred yards or two of the point to be assailed, they raise a loud but discordant yell, and rush forward. The advance of their columns is, moreover, covered by a perfect cloud of *tirailleurs*—or skirmishers—who press on, apparently in utter confusion, but with every demonstration of courage; who fire irregularly, it is true, but with great rapidity and precision; and who are as much at home in the art of availing themselves of every species of cover as any light troops in the world. The ardour of the French is, however, admirably opposed by the coolness and undaunted deportment of Britons. Our people met their assailants exactly as if the whole affair had been a piece of acting, no man quitting his ground, but each deliberately waiting till the word of command was given, and then discharging his piece."

What facing Wellington's men felt like among the French we have an account at first hand from one of those who went through the experience in the Peninsular War. One of Napoleon's officers, a captain in a line regiment, tells the story. His narrative deals with one of the earlier battles, when the British, owing to inferiority in numbers, had to stand on the defensive and await attack. It might well serve for what took place in the advance to the grand attack at Talavera.

Describing how his comrades made their advance, the French officer outlines this vividly dramatic picture:

About a thousand yards from the English line the men begin to get excited, and some to talk; pointing to the enemy and exchanging ideas in agitation. They hurry their march; the ranks begin to waver a little here and there, and get out of order. The English on their side remain silent; they are all standing stock-still, with ordered arms. In their impassive immobility they look as immovable as a long red-brick wall. And at the same time their imposing steadiness invariably produces a bad effect on our younger soldiers.

Very soon, as we get nearer, the ranks begin, by degrees, to get restive and noisy. Cries and shouts now come from some of the men; ejaculations of *"Vive l'Empereur!" "En Avant!" "À la baïonnette!"*

Next, under the same influence of excitement, a number of shakos are raised on the muzzles of the muskets in some of the companies. The whole march forward is quickened imperceptibly until the pace, without orders, is gradually increased to almost a run. The ranks are getting intermixed now, and confusion begins to set in at many points. Indeed, the general agitation threatens to become almost a tumult. And too, in their excitement, some of our soldiers begin firing off their muskets at random as they advance.

All the time the English line remains absolutely silent; standing yonder, calm and motionless. They stand there with ordered arms, drawn up as on parade; even when we are not three hundred yards away. To look at them they simply seem as if they ignore the storm that is about to break on their heads.

The contrast fast becomes unnerving:—it is, indeed, almost appalling! In our inmost thoughts each one of us cannot help feeling that the enemy are holding back their fire of set purpose. One and all realize, too, that it must fall on us with fearful effect, dealing widespread death when it does come. Our ardour begins now rapidly to cool:—the general enthusiasm is already fast evaporating. Quiet discipline and steadiness over disorder and noisiness is too palpable, too marked in its advantage; it sends a cold shiver through most of us. Some of our men now, too, begin to look behind! A terribly ominous symptom is that!

But we have not to wait much longer. The time has come!

At this moment of painful anticipation, of intense excitement, the English wall is suddenly seen to stir itself, to make a move. The redcoats, all of a sudden, all in unison, shoulder arms. We know what that means. They are making ready!

The anxiety in our ranks at the sight is cruel to witness. An indescribable "creepy" feeling that something dreadful is about to happen takes possession of us. It appears to root many of our men to the ground. More men now begin to fire; wildly, irregularly, without order, without aim, without effect.

And then—!

A moment later, all together, up go the English muskets to the shoulder. They gleam horribly in a long row as they are levelled. The next instant—immediately a blaze flashes forth, all along, close in front of us. It has come!

The enemy's volleys, steady and deliberate, precise, concentrated, pitiless, sweep havoc and death through our ranks, falling on us with crushing, overwhelming effect.

Decimated, we turn about and instinctively fall back; seeking to recover our equilibrium beyond range and re-form our ranks. Before we can draw breath three tremendous, deafening hurrahs burst forth on the air, breaking the silence of our adversaries after the volleys. And at the third hurrah they are on us: bayoneting furiously to right and left, pressing us back in a disorderly retreat, a mob of men with muskets.

Yet it is not for far. To our astonishment, they do not try to push their advantage beyond a hundred yards or so. At that distance their bugles ring out.

They halt and then retire; drawing back calmly to their former post in line, there to await our second attack. When that comes in turn, once again they stay for us, fire on us, and then charge down and drive us back!

So it goes to the end with all our attacks; till we give over, with thinned *cadres*, dispirited, exhausted, and our nerve gone.

4

The Charge of the Light Dragoons at Talavera

The last British cavalry standards ever borne under fire before an enemy are preserved in London, among the trophies of British valour displayed at the Royal United Service Institution in Whitehall, (as atime of first publication); our National Treasure-House of Victory, the British National Gallery of Heroism in Arms. Nor, among the numerous mementoes there of brave deeds done in fight, are there many so deserving of our regard. Those faded old Light Dragoon banners commemorate a story of which one and all of us should be proud. They recall to mind a gallant episode indeed in our British annals of war.

The Charge of the Light Dragoons at Talavera, indeed, was to the men of Wellington's day very much what the Charge of the Light Brigade at Balaclava is to the Victorian era.

"The heroism of the onset exceeded anything that has ever occurred in our best days of chivalry." So one of Wellington's officers said of it. "The laurels won by the survivors in that wild but gallant contest should be intertwined with cypress in respect for their devoted comrades who went boldly on, resolved to conquer or to perish."

"It seems almost miraculous," comments another of Wellington's officers, "how a man escaped."

Yet another adds this:

> We truly think that the 23rd may challenge the world to produce an instance of greater effect produced on a well-disciplined enemy by so small a body of men.

It was both magnificent and war; differing in that from what the

French General Bosquet remarked, as he sat watching the Charge at Balaclava. Costly in life in proportion to the numbers of the regiment as the Talavera charge was, at any rate there nobody "blundered." We have Wellington's own word as to that. There was no misunderstanding of orders in the Talavera charge of the Light Dragoons.

"I don't know why it was supposed," wrote Wellington, "there was any mistake. A few hundred cavalry charged a division of infantry formed in squares of battalions. They did not succeed in breaking these squares or columns; nor could they have succeeded probably if they were as many thousand as they were hundreds. They did succeed in deterring the French from making their attack upon the key of our position. 'But they sustained great loss!' To be sure they did: and for what purpose were they there if not to sustain loss, if such loss was necessary?"

Talavera (the battle took place on July 27 and 28, 1809) was, as has been said, one of the very hardest fought fights in which the British Army was ever engaged. We have it in Wellington's own words, indeed, that on the occasion, had our Spanish allies done their duty, "it would have been as great a battle as Waterloo."

The Charge of the Light Dragoons took place towards four o'clock on the afternoon of the second day of battle. It was just at the time when, in the centre of the battlefield, Marshal Victor was delivering his third and final grand attack in force.

Two dense masses of French troops, the divisions of Villatte and Ruffin, with a grenadier brigade in rear, were seen on the move towards a valley to the left centre of Wellington's position. They were apparently aiming, under cover of a furious cannonade, to turn the British flank on that side, and work round Hill's men posted on the Cerro de Medellin. Wellington up to then had not posted troops in the valley, or on the wooded Segurilla ridge beyond it, farther to the left, which overlooked and commanded the valley. The locality had seemed hitherto too distant to affect the issue of the battle; but as the new French move developed, it became apparent that the enemy were turning their attention to a serious move in that quarter.

A Spanish division was first sent across the valley to occupy the nearest ridge beyond, and keep back the French skirmishers, who were making for it. Then, when two heavy columns, well in advance of the third, and mostly infantry, were seen moving in front across the valley, the British cavalry were ordered to push towards the valley and occupy it, so as to hold the enemy in check.

Wellington, who had been watching them from the hill of Medellin, the left centre of the British position, on seeing Victor's main attack beaten back, sent word for the cavalry to charge. "As they neared the foot of the Cerro de Medellin a roar of cheering from the centre told Wellesley that all was safe in that quarter. Thereupon, crossing quickly to the reverse side of the Cerro, he sent orders to Anson's brigade to charge the French infantry on the plain."

General Anson, with the Third Cavalry Brigade, made up of two regiments of light horse, the 23rd Light Dragoons, and the 1st Hussars of the King's German Legion, arrived in the vicinity first. The Heavy Cavalry Brigade followed to support them, but were at some distance in rear.

As the Light Cavalry Brigade reached the valley, the headmost of the French columns was getting into position to open their flank attack. They were coming on with skirmishers pushed well out ahead, advancing at a sharp run with drums beating. The order to Anson was to charge the enemy the moment an opportunity offered. It was taken as definitive, and the Light Cavalry obeyed at once, making toward the nearest of the French columns, a division of some 7,000 men.

The enemy, on their side, quickly halted in their advance, after which, as a safeguard, the French took post with their battalions drawn up in squares. They strengthened themselves on one side by occupying a small farmhouse with sharpshooters. Immediately after that the second French division closed in and formed in support near at hand, a little in rear to one side, *en échelon*, and also throwing its battalions into squares, which bristled all over, in like manner, with bayonets to keep the cavalry off.

The ground in front of Anson's horsemen was fairly open to look at, although rough and broken on the surface—a stretch of valley covered knee-deep with long, rank, waving grass, awkward ground for cavalry to charge over. There had been no opportunity of reconnoitring it beforehand or of getting an idea what pitfalls and obstacles the tall grass might not hide. But there was the explicit order from Wellington to charge the enemy in front, and the ground appeared to be fairly level.

The order was obeyed forthwith. Lieut.-Colonel Seymour, in command of the 23rd, ranged his men for attack, forming up the Light Dragoons on a front the width of two squadrons. That, owing to clusters of cork-wood trees here and there on the near side of the plain, was all there was room for from flank to flank. The Light

Dragoons took the right of the brigade; the Hanoverians, formed in similar order, took post on the left.

Then General Anson gave the word for all to go forward. The trumpets clanged out, and, moving first at a trot, the whole brigade started off.

The 23rd went forward in two lines, each of two squadrons, and each squadron with, in the front rank, the cornet carrying its standard. In that manner the four flags now at Whitehall were borne into the fight. Ahead of the left wing of the Light Dragoons, two or three horse-lengths in advance, rode General Elley, one of Wellington's staff, mounted on a grey charger. He led the way, his charger and white-plumed cocked hat and scarlet coat, conspicuous to all, contrasting vividly with the black leather, dark fur-crested helmets and blue jackets of the Dragoons, all mounted on dark brown horses.

As they started off they had to ride past the hill on which stood in line the infantry of the Second Division. The troopers as they passed raised a wild shout of exultation, cheering across to their comrades on the hill, sabres flashing in the sunshine as they were brandished at arm's length, and getting back in answer rousing cheers from the infantrymen. "Never was anything more exhilarating or more beautiful," says one of the infantry officers, looking down from the hill, "than their commencement of this advance."

Immediately after that, as they cleared the base of the hill, the horsemen came under fire from the French artillery in front, the cannon-balls knocking over a number of men and horses. A few moments later the bullets of the French sharpshooters began to whistle among them. That also galled them a good deal, and there were many empty saddles. After that, without order given, the pace quickened to a canter, and from that to a gallop. In a few minutes all began to race forward, the men in a state of high excitement, eager to get hand to hand with the enemy. They had from the start about three-quarters of a mile to ride over.

They got to within 150 yards of the enemy; the Light Dragoons making for the largest French square, comprised of three battalions of the 27th Light Infantry, charging directly at it, the Hanoverian Hussars making at two smaller squares, which stood at one side of the large square, a little way to the rear. There the 24th and 96th of the Line were posted, two regiments whose ranks had been a good deal thinned after severe punishment in the early morning attack that day. But, as they all neared the enemy, at almost the last moment, with startling abruptness, there came a sudden check—"an unforeseen chance of war." It made all the difference, in the outcome, to the charge and to the fate of the 23rd.

Suddenly, General Elley, right ahead of them, was seen to pause; then to pull his horse together and make a great bound forward over some unexpected obstacle. Apparently he cleared it with difficulty and landed on a lower slope, across some chasm or pit as it seemed: it was impossible for those following in the high grass to tell what it was. The next moment the general was seen to be reining back his hardest; pulling his horse back on to its haunches; under a blaze of shots from the nearest French skirmishers. The general swung round sharply and with his cocked hat in hand appeared to be gesticulating frantically, trying to wave back the nearest troopers, to stop them and the rest close behind. All could see that he was shouting his loudest, but the noise of the enemy's shots, and the clash and turmoil and tramping of the horse-hoofs, prevented a word from being heard. There was, of course, no time to do anything; no chance even to check the pace. Within three seconds the headmost troopers, galloping in a mass, close together, knee to knee, were up with the general.

Instantly they learned what the warning was for. A wide ravine or watercourse, the bed of a mountain-stream, with steeply sloping sides some eight or ten feet deep and half a dozen yards across, suddenly confronted them. It had been hidden completely from view up to then by the long grass: until, in fact, the first horsemen were actually on the brink. It was too late to pull up, and amid a frightful scene the leaders rode headlong down into the hollow.

Colonel Seymour and the front rank of the leading squadron on the left plunged into the ravine, but, though half the horses and men came down at the bottom, many kept their footing, and, scrambling across, cleverly began to climb up the farther slope. The troopers of the rear rank met with disaster. They came down in a rush on top of those already fallen. Tumbling over them at the bottom in a moment, almost every man was flung out of his saddle and lay stretched on the ground, struggling for life, mixed up and jammed in the middle of a heaped mass of fallen horses, some maimed and with broken limbs, all terrified, confused and snorting, and lashing out frantically with their heels.

Some of the troopers cleared the stream, some swerved in time and refused the leap, others scrambled in and over at a less difficult part; but many fell, horse and man, into the trap and were crushed by the rear rank falling on top of them. There were several broken necks and scores of broken arms and legs in the leading squadron.

Such was the terrible misadventure that befell the headmost squadron of the Light Dragoons.

The second line got warning by seeing the inexplicable disorder into which their fellows had fallen. They slackened pace, but were borne into the confused mass at the ravine before they could bring themselves to a stand."

At the same moment the front face of the nearest French square opened fire in volleys.

Elsewhere along the line the Hanoverian Hussars, up to then galloping forward parallel with the 23rd, stumbled on the perilous trap at almost the same moment. But, as it proved, with better fortune. The ravine at that point was, as it happened, both less deep and its sides less steep;—yet offering a sufficiently formidable obstacle for charging cavalry. Some of the Germans managed to pull up just in time, "but many troopers were unhorsed and others, although keeping their saddles, could not manage to scramble up the farther side of the ravine. The rear squadrons came up to add to the confusion, and reined up among the survivors." Most of them struggled across the ravine, and, hastily forming in loose order, went at the French square nearest them. Luckily for the Germans their enemy did not begin firing until after the Hussars had rallied across the ravine. The Hussars then made a dash at the French square, but were beaten back by musketry and recoiled in some confusion, after which they recrossed the ravine and rode back to the shelter of the hill in rear. Many of them had done their best and fell, shot down close in front of the French bayonets.

According to Napier's amazing tale, the German Colonel, Arentschild, stopped his troopers on the brink of the ravine, made no attempt to cross it, and then, exclaiming in broken English: "I will not kill my young mans," calmly trotted back to his former position. Napier, however, was badly misinformed. He was not there to see what happened; and his story is a cruel libel on a good and gallant soldier of tried courage and ability.

This, meanwhile, was taking place with our own fellows of the 23rd Light Dragoons, at their point of passage, higher up the ravine. In spite of what had befallen their leading squadrons, the rest of the

23rd managed to get across.

The uninjured among the troopers who had been unsaddled in the disaster, getting hold of their horses again, remounted and attempted bravely to get at the enemy on their own account. Only the maimed and badly injured remained behind on the ground in the ravine. Extricating themselves from the confusion the remnant of the troopers of the first and second squadrons scrambled up the steep slope on the farther side as best they could and then made an attempt to rally and re-form on the level. As they topped the rise and were striving to get into line, the French square in front blazed off a furious volley into them; but in spite of the bullets the troopers did their utmost.

Regardless of the French musketry the survivors of the two squadrons rallied and attempted to charge the square right in front. Galloping forward, with forlorn-hope desperation, they rode to within twenty yards of the French bayonets. But to go farther was impossible. Another crashing discharge from the French square burst on them. The volley struck down *en masse*, dead or dying, two-thirds of those who had struggled over the ravine.

> They stopped short in their career; the whole plain was instantly dotted by riderless horses galloping off and men straggling to the rear, while a wide heap, as seen from the hill, marked where the slaughtered lay.

So describes an officer, watching the effort of the Light Dragoons, from among the infantry on the hill in rear. The last volley sealed the fate of the survivors of the leading squadrons. The few men left turned away, some to get back over the ravine to the British lines, a small handful to join the right wing of the regiment, which had formed the second line in the charge. Rallied by General Elley, the right wing of the 23rd was about to make an attempt by itself.

The men of the two squadrons of the right wing had struggled across at a place that was somewhat less steep than that in front of the others, and where there were no French immediately facing them. Major Ponsonby and fewer than twenty of the survivors of the others joined them. All together, the brave fellows, numbering in all fewer than 200 troopers, made their effort to get the enemy within reach of their swords. They went charging their hardest at the nearest square. But, as elsewhere, the task of breaking in proved impossible. They had to swerve off before the front row of the bayonets.

After that, galloping their hardest, they went racing past, through the midst of the enemy. Going through between the larger French square and the sharpshooters in the farmhouse, they pressed on along the flank of the next square. Again, though it was impossible to find an opening on the flank or in rear.

At the same time undoubtedly some lives were saved by this ride through.

Dashing into the midst of the enemy between the squares, they muzzled the French for the moment, balking their volleys. The men in one square dared not risk opening fire lest they might hit those in the adjoining square. There was, though, all the same, some shooting. Several muskets were discharged from the farmhouse at the troopers as they tore past, just outside the impenetrable wall of bayonets, and several of the British dragoons fell to the shots.

Without checking speed, the band of heroes went careering forward, cheering and shouting; their sabres flashing in the sun; intent only on finding a gap to break in among the bayonets. But they found none. The enemy's ranks confronted them solidly and massive on all sides; the infantrymen standing closely locked-up, and presenting everywhere a triple-tiered array of glistening points—absolutely invincible.

On raced the intrepid horsemen headlong, rushing past like a whirlwind amidst the astonished French, whose officers, as some themselves said later on, gazed at them with wonder, hardly realizing what was taking place. "They are mad!" "It is *aquardente*—brandy!" said some. Others, among these Marshal Victor himself, watching the charge through his telescope, from on horseback, on a bluff overlooking the valley at a little distance, frankly declared that "its daring surpassed anything they had ever heard of."

Indeed, they all but captured two French generals in their furious rush—General Villatte, the commander of the division, himself, and one of his brigadiers, General Cassagne. The two had got to the spot just before, but had not been able to get inside the square of the 27th for which they had made. There was, though, no time for the racing horsemen to take prisoners; their own immediate position was too precarious to allow for that.

The dragoons galloped on between the squares, and then beyond them into the open: only to meet fresh foes. There, as they cleared the infantry, they suddenly came upon some French cavalry, part of Merlin's division in support of the squares. The cavalry were halted and drawn up to bar their way. They were a corps of green-jacketed horsemen, the 10th Chasseurs. The Light Dragoons rode at the *chas-*

seurs without pause or checking pace, and the greencoats opened out before the blue. The "French troopers gave back and loosened their files, opening out as the 23rd came up." The British dragoons broke through them at once and rolling the *chasseurs* aside, galloped on at a second line of cavalry just beyond. Still more enemies were awaiting the Light Dragoons. A second French *chasseur* regiment, the 26th, at that moment came up at a trot. Without pausing, without slackening pace, the gallant 23rd went straight at them. They struck into them full in front, and broke into them and through again.

That was all that our splendid Light Dragoons could do. Their bolt was shot. The end was now at hand. The horses were blown: the men were spent with their fierce exertions. For a moment an attempt was thought of, to charge their way back again as best they could, between the squares as they had come; but that was madness—sheer impossibility. Yet it was about to be dared. In the act of trying to rally and make the desperate effort, they had to meet yet more enemies. No respite was given them, hardly breathing space. Suddenly another French regiment appeared in their front, the Westphalian Light Horse, brawny-armed Germans from the Rhineland, and well mounted—dangerous foes for any cavalry to cross swords with at any time, with men and horses in full strength and fresh.

The collision finished off the 23rd Light Dragoons. They pluckily faced the Westphalians, and at first tried to stand up to them and make a fight for it:—but the odds were overwhelming. For a few instants there was a clash of steel as they held the enemy off, at bay—then all was over! The wing squadrons of the 10th and 26th Chasseurs, which had swung apart as the men of the 23rd plunged through, came wheeling round in rear of them and closed in at their backs.

That was the *finale*.

The exhausted men and horses were trapped and quickly settled with;—killed or unhorsed and disarmed and made prisoners in the midst of five times their numbers.

A scanty group of the best-mounted troopers and some officers, General Elley and Major Ponsonby among them, turned away to try and escape as best they could. They made a forlorn-hope dash for it, to gain a wooded hill towards the rear of where they were. Shots were being fired at the French from there, and they could see some white-coated Spanish infantry in position. They made the attempt, and just succeeded in saving themselves and the standards of the regiment. The survivors brought in with them to safety the four squadron standards now at Whitehall. Two hundred and seven officers and men were left on the field, dead or disabled. Three officers and ninety-seven men—no more than that—yielded themselves up as prisoners. In that way the 23rd Light Dragoons were accounted for.

Such was the Charge of the Light Dragoons at Talavera,—a piece of service that was of immense value to the rest of the army and Wellington. It held fast and stopped a threatening French flank move, and gave the British leader time for important dispositions elsewhere. Its moral effect on the enemy at the same time was of high importance. "The whole of Villatte's and half of Ruffin's divisions," in Napier's words, "were paralyzed by the charge of a single regiment."

To the enemy, indeed, as we are told, the charge seemed an astonishing feat of intrepidity. The heroic daring of the exploit seemed to appeal with unusual force to the French. And nothing could be more chivalrous than the friendly reception which the enemy at Talavera, from Marshal Victor downwards, accorded to the surviving officers and men of the 23rd whom the fortune of the closing fight placed as prisoners in their hands. The marshal himself sent his senior *aide-de-camp* next morning to invite the three officers taken prisoners to his headquarters. The *aide-de-camp* was charged with a message to the effect that the Marshal "particularly desired to make the acquaintance of the men who had led so daring a charge."

When they were brought before Victor he complimented them highly on their "magnificent gallantry." "Their conduct," he said, "was never equalled." As a proof of his regard, the chivalrous Marshal offered that if they should wish to be exchanged he would forward a flag of truce making the proposal to Wellington that afternoon:—and he did so. General Villatte, whose infantry column the first squadron had tried to charge, and who had his own narrow escape in the midst of the fight, was yet more outspoken in his admiration. Villatte in addition treated the captives with the most marked kindness, and during the three days that they were prisoners of war in the French camp, he went out of his way to send the officers their meals from his own table, "with abundance of wine." His *aide-de-camp* (Captain Chollet) further visited them twice a day, to see that they wanted for nothing, and three surgeons attended by order twice a day to dress their wounds.

In the outcome the surviving captives were permitted quietly to withdraw themselves one night a little later, when Marshal Victor moved his camp, and rejoin Wellington, being thus spared the long and toilsome journey to France as prisoners of war.

5

Fifty Miles in Twenty-Two Hours: the Mid-Summer March of the Light Brigade

Many and celebrated were the achievements before the enemy of Wellington's famous "Light Division," "The Division," as they proudly styled themselves. The active valour under fire shown by them on almost every battlefield of the war;—at Busaco, at Fuentes de Onoro—there is no such place as "Fuentes d'Onor," as blazoned on so many regimental flags, the "e" of the "de" is never elided in Spanish, and the misspelling of the name "Onor" was due to some War Office clerk of the period—at Ciudad Rodrigo, where their leader, the fiery, impetuous Craufurd fell, sword in hand, meeting a true soldier's death, at Badajoz, amid the rugged heights of the Coa, the Sierras of the Portuguese border, the barren uplands of Central Spain; the crags and dark ravines of the Pyrenean passes; their magnificent war-record has never been outdone by any soldiers the world has seen.

And yet, perhaps, it is an achievement of another kind that has stamped the reputation of the Light Division most deeply in the minds of soldiers—their matchless feat of fortitude and stern endurance in Wellington's first great campaign; their march to join the army at Talavera.

It was in mid-July, 1809, at the very hottest time of the year; in the hottest weather of an exceptionally hot summer; and in the hottest country of Europe.

The "Light Brigade "was their official style in July, 1809. They had not yet had their organization completed to its strength of a division. That took place in the following year, when they assumed their since immortalized title of the "Light Division." The three regiments were those that Sir John Moore had personally trained in Shorncliffe Camp in 1804: the First Battalion of the old 43rd, or Monmouthshire Light Infantry (now the First Battalion Oxfordshire Light Infantry); First Battalion of the old 52nd, then, as now, known as the Oxfordshire Light Infantry (they today form the Second Battalion of the Regiment); and the old First Battalion of the 95th Rifles, now the First Battalion of the Rifle Brigade. Their work in Spain stands to all time as Sir John Moore's diploma, assuring him his niche in the Temple of Fame as a leader in arms and an Organiser of Victory; as the master who formed the school in which were trained some of Wellington's ablest lieutenants, such as Rowland Hill and Graham, Hope, and Paget, and Robert Craufurd.

The Light Brigade, together with the famous "Chestnut Troop" of the Royal Horse Artillery, a force in all some 3,400 officers and men—to be exact, according to the official "states," 3,379 of all ranks in the three infantry regiments, and 162 artillerymen of all ranks—under their brigadier, Major-General Robert Craufurd, arrived in the Tagus on June 28. They had to get together their transport before joining Wellington and the main army, then on the march to co-operate with the Spanish armies in the field and compel the French to quit Madrid. It was one of Wellington's standing orders that no corps was to join him in the field until completely supplied with its own transport and field service equipment, from baggage-mules and ammunition-carts down to camp-kettles.

"We were busily employed," writes one of the officers of the Light Brigade, "from the moment of the arrival on June 28 to July 2 in purchasing horses, mules, and donkeys, pack-saddles, cigars, and various other odds and ends indispensable in campaigning. We were to proceed without delay to join Sir Arthur Wellesley, who was at this time in Spanish Estramadura."

They were as efficient a set of soldiers as the British Army ever had, a *corps d'élite* in the best sense—practically all veterans.

> Each regiment was nearly 1,100 strong, and there were many hundreds in each battalion to whom the smell of gunpowder in earnest was no novelty.

"They had served," says one of the 95th Rifles, speaking of his own corps, "with Nelson at Copenhagen, with Auchmuty at Monte Video, with Whitelock in the ill-fated and bloody business at Monte Video, with Sir Arthur Wellesley at Roleia and Vimiera, and with the ever-to-be-lamented Sir John Moore at Corunna. If, therefore, they were not veterans in age, they had at least some claim to the appellation from their services."

To avoid at the outset the long and wearisome tramp along the river bank to the army base at Santarem, some fifty odd miles up the Tagus, Craufurd elected to carry men of the Brigade as far up as possible by boats, to the village of Vallada, which would save forty miles of marching. The baggage and transport animals meanwhile would be coming on by road to Santarem.

"About midnight on the 2nd of July," as related by an officer of the Rifles, "the tide serving to take us up the river, we were put into flat-bottomed boats and launches, and the tedious operation of towing us against the current commenced. After twenty-four hours spent in this bewitching manner, every man's legs being terribly cramped by being crammed so tight into the boats, we reached Vallada, near which place we bivouacked on the banks of the river. I never entertained the smallest doubt that all the frogs in the Peninsula had assembled by common consent to welcome us to Portugal: for such an eternal croaking I never heard before or since! It failed, however, to spoil our night's rest, as sleep the previous night had been out of the question, owing to our being constrained to sit upright in the boats."

After a few hours' rest at Vallada they pushed on to Santarem, where Craufurd halted for three days until the baggage and commissariat animals from Lisbon had come up. Thence the regiments marched on independently, starting on successive days, for Castello Branco; a week's continuous tramp. The weather was broiling, and their way took them across a tract of country which had been ruthlessly devastated some months before by the French; a waste now of desolate and ravaged fields, ruined and plundered villages and sacked towns. "Owing to the suffocating heat our march was mostly at night, or very early in the morning. We started usually just after midnight and finished by 8 or 9 a.m., and rested during the heat of the day." "We harnessed for the night's march and poked our way in the dark" is another descriptive touch. For rations "we had tough beef, perhaps only killed a few hours before, boiled into an *omnium gatherum* with an onion or two, some rice, and a mouldy ship's biscuit."

At Castello Branco, a squalid town, "extremely dirty, with narrow streets, and where tens of millions of flies were disporting themselves," the brigade closed up and reunited.

ROYAL ARTILLERY ON THE MARCH

With all Craufurd's endeavours to mitigate the hardships of the march, the men had already suffered severely from the stifling oppressiveness of the weather. The heat was so great that "brain fever made fearful ravages in our ranks, and many men dropped by the roadside and died. Two men of the 52nd"—so one of the soldiers in the column relates—"unable to continue facing the sufferings we daily endured, actually put a period to their existence by shooting themselves."

Starting off at midnight on July 17, they then had ten days of continuous hard marching, from twenty to twenty-five miles each march, "toiling through many places of barren and desolate country, parched and uninteresting." The men, wherever it was possible, rested during the heat of the day, bivouacking in the open under hastily-put-together shelters of leafy boughs, or on the outskirts of woods near the road. What villages and small places they passed, where provisions might have been procurable, had been ravaged and destroyed by the enemy; on all sides were burned-out, roofless cottages.

Owing to the exhausting weather Craufurd, on the 23rd, halted for twenty-four hours at Coria, after covering forty miles in the previous two days. The brigade then started again, under a broiling sun, for four days' continuous marching to Naval Moral.

Two and a half miles an hour, with five or ten minutes' halt every hour and a half, and fifteen miles as the normal limit of the march, was, according to Wellington's army orders, the rate of marching for troops on independent service. Craufurd, after leaving Santarem, never marched less than twenty miles between bivouacs—more often twenty-five. The road in places was as bad as possible: here, along steep and rocky tracks through narrow ravines; there, over arid desert plains and heavy sand; occasionally, "for miles through wide and thick forests of ilex and cork."

The weather by day, when the sun was not beating down in torrid fierceness, was sultry, with a steamy heat; the air at night, breathless and close and oppressive. Every soldier had on the heavy felt, tall, brass-bound *shako* of the period, and was wearing his thick English clothing, coat closely buttoned up to the neck, with, strapped tightly over the chest, a mass of belting and buckles and elaborate accoutrements, and heavy leather *cartouche*-box and pouches holding eighty rounds of ball ammunition.

On his back each man had to carry a load of upwards of half a hundredweight dead weight—knapsack and kit, spare shoes, rolled greatcoat, blanket, and camp-kettle, three days' provisions of ship's biscuit and beef, his musket and bayonet (weighing over twelve pounds). The normal full load of a lightly clad or naked West African or Chinese *coolie* is fifty pounds, and the Roman legionaries of Caesar's campaigns, who are always cited as the stock examples of heavily-burdened soldiery, carried in war-time no more than fifty pounds of total weight—arms, armour, kit, and other "*impedimenta.*"

No tarrying by the way was allowed, no slacking off. Angry grumblings in the ranks there might be, and there were many at times, men complaining that they were being pressed beyond endurance; but, in spite of everything, the indefatigable brigadier kept them on the move, maintaining throughout along the line of march a rigid and iron discipline. "No man, on any pretext whatever," says one of the 95th, "was allowed to fall out of the ranks without a pass from the officer of his company, and then only for indispensable causes. Even when almost dying with thirst, we were compelled to pass springs of the finest water by the roadside untasted."

To fall out without leave, indeed, was, according to the brigade order issued on July 10, a court-martial offence. "Every man," ran the order, "who quits the ranks without having received a ticket from the commanding officer of the company, or having left his arms and pack with his company, as the case may be, must be brought to a court martial. If ill, he must be tried as soon as recovered; but if not ill, it must be done on the drum-head, as soon as the regiment arrives, or as the man comes up, and the punishment be inflicted as soon afterwards as circumstances will permit." If nothing else was at hand, any wayside tree would serve to tie up a man to and give him a flogging.

The men had to keep up. No excuses except incapacitating illness were accepted. A few of the soldiers, we are told, now and again attempted to "lie down, or rather, fall down, and say positively they could not go farther," but they were made to get up and hobble along somehow, assisted for the time by comrades carrying their muskets and part of their kit.

By orders specially issued to each regiment at Santarem, captains and officers commanding companies marched in rear of the men; the majors had their posts each in rear of his wing. Lieut.-colonels were to keep moving from point to point along their battalions and have all under constant observation. The Brigadier himself rode about meanwhile everywhere having his eye on everybody, and letting them know it.

During the second part of the march they were on reduced rations. "Half a pound of bread was served out on the 27th, which was instantly consumed, as since our departure from Coria we knew of such a thing only by name." Before that, once or twice, when halted near cornfields, "the men had filled their haversacks with the green ears, which they boiled at the next bivouac"; that and rations of ship's biscuit with commissariat beef had been the general fare.

While in bivouac at Naval Moral the first rumours from the front began to arrive. "On the evening of the 27th, vague rumours reached us at Naval Moral relative to the hostile armies. We knew nothing further than that Sir Arthur Wellesley and the Spanish General Cuesta had united their forces in the plains some leagues in our front, and as the French, under Marshal Victor, the Duke of Belluno, were known not to be far distant from the allied army, a general action might be daily expected."

Naval Moral is not far from the little town of Malpartida de Plasencia, where during that night the definite news came in that a battle had taken place, and that Wellington had been defeated.

"We bivouacked near Malpartida de Plasencia," says a soldier in the ranks of the 95th, "when a report reached our corps that a battle had been fought at Talavera, and that the English had been beaten and dispersed. Although, I believe, few of us gave credit to the story, still it created some uneasiness among men and officers. Its only effect, however, upon our brigadier was to make him hurry forward with, if possible, increased speed. Our bivouac was broken up. We got under arms, and leaving the sick of the brigade (some fifty in all) behind us in the town, under charge of a subaltern from each regiment, we commenced one of the longest marches, with scarcely a halt or pause, in the military records of any country."

Plasencia was a four days' march from Talavera in ordinary conditions and ordinary weather, a distance of some sixty-three miles—the distance in England, speaking roughly, between London and Dover, or between York and Liverpool. It was traversed by the Light Brigade on foot in twenty-six hours. Not only that, but the final spurt came on the top of the incessant hard marching of the previous days. They had, indeed, only just got to their bivouac near Plasencia, after marching twenty miles on end during the past night, when they were ordered to turn out and start, hot-foot, for Talavera.

Distant firing began to be heard soon after they set off again. The effect of it was to incite Craufurd and all the Brigade to redoubled exertions.

"Before day dawned," to quote one of the officers, "we were off again, and ere long something like a distant cannonade was heard. Our suspense and anxiety can easily be imagined, aware as we were of the proximity of the hostile armies to each other. We arrived at Oropesa at midday, where General Craufurd considered a short halt necessary. He then directed the commanding officers of regiments to select and leave at Oropesa such men as they thought incapable of enduring the forced march which he determined to make, and not to halt until he reached the British army which was known to be engaged in our front, as the distant but unceasing cannonade plainly announced. Having rested his brigade in this burning plain, where water was not to be procured, General Craufurd put us in motion towards Talavera de la Reyna."

The weakest men were left at Oropesa, together with the baggage-mules and tents, and then, after hastily cooking a meal, the Brigade was off again.

One and all were in "the highest degree of feverish anxiety and excitement. The one only feeling was to push forward to throw our mite into the scale and to lend a helping hand to our brothers-in-arms."

We soon met *wounded* Spanish soldiers, and Spanish soldiers *not wounded*, bending their course in a direction *from* the field of battle. I regret to say that stragglers from the British army, some without a wound, were also taking a similar direction to the rear. As they passed our column they circulated all sorts and kinds of reports of a most disheartening nature. 'The British army was utterly defeated!' 'Sir Arthur Wellesley was wounded,' and by others, 'he was killed.' All was suspense and uncertainty. One thing was nevertheless certain—that the cannonade continued without cessation.

"The road," relates Captain George Napier, who also describes the meeting with the runaways, "was crowded with cowardly fugitives—Spaniards innumerable, and lots of English commissary clerks, paymasters, sutlers, and servants, to say nothing of a few soldiers and officers who said they were sick—all swearing the British army was cut to pieces. How we did swear at them and hiss every fellow we met!"

"These men, we learned," says one the Rifles, "were part of General Cuesta's army which had been beaten on the 27th, and who chose to give the most disastrous account of the English army, which they stated was completely destroyed. We could not but remark that these Spaniards, who we knew to be a disorganized crew, had not forgotten to help themselves to plunder in their flight, as most of them carried some article or other to which they could have little claim, such as ham, cheese, and fowls. Some, although infantrymen, rode on excellent horses, while others drove mules, carrying sacks of flour, etc. Never was seen such a thoroughly demoralized wreck of an army."

The Spaniards belonged to some newly-raised regiments, who early on the previous evening had bolted in a sudden panic, abandoning the position they held at the sight of some French cavalry coming towards them, though still a quarter of a mile off. Many of the runaway's had been rounded up by their own cavalry, who were sent after them, and brought back to be decimated later; shot in public as cowards, one man in every ten. The others bolted off through the British camp, plundering right and left, and carrying off with them in their flight several frightened commissaries, and sutlers, "and at least one combatant officer." They hurried along in a wild panic until they met Craufurd's men, to run the gauntlet of their hisses and curses.

Throughout that afternoon and evening, and far into the night, the Light Brigade held on their way, marching their hardest and fastest. All the afternoon heavy firing was heard continuously in the distance ahead from the direction of the high ground in view towards Talavera. That at least was to the good. Fighting was then still going on! Their comrades, it was evident, were not done with. "The constant cannonade heard in front was a stimulus which had a most beneficial effect, and made the men forget for the time their extraordinary fatigue." Coat-collars were opened; chest-straps were loosened or unbuckled, as one and all stepped out more briskly than ever; flinging themselves forward as they pounded along at quickened speed through the heavy sand of the plains of Central Estramadura.

Wherever the ground was sufficiently free from obstructions, in spite of the intense sultry heat, they covered it at six miles an hour, using a pace which Sir John Moore had devised originally, and tried at Shorncliffe. That was to take three steps at a quick march, alternatively with three steps at the double, running. The expedient proved its value now as an ideal method of getting over country speedily.

"We certainly should have found a much greater difficulty in accomplishing it," to quote, also, from an officer's letter home, "had we not met several wounded British officers riding from the field of action, who told us what was passing when they left. Every man seemed anxious to push on, and all were in high spirits, hoping soon to be on the field of battle, and to be assisting their brave countrymen."

Not until two hours before midnight did the indefatigable brigadier permit a halt to be called, even for five minutes. All had kept up without a check: only seventeen men of Craufurd's 3,000 and odd soldiers fell out along the way. They had now to stop for a brief respite from sheer exhaustion during that close and steamy, airless July night. They halted close beside a cattle-pond, to rest for a short time and snatch a few mouthfuls of what provisions they had in their haversacks.

Water,—a drink of any kind, anything to quench their burning thirst,—was their urgent need. Foul and repulsive as the pond-water looked, it sufficed for the parched and perspiring soldiers.

> We pressed forward until ten o'clock at night, when, having reached a pool of stagnant water near the road, in which cattle had been watered during the summer and where they had constantly wallowed, a halt was ordered.... The whole brigade, officers and soldiers, rushed into this muddy water and drank with an eagerness and avidity impossible to describe.
> After a short repose on the banks of this horse-pond, we again got under weigh, and without another halt joined the British army in its position at Talavera.

In that last stage thirty miles were covered without a stop.

They were in sight of the white houses of the town of Talavera early on the morning of the 29th, and within a short time of that they learned the actual state of affairs.

> As we advanced nearer to the scene of action the reports became less formidable, until the heights of Talavera burst upon our sight, and we hailed, with three loud huzzas, the news that the British, in the action the preceding day with the French, had been victorious!

They cheered their heartiest for their lucky comrades: for themselves they were poignantly and bitterly disappointed. After all their rough trial, their extreme exertions, they had reached the scene too late! "After all our efforts we arrived on the field of battle just soon enough to be too late!" From Craufurd himself downwards the keenest and most intense regret was the one feeling among all. Why had they made those halts during the earlier portion of the march?

"Could General Craufurd," continues the same officer, "have foreseen that by those halts his brigade would have arrived *a few hours too late*, I feel thoroughly convinced that he would have pushed on *pêle-mêle* without a single halt between Santarem and the field of battle."

Yet they had done their best. "Our Brigade did all that men could do to reach the field of action in time." They were in the immediate neighbourhood of the field of battle between six and seven o'clock, and thereupon they announced their approach to Wellington's camp in style. "Our bugles struck up merrily as we crossed the field of battle early in the morning on the 29th of July."

Craufurd had already reported his arrival to Wellington. He declared his men ready to proceed forthwith on any service to which they might be told off, regardless of the experiences they had just gone through.

"In the last twenty-four hours," says an officer, "I had only six ounces of mouldy bread and some bad water. . . . in which time we marched fifty-two miles, resting three hours on the ground." The brigadier was taken at his word. The sturdy lads of the Light Brigade at once passed through the camp to the outposts to assume charge there. They pushed out their own sentries to within gunshot range of the position across the little River Alberche, to which the French had withdrawn during the night, while the men not required at the outposts lent invaluable aid to their wearied comrades who had taken part in the battle by searching for and bringing in the wounded from all over the field.

6

The Astonishing Adventures of Wellington's Chief Scout

No man of all the British army in Spain probably went through more adventures and rendered his country more useful service than did the officer who filled the *rôle* of Wellington's chief scout, Colonel Colquhoun Grant. He lived to be a general and a Knight of the Bath.

A soldier born was Colquhoun Grant; no finer fellow ever wore the King of England's uniform; the *beau ideal* of a British officer and gentleman. This is what was said of him by one who knew him intimately as a relative:

> Equal to most officers of the Peninsular army in military capacity, he far surpassed everyone I ever met for the milder virtues of the Christian soldier, and for all that was amiable, kind, and benevolent in disposition. Colonel Grant was devotedly fond of his profession. He entered the Army at a very early age, having, I believe, hardly completed his fifteenth year.

The fascinating and romantic tale of his career in Spain cannot be better told than in the words of those who served with him before the enemy. General Napier, the historian of the war, was among them. He speaks of Colquhoun Grant in these words; writing in a personal memorandum he once sent to the then Duke of Cambridge:

> In the Peninsular War he was selected by the Duke of Wellington as one of his exploring officers, men of whom the duke in after-times said: 'No army in the world ever produced the like.' I say exploring officers, because Grant was also employed to

conduct a great portion of the secret intelligence; and it might be erroneously supposed he acted personally as a spy. There *was* a Grant who did so, and a very remarkable man he was: but Colquhoun Grant, though he repeatedly penetrated the enemy's line, and even passed days in their cantonments, was always in uniform, trusting entirely to his personal resources; and with reason, for his sagacity, courage, and quickness were truly remarkable, indeed, scarcely to be matched. As conductor of the Secret Intelligence, Grant, besides his own personal exploits, displayed a surprising skill. I have seen letters from *alcaldes* and other agents of his from all parts of Spain, conveying intelligence rare and useful; and it is worth noticing that he told me that his best, and, indeed, his only sure spies, were men who acted from patriotism, and would not accept money. His talent in discovering them was not the least of his merits."

"Colonel Colquhoun Grant," to add another officer's testimony, "had a singular talent, not only for the acquisition of languages, but of the different dialects of languages. He was a proficient in those of all the provinces of Spain; was intimately acquainted with their customs, their songs, their music, and with all their habits and prejudices. He was, moreover, an enthusiastic admirer of the Spanish character; was well read in all their popular works; he danced even their national dances most admirably. With such qualifications and predilections so flattering to the national sentiment of the Spaniards, in union with a character of the most rigid morality, it will not be surprising that he was a favourite with them; particularly with their priests and peasantry, who spread his name and character so widely, and were so devotedly attached to him that in most critical situations, and when surrounded by posts of the French army, he was at all times secure.

"In collecting accurate information of the French army, as he informed me, and as was well known to Lord Wellington, he was occasionally in their rear, where he obtained exact intelligence, not only of their numbers and equipment, but of the description of their troops, the manner in which their cavalry was mounted, the number and equipment of their guns, the state of their supplies, etc. He was acquainted not only with the character of each superior officer, but of that of each commandant of battalion. The hairbreadth escapes which he had were numerous: sleeping frequently in the fields under any shelter, or, as it frequently happened, without any, and in all kinds of weather, which he had done for two or three years. But, as he said, he always felt secure when in Spain, where one *padre*, or peasant, passed him on to another, all emulous to serve, and in admiration of the character of '*Granto Bueno*.'"

How Colquhoun Grant fell into the hands of the enemy during the Salamanca campaign, and the amazing series of strange happenings by land and sea that resulted, until at length he once again joined Wellington, equals anything, perhaps, in the pages of adventurous fiction. He had previously, more than once, been within an ace of being captured; on one occasion, indeed, at Caçeres in 1810, some of Foy's men so nearly got hold of him that he only got clear by jumping from a window and running off in his shirt, leaving his papers and his horse behind him. Of his capture, we had best let the tale be told by brother-officers who were on service in Spain at the time.

"When Marmont came down on Beira in 1812," says Napier in his personal narrative, "the Duke of Wellington's operations and designs were seriously affected, because, from the Spaniards' conduct, Ciudad Rodrigo was in great danger of being taken by a *coup de main*; and Almeida also, from its weakness, was in a like danger. The rapidity necessary to succour these places was very embarrassing. In this difficulty, Colquhoun Grant daringly entered the enemy's cantonments, and then perseveringly hung upon his flank, watching his every movement; counting his numbers; and, finally ascertaining that his scaling-ladders were left in Tamames, he assured the Duke that no coup de main was designed, and that Marmont's force was not such as to menace a serious invasion of Portugal. Thus time was given for arrangements which accident alone prevented being fatal to the French army."

It was immediately after this that Colquhoun Grant fell into the enemy's hands. That came about in this way, as Napier tells the story:

> Attended by Leon, a Spanish peasant, faithful and quick of apprehension, who had been his companion on many former occasions, he reached the Salamanca district, passed the Tormes during the night in uniform, for he never assumed any disguise, and remained three days in the midst of the French camp. He thus obtained exact information of Marmont's object, of his provisions and scaling-ladders, making notes, which he sent to Wellington from day to day by Spanish agents. The third night, some peasants brought him an order worded thus: 'The notori-

ous Grant is within the circle of the cantonments, the soldiers are to strive for his capture, and the guards will be placed in a circle round the army.' Grant consulted the peasants, and before daylight entered the village of Huerta, close to a ford on the Tormes, where there was a French battalion, and, on the other bank of the river, cavalry *vedettes*, patrolling back and forward for the space of 300 yards, yet meeting always at the ford.

At daylight, when the soldiers were at their alarm-post, he was secretly brought, with his horse, behind the gable of a house, which hid him from the infantry, and was near the ford. The peasants, standing on loose stones, spread their large cloaks to hide him from the *vedettes* until the latter were separated to the full extent of their beat. Then, putting spurs to his horse, he dashed through the ford between them, received their cross-fire without damage, and reaching a wood, baffled pursuit, and was soon rejoined by Leon.

Grant had before ascertained that ladders for storming Rodrigo were prepared, and the French officers openly talked of doing so; but desiring further to test this and ascertain if Marmont's march might not finally be for the Tagus, wishing also to discover the French force, he placed himself on a wooded hill near Tamames where the road branched off to the passes of Rodrigo. There, lying *perdu* while the army passed in its march, he noted every battalion and gun, and finding all went towards Rodrigo, entered Tamames, and found the greatest part of their scaling-ladders had been left there, showing that the intention to storm Rodrigo was not real. This it was which had allayed Wellington's fears for that fortress when he sought to entice Soult to battle.

Marmont passed the Coa, but Grant preceded him, with intent to discover if his further march would be by Guarda upon Coimbra, or by Sabugal upon Castello Branco. To reach the latter it was necessary to descend from a very high ridge, or rather succession of ridges, by a pass at the lower mouth of which stands Peñamacor. Upon one of the inferior ridges of this pass he placed himself, thinking the dwarf oaks which covered the hill would secure him from discovery; but from the higher ridge the French detected his movements with their glasses; and in a few moments Leon, whose lynx eyes were always on the watch, called out: 'The French! The French!' Some dragoons came galloping up; Grant and his follower darted into the wood for a little space, and then, suddenly wheeling, rode off in a different direction. But at every turn new enemies appeared, and at last the hunted men dismounted, and fled on foot through the low oaks.

Again they were met by infantry, detached in small parties down the sides of the pass, and directed in their chase by the waving of hats on the ridge above. Leon fell exhausted, and those who first came up killed him, in despite of his companion's entreaties: a barbarous action!

Grant they carried to Marmont, who invited him to dinner, and the conversation turned on the prisoner's exploits. The French marshal said he had been long on the watch, knew all his captive's haunts and disguises, and had discovered that only the night before he slept in the French headquarters, with other adventures which had not happened. This Grant never used any disguise; but there was another Grant, also very remarkable in his way, who used to remain for months in the French quarters, using all manner of disguises; hence the similarity of names caused the actions of both to be attributed to one. That is the only palliative for Marmont's subsequent conduct.

Treating his prisoner with apparent kindness, Marmont exacted from him an especial *parole*, that he would not permit a rescue by the *partidas*, while on his journey through Spain to France. This secured his captive, though Wellington offered 2,000 dollars to any guerilla chief who should recover him. The exaction of such a parole was a tacit compliment to the man; but Marmont sent a letter with the escort to the Governor of Bayonne, in which, still in error as to their being but one Grant, he designated his captive as 'a dangerous spy who had done infinite mischief,' and whom he had not executed on the spot out of respect to something resembling uniform which he wore. He therefore desired that at Bayonne he should be placed in irons and sent to Paris. This was so little in accord with French honour, that before the Spanish frontier was passed Grant was made acquainted with the treachery.

Apparently, while still a prisoner at Marmont's headquarters, he had at least once fallen foul of the French Marshal. What took place is related by the colonel's brother-in-law, to whom Grant told the story.

"Unable," says Sir James McGrigor, "by sifting to get much information from him respecting the British army, the Marshal treated him somewhat harshly, and said, 'It is fortunate for you, sir, that you have that bit of red over your shoulders (meaning his uniform); if you had not, I would have hung you on a gallows twenty feet high.' The colonel answered: 'Marshal, you know I am your prisoner; and, recollect, I have given you my *parole*, but hitherto I have not been treated as an officer on *parole*.' The marshal desired the French officer, who had conveyed Colonel Grant to his presence, to lead him away, and he was brought to a quarter which had been assigned to him, and was strictly guarded. Not only was a French sentinel placed at the door of his apartment, but an officer was placed in his room.

"Of this he complained greatly; and the French officers, who were daily appointed for this duty, all felt for a gallant officer, and did their duty lightly, leaving the apartment when anyone called upon him. He was visited by several of the principal inhabitants of Salamanca, to whom either by character or personally he was known. In fact, the whole population of Salamanca and its neighbourhood admired his deeds and hairbreadth escapes, and were much troubled over the annoyance he had been put to by the French, whom they cordially hated.

"One of his most frequent visitors was Dr. Curtis, head of the Irish College at Salamanca, from whom I had these particulars. The frequent visits of Dr. Curtis to Colonel Grant gave great offence to Marshal Marmont, who sent for the reverend gentlemen. As Dr. Curtis related to me, the marshal behaved very harshly to him, and threatened him much if he did not reveal what he said he was in possession of—*i.e.*, the secrets of Colonel Grant. He said: 'You frequently visit the English colonel.'

"He replied: 'I do,'

"'How is it possible, sir, that you do so without having some purpose, some business therein?'

"He replied: 'The Holy Catholic religion, which you, marshal, and I profess, enjoins us to succour the distressed, to visit the sick and prisoners, and to administer consolation to them.'

"The marshal rejoined: 'He is not of your religion, he is a heretic, a Protestant.'

"Dr. Curtis replied: 'We are both Christians, we follow the precepts of our Saviour; and he is my countryman.'

"The marshal said: 'That is false, he is *Écossais*, and you *Irlandais*. You shall immediately go to prison unless you reveal to me secrets which I am informed the English colonel has confided to you, and which it is material to the interests of the Emperor that I should be put in possession of.'

"He did not throw Dr. Curtis into prison, but he treated him most harshly, expelled him from his college, and took possession of his furniture and a valuable library.

"Even at this time, in Salamanca," continues Sir James, relating what Colquhoun Grant told him of himself, "Colonel Grant continued to convey much valuable information to Lord Wellington; and in this manner: whenever the weather was favourable, he was permitted to walk out. On such occasions some of the Spanish peasants who had been employed by him got near to him, and he put into their hands, on small twisted pieces of paper, such information as he had collected; and they, as Lord Wellington afterwards informed me, carried these to headquarters, where they always received handsome rewards. I have reason to believe that the priests organized these messengers, trustworthy, hardy fellows, for this very dangerous vocation.

"Not long after this, although Colonel Grant had given his *parole*, so formidable did he appear from the attachment to him of the priests and peasantry, and so universally was he known and admired by the Spaniards, that, when Marmont sent him off to Bayonne, it was with an escort of 300 men and six guns! So fearful was he that a rescue might be attempted by the guerillas and peasantry!"

As a fact, his rescue had been arranged for by Wellington. Wellington had sent word to Grant not to give his *parole* while in Spain, and had settled terms with several guerilla leaders to attempt a rescue at certain points between Salamanca and Bayonne. But Colquhoun Grant had already given his *parole*, and on learning of the scheme declined to take advantage of it.

This is what happened to Colonel Grant at Bayonne, and how he got away there from his escort.

"On the way," as Colquhoun Grant told his brother-in-law, "he entertained the French officers with several of his exploits, and the manner of his escape when some of his hearers were in pursuit of him at different places. Gallant men themselves, they admired his courage and address, but," adds Dr. McGrigor (Sir James was Principal Medical Officer to Wellington's army), "whether any of them connived at his escape, or not, I never could learn from Colonel Grant.

"When the party arrived at Bayonne, it was in the evening; they halted in a place or square, and all busied themselves in procuring billets. Grant, finding himself alone, walked off, found his way to a place from whence the diligence started, took his place to Paris as an American, and soon after left Bayonne. When he was missed, he did not exactly know; but, as he afterwards heard, as soon as he was missed, parties of horse and foot were sent in search of him, the police and infantry soldiers searched every corner of Bayonne and of the environs, and parties of light cavalry scoured the whole country in the direction of the Spanish frontier, making sure that he would endeavour to get through to Spain, where he had so many friends. The search for him was long continued, but no Colonel Grant was to be found. He had, in the meantime, arrived in Paris; the last place in the world where they would have thought of looking for him!"

He had, indeed, got away from Bayonne by sheer audacity and coolness, according to another version of the manner in which he escaped:

> At Bayonne, in ordinary cases, the custom was for prisoners to wait on the authorities and receive passports for Verdun. This was done; the letter was purposely delayed, and Grant with sagacious boldness refrained from escaping towards the Pyrenees. Judging that if the governor did not recapture him at once he would entirely suppress the letter and let the matter drop, he asked at the hotels if any French officer was going to Paris, and finding that General Souham, then on his return from Spain, was so bent, he introduced himself, requesting permission to join his party. The other readily assented, and while thus travelling, the general, unacquainted with Marmont's intentions, often rallied his companion about his adventures, little thinking he was then an instrument to forward the most dangerous and skilful of them all.
> In passing through Orleans, Grant, by a species of intuition, discovered a secret English agent, and from him received a recommendation to another in Paris. He looked upon Marmont's double-dealing, and the expressed design to take away his life, as equivalent to a discharge of his *parole*, which was, moreover, only given with respect to Spain. Hence, on reaching Paris, he took leave of Souham, opened an intercourse with the Parisian agent, and obtained money. He would not go before the

police to have his passport examined, but took lodgings in a public street, frequented the coffee-houses and visited the theatres boldly, for the secret agent, intimately connected with the police, soon ascertained that his escape had been unnoticed.

As a fact, no less extraordinary than the experiences he had gone through, were those that Colquhoun Grant met in Paris.

"On his arrival," to take up the version of the story as the colonel himself told it, "he found his way to the house of Mr. McPherson, an eminent jeweller and a worthy Highlander, of whose kindness to his countrymen he had heard much. This old gentleman had been many years a resident in Paris. During the time of the Revolution he had been thrown into a dungeon by Robespierre, and had been doomed to the guillotine, but had escaped that death by the death of the monster Robespierre himself.

"While with Mr. McPherson, as an American, and with an American passport, Grant moved freely about Paris; made it a point to be present at all the reviews, and by entering into conversation with various individuals, whom he met out of doors and at Mr. McPherson's table, got correct information of the reinforcements sent to all the armies, particularly that of Portugal. At Mr. McPherson's he frequently met a gentleman with whom he contracted some degree of intimacy. These two gentlemen, as acquaintances, became most acceptable to each other, and Grant gained very much valuable information from him; and, extraordinary as it may appear, he continued to convey that information to Lord Wellington!"

"I do not exactly recollect," Sir James McGrigor adds on his own account, "where the British army was at the time in Spain; but one day, when I was with Lord Wellington on business, a day on which the mail for England was being made up at headquarters, Lord Wellington, addressing me, said: 'Your brother-in-law is certainly one of the most extraordinary men I have ever met with. Even now, when he is in Paris, he contrives to send me information of the greatest moment to our Government. I am now sending information of his to ministers, of the utmost value, about the French armies in every quarter; information which will surprise them, and which they cannot by any possibility get in any other way: and what is more, which I am quite sure is perfectly correct. Go into the next room, and desire Fitzroy (Lord Fitzroy Somerset, afterwards Lord Raglan) to show you the information from Grant enclosed in the dispatch to Lord Bathurst.'

"About this time his friends, whom he met at Mr. McPherson's, told that gentleman to desire Grant to discontinue going to the reviews; and further, that he must remain quiet for some time, change his appearance if possible, and get a different passport. All this was accomplished. He assumed a different appearance, and got another American passport, that of an American gentleman recently deceased in Paris (one Jonathan Buck). But McPherson was further informed that the police were secretly making inquiries for him; and it was decided that he must leave Paris. He did so, and got to the coast, off which he learned that a British man-of-war was stationed."

There, at a seaport at the mouth of the Loire, Colonel Grant first took a passage in an American ship, but its departure was unexpectedly delayed. As the best thing to do he frankly told his situation to the captain, who desired him to pass himself off as a discontented seaman, gave him a sailor's clothing with forty dollars, and sent him to lodge the money in the American consul's hands, as a pledge that he would prosecute for ill-usage when he reached the United States. This being the custom, the consul gave him a certificate to pass from port to port as a discharged sailor seeking a ship.

Colquhoun Grant immediately decided on making his attempt in another way.

A promise of ten *napoleons* induced a French boatman to row him in the night to a small island, where, by usage, English vessels watered unmolested, and, in return, permitted the few inhabitants to fish and traffic without interruption. The masts of the British ships were dimly seen beyond the island, and the termination of all Grant's toils seemed at hand, when the boatman, from fear or malice, returned to port..... The money promised was Grant's all, and the boatman demanded full payment; but with admirable coolness he gave him one piece and a rebuke for his misconduct. The other threatened a reference to the police, yet found himself overmatched in subtlety. His opponent replied that he would then denounce him as aiding the escape of a prisoner of war, and adduce the price of his boat as a proof of his guilt.

The indomitable nature of the man, however, was far from being daunted by the difficulties and dangers that at that moment surrounded him.

On being put ashore, he determined not to stay where he was.

He learned that not many leagues from where he was a French marshal of Scottish descent (Marshal Macdonald, the hero of Wagram), a relation of his mother's, had his seat, and he determined to make for it. He travelled the whole of that night, and during the following day remained concealed in a dry ditch overhung with weeds. He resumed his journey the following night, and on the next day reached the mansion of the Marshal. On obtaining an interview with him, and explaining the object of his visit, the marshal immediately acknowledged the relationship, and ordered refreshments for him; but said he did not think it would be safe for him to prolong his stay in his house. The marshal, however, lent him 100 *louis*, with which he returned to the port he had left, where he hired another fishing-boat.

An old fisherman and his son now undertook to take Colquhoun Grant out to a British ship, and they faithfully performed their bargain; but for the moment there were no cruisers near the port. However, the fisherman caught some fish, with which he sailed towards the southward, having heard of an English ship-of-war being there. A glimpse was obtained of her, and they were steering that way when a shot from a coast-battery brought them to, and a boat with soldiers put off to waylay them.

At the crucial moment when the sail was lowered to be coiled round the mast, the fisherman put Grant upright close to the mast, twisting the sail round him so that he was effectually concealed. The soldiers jumped on board, searched everywhere, and even probed several parts with their swords. They did not, however, discover Colonel Grant.

The soldiers, it turned out, had been sent to search for contraband, and also to warn the fisherman not to pass the battery because an English vessel (the one they were looking for) was off the coast. The old man bribed the soldiers with some fish to let him pass, assuring them that he must go on with his son, or his family would starve; saying also that he was so well acquainted with the coast that he could easily escape the enemy. Being desired to wait till night and then depart, he, under pretence of avoiding the English ship, made the soldiers point out her moorings so exactly that when darkness fell he ran her straight on board, and the intrepid Grant stood at length in safety on a British quarter-deck.

In England he got permission to choose a French officer for an exchange, that no doubt might remain as to the propriety of his escape; great was his astonishment to find in the first prison he visited the old fisherman and his son, who had been captured, notwithstanding a protection given to them for their services! Grant, whose generosity and benevolence were as remarkable as the qualities of his understanding, soon obtained their release, sent them with a sum of money to France, returned to the Peninsula, and within four months from the date of his first capture was again on the Tormes, watching Marmont's army as before!

※※※※※※

At Waterloo Sir Colquhoun Grant, as he had by then become, as Major-General, commanded Wellington's 5th Cavalry Brigade. He had five horses shot under him during the battle.

This authentic anecdote, told of him in later years when serving in Ireland, may round off our narrative of the adventures of this extraordinary man:

> Sir Colquhoun Grant, we are told, being in command at Clonmel, gave offence in some way to an honest shopkeeper, named Mulcahy, who struck the General on parade, in presence of his whole command. Some officers ran forward to seize the delinquent, but Sir Colquhoun interposed, declaring that he had been the aggressor, and as the gentleman thought proper to resent his conduct in so gross a manner, it remained for him to seek the usual reparation. 'Oh!' exclaimed Mulcahy, 'if it's for fighting you are, I'll fight you: but it shall neither be with swords nor pistols, nor anything else but my two fists.'
> And fine big mutton fists they were, sure enough, notes the recorder of the story. 'Well, then,' replied the gallant Sir Colquhoun, 'with all my heart. By insulting you, I have put myself on a level with you, and of course cannot refuse to meet you on your own terms. Come along, sir.'
> The men were dismissed, and General Grant, accompanied by his adversary and some mutual friends, repaired to the messroom, where he very speedily closed up Mr. Mulcahy's peepers, and sent him home perfectly satisfied. That was the proudest day of Mulcahy's life, and many a time did he boast of 'the black eye he got from a K.C.B.,' as if it were an honourable ordi-

nary emblazoned upon his *escutcheon*. 'Ever since that morning,' would he say also, 'let me meet Sir Colquhoun Grant where I might, in town or country, among lords or ladies, dressed in plain clothes or dizened out in gold and scarlet, he would give me his hand and say, "How are you, Billy?"'

7

Some Daring Exploits of Wellington's Other Famous Scouts

Colquhoun Grant stands by himself, foremost of all among Wellington's intelligence officers. But, at the same time, there were others, some of whom rendered notable and distinguished service on the same lines. They were, of course, as has been said, totally distinct from Wellington's secret service agents, or spies, of whom a large number were continuously at work all over the country. "Lord Wellesley," says Napier, "had to keep in his pay a numerous band of spies, who passed most of their time within the French lines. Among them was Sobral, a Spanish Councillor of State, who lived at Victor's headquarters, while Fuentes, a guitar player of celebrity, upon whom no suspicion of military intelligence rested, was allowed to pass in and out of Madrid as he liked. The best and cleverest of Lord Wellesley's spies were Spanish gentlemen, *alcaldes*, and occasionally peasants, who disdained rewards, held danger in contempt, and were deserving of praise for their boldness, talent, and virtue."

On the border line was the Captain Grant who, as has been told, some of the French officers tried to identify with Colquhoun Grant. He was John Grant, at one time an officer in the 4th Foot, then a captain of Caithness Militia, and during the war a lieut.-colonel in the Portuguese service. Working by himself, sometimes in uniform, oftener disguised—he could speak Portuguese fluently—he mostly frequented the Tagus Valley, and was indefatigable in supplying Wellington with useful information. On one occasion, indeed, in the earlier part of the war, he even intercepted a batch of important private letters from Napoleon to King Joseph, and sent them to the British headquarters.

Another man of much the same type was a German officer, Rumann by name, a captain in the 97th, who, in like manner, was continuously on the move on his own account in the country between the Douro and Salamanca, and forwarded reports to Wellington that frequently proved of great importance.

Of the intelligence officers attached to the headquarters' staff and employed openly at the front, one of the most brilliant and distinguished was Captain Somers Cocks, of the 16th Light Dragoons—killed in action at Burgos, and mourned by the whole army. He did his work for the most part with a small escort of picked troopers of his own regiment, and is described as being unmatched for his vigilance and sagacity of observation, and the skill and daring he showed in getting hold of information.

Colonel John Waters, whose exploits and adventures as a scout rank second only to those of Colquhoun Grant, was in like manner on the Headquarters' Staff. He was a Welshman by birth, the grandson of a High Sheriff of Glamorganshire, and personally a great favourite, owing to his singleness of heart and amiability of disposition. With that he was one of the most energetic and active of soldiers, ready-witted, and gifted with remarkable shrewdness and an exceptional talent for languages, together with the knack of understanding and getting on with foreigners. He had learned to speak both Portuguese and Spanish like a native—an acquirement to which he owed the fortune that attended his career. He was a captain in the Royal Scots when he got his first chance of making his mark, by saving Sir John Moore's army from total destruction—from being trapped and captured *en bloc*.

At the moment of the fateful discovery by Captain Waters, Moore's army was marching forward into the heart of Spain, full of confidence and high hopes, and with every expectation of carrying out a triumphant campaign. According to Moore's latest advices up to that moment, received from the British Minister in Spain, the Spanish patriot armies, whom Moore was on the way to assist, were holding their own successfully, and Madrid was waiting to welcome the British columns with open arms.

Captain Waters, acting as an *aide-de-camp* with the cavalry, was scouting by himself far in advance of the army. While so doing, at the village of Valdestillos, near Sahagun, to the north of Valladolid, he intercepted a dispatch of the utmost urgency from Marshal Berthier, Napoleon's chief of the staff, to Marshal Soult. It announced that the Spanish armies Sir John Moore was marching to join had been defeated and scattered, and that Madrid had surrendered, and had been in the complete possession of the French for the past ten days. Napoleon himself, the dispatch stated, was rapidly moving at the head of greatly superior forces to attack Moore's army, and orders had been sent to the other French armies in Northern Spain to concentrate and close round the British so as to hold them fast, enormously outnumbered, as in a net. Soult was to push across so as to cut off Moore's retreat and bar him from reaching the coast.

The dispatch fell into Captain Waters's hands by a strange chance. It had been sent in the care of a young French staff-officer, riding, very imprudently, without an escort. He had ridden safely for over 150 miles until he reached Valdestillos, where he halted at the posting-house—the village inn—to get a fresh horse. The villagers, as it befell, were celebrating a local festival on that day and holding revel, and dancing in front of the inn at the moment the French officer rode up. In a loud and arrogant tone he called for the innkeeper. The man was dancing among the rest, and shouted back to the officer that he would have to wait: he was going to finish his dance first.

The French captain lost his temper, swore at the Spaniard, swung himself out of his saddle, and striding in hot anger into the middle of the dancers, roughly laid hold of the innkeeper and tried to drag him away to go and get the horse. The man resisted, and the girl he had been dancing with joined in the scuffle. She freed her partner, shoving back the officer, who in a fury shouted in her face a brutal insult. Whipping out a knife from her garter for answer, the girl stabbed the young Frenchman to the heart then and there. The dead man's valise was searched and the dispatch was found. As that took place Captain Waters came riding up.

The document was of little use to the Spanish peasants, who had no idea of its importance, nor thought of the British general in the matter. They would, however, not part with it. Captain Waters had to use all his arts of cajolery to get them to give it up to him. The innkeeper refused to let it go for less than twenty dollars. Captain Waters paid that sum, and at once rode off with his find. "The accidental discovery thus obtained was the more valuable," we are told, "as neither money nor patriotism had induced the Spaniards to bring in any information of the enemy's situation."

That was Captain Waters's first piece of important service. His second was performed just six months later. He had then got his majority in his regiment, and had been attached to the reorganized Portuguese army, with the local rank of Lieut.-Colonel. It took place at Oporto, where, as has been related, Colonel Waters, by finding the boats for Wellington to cross the Douro and seize the key of the position occupied by the enemy, the Seminary buildings, enabled the British army to achieve its first great success in the war.

Wellington, after Talavera, had Colonel Waters transferred to the Headquarters' Staff, making a special application for him to the authorities in England. "I have employed him," wrote Wellington, "in several important affairs which he has always transacted in a manner satisfactory to me, and his knowledge of the language and customs of the country has induced me to send him generally with the patrols employed to ascertain the position of the enemy, in which services he has acquitted himself most ably."

Betweenwhiles, when not on scout among the French outposts, during the months that the British army lay in the Lines of Torres Vedras, and was watching Masséna after that marshal's withdrawal into Eastern Portugal, Colonel Waters found occupation as huntsman and earth-stopper to Wellington's pack of hounds, and so he continued to employ his leisure on other occasions later, during the intervals of the fighting whenever the army was in winter-quarters.

It was while Masséna was falling back before Wellington in the final stages of his retreat from Portugal that Colonel Waters performed a fine exploit of coolness and pluck—his daring escape, after being taken prisoner, from the midst of the French army in broad daylight. He had had, a short while before, a preliminary adventure, characteristic of his nerve and promptness in emergency.

On that occasion, with a brother staff-officer, a captain in the 3rd Guards, he was one morning tracking the French close on Masséna's heels, dodging from point to point beside the road along which the enemy were retreating, as the pair kept up with and watched the French rearguard. At one point where steep ground on that side stopped them, the two coolly descended to the road, and rode along it a short distance in rear of the last of the French regiments. They had not observed on the road three French *gendarmes*, men belonging to a picked corps of old soldiers, whose duty it was to patrol roads in war, safeguard convoys, and check straggling on the line of march. Colonel Waters and his companion, it would seem, first discovered the *gendarmes* on casually looking back. It was an awkward discovery, but the colonel promptly formed a plan for getting out of the fix.

The two British officers had on blue *surtouts*, the everyday wear of the staff, and they realized that the *gendarmes* took them for French officers. Slowing their horses down to a walk, they gradually let the three men nearly overtake them. Then they wheeled round their horses sharply, and grappled two of the Frenchmen before they could use their weapons.

The two *gendarmes* were roughly unhorsed and flung to the ground, where they lay, apparently stunned by the fall. The third man spurred up his horse to escape and galloped off by a side-path. Both officers went after him, but they could not catch him, and he disappeared in a ravine. Then they went back quickly to the other two, but the Frenchmen had had time to recover their senses and had gone, leaving their horses behind. Taking possession of the two horses, Colonel Waters and his companion, each leading his captive by its bridle, rode back until they rejoined headquarters.

On another day, while again scouting close in rear of Masséna's retreating columns with a couple of dragoons, Colonel Waters came across a small French baggage-guard following quite close to the main army. With ready boldness the three pounced down upon the party, taking it by surprise. They beat off the escort of soldiers, sent them flying, and, after ransacking the baggage, galloped away before the nearest French troops could come to the rescue, taking with them the best of the French mules as Colonel Waters's personal prize.

It was a short while after this, on April 3, 1811, that the colonel fell into the hands of the French. He was by himself at the time, and had crossed the River Coa and ridden up to a small bluff, whence he was watching a distant movement of the enemy through his telescope, when four French hussars suddenly stole up and sprang on him, making him prisoner. They took him before the nearest French general, Regnier, who ordered him to be taken on to Salamanca, Masséna's headquarters. His *parole* was offered to Colonel Waters, but refused: he would take his chance, he said, with some other British prisoners whom the French were sending in the same direction. The only favour he would ask was to be allowed to ride his own horse. It was one of the two horses which he and his Guardsman friend had taken from the *gendarmes*. "Dragon" was the name that Waters had given the horse.

There was some difficulty over the horse at first. Some of the French recognized Dragon as having been one of their own animals, and Colonel Waters was closely questioned how he had come by the horse. He explained briefly that it had been fairly captured, but gave no details. The three *gendarmes*, as it happened, on regaining their comrades had made up a story that they had been ambushed and attacked by a dozen English soldiers at once, who had overpowered them by force of numbers and taken their mounts from them. Waters's statement was accepted without further inquiry being made, and his request to be allowed to ride Dragon until he got to Salamanca was granted, and he was taken off to commence his journey with the train of other prisoners. He had, though, made up his mind to escape at the first opportunity that offered; which was why he had refused to give his *parole*.

Meanwhile Wellington had heard what had happened from some French prisoners, captured by our cavalry on the day after Colonel Waters's misadventure. Waters had, of course, been speedily missed, and the French prisoners were questioned as soon as they were brought in. They had seen, they admitted, such an officer as was described to them among the captives in General Regnier's camp—"a fair-haired, blonde man, wearing a small cocked hat." The news was a blow to Wellington. "His loss," he wrote of Colonel Waters in his next dispatch to England, "is severely felt." But in a very short time a spy brought in the intelligence that Waters had refused to give his *parole*. Wellington understood what that meant. "Colonel Waters will not remain long in the hands of the enemy!" he cheerfully remarked when refusing to have the captured officer's baggage forwarded to the French outposts under flag of truce—an act of convenience and courtesy usual on both sides when officers of rank were taken prisoners. Wellington proved to be justified in his expectation of again seeing Colonel Waters at headquarters before very long.

The prisoner had, for his part, lost no time in arranging for an escape. He kept a watchful eye over Dragon first of all, managing somehow to retain the horse under his own personal care by night and day. As he took careful note, the French *gendarmes* of his escort, whenever they halted on the road at night, turned their horses out to graze in the nearest fields. Colonel Waters contrived to prevent Dragon being fed on green fodder, and secured a supply of oats instead. He had his own reasons for that arrangement.

At Ciudad Rodrigo, where the prisoners stopped for a couple of days, he was kept in confinement; but a Spaniard of his acquaintance, whom Waters had befriended on some former occasion, was able to get access to him privately. The Spaniard offered to do anything in his power to assist the colonel. "Only get me a new pair of very sharp rowels to my spurs, that is all I want!" was the answer. It was done, and the rowels were smuggled in and received by Colonel Waters that night. It was just in time. The prisoners were all marched off in company with a column of infantry at seven o'clock next morning.

The opportunity for escape the colonel had anticipated and was watching for offered itself as they were nearing Salamanca at noon on the day following. It was very hot weather, under a broiling sun, and after crossing a wide and shelterless plain they had reached the edge of a large wood. The column halted there, and the soldiers were allowed to lie down. Most of the mounted *gendarmes* of the escort with the prisoners also got off their horses to take a rest. That gave the chance Colonel Waters wanted. He managed to delay getting down from his horse for a moment. Then he turned Dragon round and using his new rowels with effect rode off at his hardest.

He met with a mishap as he started off by riding into a tree, which knocked off his hat, but the collision did not check him for many seconds. He was quickly clear of the wood and riding out across the plain. So sudden and totally unexpected by the French was his dash off that he had got a fair lead before pursuit began.

The chase was taken up hotly. Like a pack of hounds in full cry, the *gendarmes* came after their prisoner, careering at a pelting gallop. The plain extended for some miles, bare and open for the most part, and the road over it was thronged by columns of French infantry on the march, following each other along and beside it. Waters had to get past them, a hatless fugitive, galloping furiously, with behind him, riding also at their hardest, several chasing gendarmes. Some of the men in the regiments, as the chase swept by, levelled their muskets at him and fired, but not a single one of the bullets fortunately hit either him or Dragon. Others, of more sporting instincts it may be, gave him a cheer as he sped past, or called out mocking words of encouragement. At any rate, he got by all safely.

For one moment at the first it had seemed likely to go badly with the fugitive. Dragon was a slow beast, as Colonel Waters had found out before. His want of speed let several of the *gendarmes* get close up at the outset of the chase, so near, indeed, that at one time, not very long after the start, two or three of them were close on Dragon's heels. For some reason, luckily, none of the Frenchmen thought of using their pistols. Their quarry meanwhile was able to keep just ahead, for Dragon, at any rate, proved a good stayer. Then, as the chase proceeded, thanks to Colonel Waters's forethought about the oats, the pace began to tell on the French pursuers. Dragon shouldered his way steadily on, untiringly, without faltering, while the grass-fed horses of the dragoons began to get blown.

The pursuers were dropping back more and more and tailing away, when, seeing a wooded hollow at a little distance on the farther side of the road, Colonel Waters made for it. He had to attempt a daring dash between two French columns on the march, but he risked it, and got through unscathed. Neither man nor horse had been touched by a bullet all through. Crossing the road rapidly, Waters got to the wooded hollow and dipped down into it. Then, plunging into the thick bushes and underwood, he finally vanished from the view of the French.

From there he managed without molestation to make his way round by a rough cross track among the mountains to Tamames, which place he reached an hour before the following midnight. Fuentes de Onoro was reached in thirty-six hours from Tamames, after which all that remained was for the escaped Colonel to report his return to Wellington at headquarters.

So ended one of the most exciting adventures of its kind perhaps that a British staff-officer ever experienced in the war.

One is rather sorry to hear that Colonel Waters sold Dragon not long afterwards. Wellington himself was surprised at it, and asked the reason why. "Because, my lord," was the answer, "I was very near being taken again on him when with your lordship at the Battle of Fuentes de Onoro. That would have been awkward, as the horse is known to the French." On the occasion at Fuentes de Onoro, a bold charge of French dragoons into the heart of the British position all but surrounded Wellington and his Staff, who had to ride their best to get back into safety, with some of the enemy only a few yards off, almost among them indeed, and racing to head them off.

Colonel Waters in his career missed none of the great days of the war. He acted as Wellington's adjutant-general at the final attack on Badajoz and again at Salamanca; and after that he did good service on the staff at Vittoria. He was wounded, in the Pyrenees, while receiving a personal order from Wellington; for the first and only time in the war. He was struck on the head, on the temple, by a bullet that went through his hat. It was the narrowest of escapes, but the light-hearted colonel did not let his wound keep him long among the casualties. He turned up, cheerful and smiling as usual, at headquarters a couple of days later, and presented himself before Wellington, as ready for anything he might wish him to do. "Your head, colonel, must be as hard as a rock," was Wellington's comment as he warmly welcomed his invaluable subordinate.

Again, in the campaign against Soult, in Southern France, once more Colonel Waters found opportunities of making himself useful in his old work of ferreting out the intentions of the enemy. "We have found since crossing the French frontier," says one of our cavalry officers, "that he has not lost his talent in coming into so new a field. He is constantly in rear of the French army, and ever bringing the best information, and his quietly withdrawing from headquarters and subsequent absence of a few days is ever the fore runner of satisfactory news respecting the enemy's force and movements."

Colonel Waters was on the Staff at Waterloo in due course. During the latter part of that battle, on Sir Edward Barnes, "our fire-eating Adjutant-General," and his successor, General Elley, of Talavera fame, being both incapacitated by wounds, he had the distinction of filling the post, and his signature stands at the foot of Wellington's official return of the killed and wounded at Waterloo.

To conclude: Sir John Waters, K.C.B., as he became, was for his services in the Peninsular War, awarded the Gold Cross, with four clasps for the Battles of Nive, Nivelle, Orthez, and Toulouse, the Cross itself being inscribed: "Badajoz," "Salamanca," "Vittoria," and "Pyrenees."

8

Wellington the War Lord in the Field

Here is a look round behind the scenes: a flying glance, as it were, at Wellington himself and life at headquarters in the intervals of the fighting.

To begin with a glimpse at the personality of the "Commander of the Forces," as was Wellington's official designation throughout the Peninsular War. He was then between forty and forty-five years of age, a man of middle height, slightly built but wiry, with a long face and prominent aquiline nose. That nose the whole army knew and welcomed the sight of when hard fighting was on hand, as eagerly as ever Napoleon's men looked out for the little cocked hat and *redingote gris*. "The sight of his long nose among us on a battle morning," says one officer, "was worth 10,000 men any day of the week !" Among the men one of his names was, "Arty, that long-nosed—that licks the *Parleyvoos!*"

Endowed by Nature with an iron constitution, no climate or season seemed to affect Wellington, and he kept himself at all times in condition by hard training; ever keenly on the alert and active in mind and body. He could do with very little sleep as a rule, and had the invaluable faculty of being able to snatch moments of rest at any time: on the battlefield, indeed, on occasion; as at Talavera, when he lay down and took a nap in the lull during the fighting on the second day, while King Joseph and his two marshals were wrangling about the next attack; also at Salamanca, after he had given Pakenham's Third Division its orders, while waiting for Marmont to commit himself to his fatal move.

At Talavera:

Wellesley and Cuesta had arranged to meet at the central redoubt between their armies; Cuesta failing to appear, Wellesley dismounted, lay down his cloak, and slept calmly till he should appear. He slept so till noon.... At that drowsy hour the French drums began to roll, announcing that the King of Spain and the Indies had made up his mind.

At Salamanca:

> His battle-front was ready, but Marmont's attack was still two miles' distant. 'Watch the French, Fitzroy,' he said to his *aide-de-camp*, Lord Fitzroy Somerset, 'I am going to take a rest; when they reach that gap in the hills wake me.' Then he lay down on his cloak on the heath among the sweet *gum-cistes* flowers and was asleep in a minute.

"His countenance was very animated; his keen, clear, violet-coloured eye full of intelligence," describes an officer. "Eyes bright and searching as those of an eagle," says one who saw him in the lines of Torres Vedras, one morning, "standing on the highest point and looking around him." In the closing years of the war, we are told, "his hair was beginning to show the slightest tinge of grey, but not so much as to detract from the youthfulness of his general appearance."

At all times Spartan severity was the rule of Wellington's life in the field, as far as he himself was personally concerned. It had been his way to keep himself in strict training from the first, indeed; to practice adapting himself to all circumstances in which he might find himself on service. When going out to India as a young colonel, for instance, he greatly scandalized the naval captain commanding the frigate he went out in (Captain Benjamin Page of the *Caroline*) by his habit of going to bed fully dressed: "turning into his cot all standing, like a trooper's horse." "Colonel Wellesley," as he then was, "explained that, as he was starting on a campaign in India, he wished to accustom himself to sleeping in his clothes; but Captain Page was not satisfied till his steward assured him that, although the colonel slept in his breeches, he took them off and tubbed before he appeared at breakfast."

This was Wellington's turnout for a day of battle, as his officers saw him in the Peninsular War:

> He was dressed in a light grey frock-coat (he always wore grey when there was a chance of active work, the colour being less conspicuous from afar than blue), a cocked hat, low in the crown, without a plume, and covered in oilskin, a pair of black

leather leggings, fastened at the sides and reaching half up the calf, protected his legs, and he wore a light steel-mounted sabre, without any sash.

Describes an officer of Light Dragoons, speaking of his appearance at other times, in particular when the army was on the march to Vittoria in the early summer of 1813:

> Headquarters sometimes dashes by us, or across our line of march, with him, who, now, like Marlborough, or the angel (I forget which) in the beginning of the last century, ' rides on the whirlwind and directs the storm,' leading, often singly, at the front. We know Lord Wellington at a great distance by his little flat-cocked hat (not a fraction of an inch higher than the crown), being set on his head completely at right angles with his person, and sitting very upright in his hussar saddle, which is simply covered with a plain blue *shabrack*. His lordship rides to all appearance devoid of sash; as, since he has been made a Spanish field-marshal, he wears on his white waistcoat, under his blue *surtout* coat, the red and gold-knotted sash of that rank, out of compliment to our allies. From the same motive, he always wears the order of the *Toison d'Or* round his neck; and on his black cockade two others, very small, of the Portuguese and Spanish national colours. His lordship, within the last year, has taken to wearing a white handkerchief instead of our black regulation, and in bad weather a French private's dragoon cloak of the same colour.
>
> I continue these details respecting our great captain (who may yet lead us to the gates of Paris), as I always found every *minutiae* of celebrated characters as much sought after by the inquisitive as the very deeds which have brought them into notice. Often he passes on in a brown study, or only returns the salutes of the officers at their posts; but at other times he notices those he knows with a hasty 'Oh! how d'ye do?' or quizzes, good-humouredly, some of us with whom he is well acquainted. His staff come rattling after him, or stop and chat a few minutes with those they know; and the *cortège* is brought up by his lordship's orderly, an old hussar of the First Germans, who has been with him during the whole Peninsular War, and who, when he speaks of him, uses a German expression, literally meaning 'good old fellow,' emphatically implying in that language at-

tachment and regard.

"His lordship," as someone else describes, "is seldom seen in full uniform; usually he wears a plain blue frock coat, a small featherless cocked hat and short cape. Often he rides about the cantonments in civilian garb, round hat and grey trousers. Indeed, nothing could be less showy than Headquarters Staff: a small group of blue-coated officers, with an orderly dragoon or two riding in the wake of the dark cape and low, glazed, cocked hat of the chief."

The studied plainness of Wellington's garb, it may be added by the way, led now and then to amusing *contretemps*. Here is one, as related by the officer of the 11th Light Dragoons, whose letters have been laid under contribution. Speaking of the year 1811, when the army was advancing up the Tagus Valley before Talavera, he tells this story:

> At Thomar, hearing that Sir Arthur was on the road, the Portuguese General, Miranda, sallied out in full dress to meet him, with a vast and gorgeous Staff, including forty-three *aides-de-camp*, expecting to meet the British General, like himself, surrounded by innumerable officers and a bodyguard. He rode on and on, however, only meeting single officers, who all appeared beneath his notice, till his continued ride at last made him doubt if he should be back in time to preside at the dinner he had prepared for the British leader and his staff at headquarters. At last his Excellency thought it well to inquire, and then he was told that he must have already met Sir Arthur. And sure enough he had, but he had never suspected that the commander-in-chief could, or would, ride without ostentation in a plain blue *surtout*, unattended by his staff, and with but a single orderly! Sir Arthur, guessing from the clatter on the road what was intended, and anxious to avoid it, on Miranda's approach had got on one side of the road, letting them all pass without notice. Highly amused at the circumstance, he quietly reached his quarters without any troublesome formalities.

This, again, is what happened when Wellington visited Cadiz in the winter after the great victory of Salamanca, to hold conference with and give advice to the Spanish Regency and Cortes, as related by another British officer:

> His entrance was expected with the most enthusiastic anxiety, the highest authorities of the country meeting him even along

his route, and conducting him in triumph along the ramparts that had been prepared for the uninterrupted passage of the *cortège* assembled to do honour to the British general. Accustomed in their own country and from the habits of the French marshals to find a commander-in-chief placing much importance in outward show or gaudy parade, the Spanish Regency and Members of Cortes met with surprise the great leader of the allied army, accompanied by Lord Fitzroy Somerset and one orderly dragoon!

To be well mounted and have a good telescope was all that interested Wellington in regard to his personal equipment. "A bold rider, who made light of a fall," he took care to be always well mounted, to which fact, indeed, on more than one occasion, he owed his preservation from capture. As a rule he rode unattended, except by his military secretary and a single orderly. The best field-glass that money could buy was another *sine qua non* for a general in command in Wellington's eyes, and the excellence of his Dollond often stood him in good stead in action. Once at least, indeed, it had a good deal to do with his winning a battle.

That was in the closing stage of the war, in the action at Sorauren, during the Battles of the Pyrenees. Wellington himself has told the story of what took place:

> A Frenchman employed as a spy came up to me and said, '*Monseigneur, voulez-vous voir le Maréchal Soult?*' pointing with his stick at a group of officers on the other side of the valley. I levelled my glass exactly as he pointed, and there, sure enough, I distinctly discerned Soult with his staff round him, several of them with their hats off and in animated conversation. He had just finished writing an order, and was giving instructions to an *aide-de-camp*, who was going off with it. As I observed him pointing towards a particular direction, where I had reason to anticipate some movement, I paid much attention to his actions, and, indeed, I saw all that was passing so clearly with my glass that I could almost have fancied I heard the *aide-de-camp* say, '*Oui, Monseigneur!*' The *aide-de-camp* presently mounted and hurried off with his order, and so convinced was I of its purport, that I immediately directed a counter-movement to be made in that quarter, which the result showed was but just in time to prevent Soult's intended operation.

Wellington adds this:

> I saw his features so distinctly, that when I met him in a drawing-room in Paris for the first time I knew him at once.

Referring to this incident, an officer of the 85th, who was looking on, adds these details:

> A crowd of horsemen arrived in our rear, the duke in his war-dress being conspicuous among them. It was then that he and Soult from opposite sides gazed at one another, each trying to divine his rival's object. The duke noticed the hurried departure of one of Soult's staff-officers towards our right, in other words the French left. He had not dismounted, though Soult did; but, turning his horse sharp round, said in tones loud enough to be heard along our line: 'Now, lads, hold your own, for there is nothing behind you'; and darted away at full speed, followed by his staff and escort in the direction that the French mounted officer had gone.... His little speech to the 85th Regiment on December 12, 1813, made them a match for twice the number of the enemy!

Of Wellington's imperturbable calmness in moments of crisis, these two instances are related by one of the officers on the Headquarters Staff:

> Once in a fog in the morning when he was pursuing the enemy he found a division of our men under Sir William Erskine much exposed in advance and nearly separated from the rest of the army, and the French in a village within a mile of where he was standing. He could see nothing. But on some prisoners being brought in he asked what French division and how many men were in the village. They, to the dismay of everyone except Wellington, said that the whole French army was there! All he said was, quite coolly, 'Oh, they are all there, are they? Well, we must mind what we are about!'

> After Fuentes de Onoro, one morning early when about to attack in order to cover the siege of Almeida, suddenly Lord Aylmer "came in to him, while he was shaving, to tell him that the French were all off, and the last cavalry mounting to be gone, the consequence of which movement relieved him entirely, gave him Almeida, and preserved Portugal. He only took the razor off for one moment and said

to Aylmer, 'I thought they meant to be off; very well!' and then another shave, just as before, and not another word till he was dressed."

This was how Wellington ordinarily spent his day in camp:

> Lord Wellington rises at six every morning and employs himself to nine (the breakfast hour) in writing. After breakfast he sees the heads of departments—*viz.*, quartermaster and adjutant-general, commissary-general, commander of the artillery, and any other officers coming to him on business. This occupies till 2 or 3 p.m., and sometimes longer, when he gets on his horse and rides till near six. This, of course, is interfered with when the troops are before the enemy. At nine he retires to write again, or employs himself until twelve, when he retires for the night. His correspondence with England and the Spanish and Portuguese governments is very extensive.

Adds another officer, speaking of the winter-quarters season of 1812-13:

> Lord Wellington reads and looks into everything. He hunts every other day almost, and then makes up for it by great diligence and instant decision on intermediate days. He works until about four o'clock, and then for an hour or two parades with anyone whom he wants to talk to up and down the little square of Frenada (amidst all the chattering Portuguese) in his grey great-overcoat.

A gallop with his hounds was Wellington's favourite form of recreation, as much as anything for strictly practical reasons, as we are told by one of the Staff. "He has a notion that it is exercise that makes headquarters more healthy than the rest of the army generally is, and that the hounds are one great cause of this." The same officer adds: "Lord Wellington has a good stud of eight hunters. He rides hard and only wants a good gallop; but, I understand, knows nothing of the sport."

An officer's letter, during the last year of the war, gives this interesting glimpse of the social side of life at Wellington's headquarters:

> Lord Wellington commemorates his old victories by dinners on their anniversaries, and does not forget those he gained in India, of which the commandant of headquarters, who shared their dangers and glories, is not a little proud. You may, therefore, rest satisfied that the honours of the headquarters of our army are

done with liberality, and, even during the most active operations, all preparation is made at the town where the baggage is quartered, in case his lordship should arrive: while, should he be detained, several mules laden with cold meat (and since we have been near the sea, with plenty of porter, and a due proportion of silver), are sent to the front.

In this connection these notes of social gatherings at headquarters from officers' diaries are in point. Records one:

April 6, 1813—Lord Wellington kept the day of the storming of Badajoz with a grand dinner yesterday; only those present at that event were invited.

May 16, 1813—Lord Wellington gave a great dinner at Frenada to Marshal Beresford on the anniversary of Albuera; a tremendous gathering and songs. I was entertained at the display of etiquette between the marshal and General Castaños (the commanders respectively of the armies of Portugal and Spain) as to who should go into the tent first; at length they went in side by side!

Apropos to that a regimental captain notes in his diary of another anniversary festivity, to which he was not invited.

July 28, 1812—Lord Wellington gave a ball in honour of the anniversary of Talavera. We dined on rations; *no* wine and *no* money!

This, again, is the account given of a festive affair while the army was in winter-quarters shortly before the opening of the Vittoria campaign. The occasion was the investiture of General Sir Lowry Cole, commanding the Fourth Division, as G.C.B. It took place at Ciudad Rodrigo.

As he has never done anything at Ciudad Rodrigo of which he is duke, Lord Wellington determined upon this opportunity to give a grand *fête* there, in the midst of the ruins: a grand dinner, ball and supper. All heads of departments, generals, public authorities, Spaniards, and English, were asked to dinner to the amount of sixty-five. The dinner and supper were half cooked at Frenada and carried over in military wagons and on mules. All the plate at headquarters was put in requisition, and there was enough to afford a change in silver at dinner. Plenty of claret, champagne and Lamego—that is, port—was sent over, etc. A caravan of glass and crockery from Almeyda, twenty-five miles off Rodrigo, from the Governor there, and from a shop just set up, I understand, there.

The whole went off very well except that it was excessively cold, as a few balls during the siege had knocked in several yards of the roof of the ballroom, and it was a hard frost at the time. Lord Wellesley staid at Frenada until half-past three, and then rode full seventeen miles to Rodrigo in two hours to dinner, dressed in all his orders, etc., was in high glee, danced himself, staid supper, and at half-past three in the morning went back to Frenada by moonlight, and arrived here before daybreak at six, so that by twelve he was ready again for business. The bare walls of the banqueting and ball room were draped with hangings, brought away from the palace of S. Ildefonzo to save them from the French; yellow damasked satin with silver borders, crimson satin and gold hangings in other rooms. The defects were concealed almost entirely.

One hole in the floor had a man near it to see no one got a leg in, and a mat was over the hole. The ladies were not very handsome, but two or three good-looking and several very ladylike in their manners. We had much drinking and toasts given on both sides at the expense of the French: 'Ferdinand the Seventh,' 'The next campaign,' 'Death to all Frenchmen,' etc. In short, several Spaniards as well as English got drunk by five o'clock in the morning, and they chaired the Prince of Orange, General Vandeleur (whom they let fall), and several others, as soon as the ladies were gone and there was nothing else to do.

French officers of rank among the prisoners found themselves now and again among the guests at Wellington's table: and under the influence of a good dinner and wine sometimes things came out informally in conversation which proved of value to the British side. This, for instance, is what happened at one such dinner, in the campaign in Southern France, after the Battle of Nivelle, where a number of the officers of the French 88th were specially invited to dine at the British commander-in-chief's table, with the set purpose this time of obtaining certain information. The officers and their regiment by a coincidence had been taken prisoners by the British 88th, the Connaught Rangers.

In the redoubt where the French 88th Regiment was captured a copy of the *Imperial Gazette* was found, containing the momentous news of the Emperor's total defeat at Leipzic. Lord Wellington, naturally anxious to hear the latest intelligence, directed one of his staff to put some questions to the chief officers of the 88th; but they would communicate nothing, sullenly declaring that they had done their own duty, and knew nothing about what was going on elsewhere.

"On hearing this," as Wellington related to Lord de Ros, "I directed they should be left alone; but I sent them an invitation to dine with me, which they accepted readily. I warned my staff to ask them no questions, but to see that they were well supplied with Madeira. Gradually they became in excellent humour and far more communicative. Watching my opportunity, I turned in an off-hand manner to the commanding officer and said:

"'*Où etait le quartier-général de l'Empereur d'après ces dernières nouvelles?*'

"'*Monseigneur,*' he replied, '*il n'y a plus de quartier-général*'

"'*Comment, plus de quartier-général?*'

"'*Monseigneur, il n'y a ni quartier-général, ni armée francaise: l'affaire est finie!*'

"Then he went on to tell me of the Battle of Hanau, of the Emperor being driven over the Rhine, and the army totally dissolved. The effect of this announcement on twenty or thirty of the principal officers of the English army round that table may be imagined, but not described!"

Our Light Dragoon correspondent tells us this of Wellington's personal *ménage* on campaign:

"His lordship has a service of plate; for the same reason (to avoid breakage) that others have metal dishes, plates, etc., in their canteen. His lordship sets a good example in his own personal baggage, scarce having anything but his clothes, boxes of papers, and a little bedstead, about twenty inches wide, without curtains, and on it a mattress of Russia leather. The whole of his baggage, including his *batterie de cuisine* for so many persons, does not require above seventy or eighty mules. Marshal Beresford has a table kept for him, according to the Portuguese custom of finding their Marshals in the field, and has, as well as the Commander of the Cavalry, a silver service. We were amused at the house of the latter this winter (1812-13) to see two footmen, as in

London, dressed in livery, and in breeches and stockings!"

As to that, indeed, more than one of the generals under Wellington kept a better table than did the commander-in-chief, as Wellington himself told one of his staff-officers on a certain occasion. "An officer of the Staff," according to the story, "who had not long joined, being one day asked to dinner by Lord Wellington, hesitated a little, and at length stammered out that, although greatly honoured by his lordship's notice, he was awkwardly situated, being previously engaged to Sir Rowland Hill. 'Go, by all means,' was the reply; 'you will get a much better feed than here.' And then his lordship added: 'As you are a stranger, I will give you some useful information. Cole gives the best dinners in the army; Hill the next best; mine are no great things; Beresford's and Picton's are very bad indeed!'"

At the same time Wellington could be unpleasant to a degree, the severest and most domineering of masters. None who crossed the Chief in angry mood was spared, whatever his rank. Haughty and self-confident to a degree by nature at all times, he showed himself impatient of anything that seemed in the least like interference with his methods or a display of independence or unauthorized initiative on the part of those under his orders. The offering of unasked-for advice, from whoever it might come, was taken by him rather as an unwarranted liberty, an unpardonable trespassing on his supreme authority. And he could express himself when out of temper in language that in its blunt outspokenness was deliberately insulting.

Even a thick-skinned, tough-grained veteran like Picton, whose own language habitually was of the roughest, would go away sometimes, we are told, after an interview at headquarters, "boiling over with rage and muttering words that could not be consigned to print." Another general, Charles Stewart, on one occasion left Wellington's presence "in such a state of nervous prostration that he broke down and wept."

This is what passed at one interview, as written down by the Principal Medical Officer of the army in Spain, Sir James McGrigor, after a bad quarter of an hour with the chief. It was after Salamanca, while Wellington was in occupation of Madrid:

"When on my arrival at Madrid," says Dr. McGrigor, "I waited on Lord Wellington he received me in the kindest and warmest manner. He was sitting to a Spanish painter for his portrait, and after receiving me, he asked me, if I was not too much busied, to sit down and give him the detail of the state of the wounded at Salamanca, with that of my journey thence. I related to him the number of sick I had met with at so many places, and their miserable state. But when I came to inform him that for their relief I had ordered up purveying and commissariat officers, he started up, and in a violent manner reprobated what I had done. It was to no purpose that I pleaded the number of seriously ill and dying I had met with; and that several men and some officers had died without ever having been seen by a medical officer. I even alluded to what had formerly happened at Talavera, and to the clamour raised in England when it was known that so many wounded and sick had been left to the mercy of the enemy. All was in vain. His lordship was in a passion . . . 'I shall be glad to know,' exclaimed his lordship, ' who is to command the army—I or you? I establish one route, one line of communication for the army; you establish another, and order the commissariat and the supplies by that line. As long as you live, sir, never do so again; never do anything without my orders.' I pleaded that 'there was no time to consult him to save life.' He peremptorily desired me 'never again to act without his orders.'"

On the other hand, Wellington knew how, on occasion, to give honour where honour was due. Witness for that the unique compliment that he went out of his way to pay to the troops who fought so well at the brilliant affair of El Bodon, near Ciudad Rodrigo, in October, 1811; in particular the Northumberland Fusiliers, the ever-renowned "Fighting Fifth," and the 77th, now the Second Battalion of the Middlesex Regiment, for their magnificent behaviour before the enemy. It was in that dashing little encounter that the "Fighting Fifth "performed the exploit, matched only by what took place at Minden, of charging cavalry with the bayonet and scattering them in rout.

"They marched up in a line," says Sir Charles Stewart, afterwards Marquess of Londonderry, who was watching them, "and firing with great coolness; when at a distance of only a few paces from their adversaries they brought their bayonets to the charge and rushed forward. Never was charge more successful. Possessing the advantage of ground and keeping in close and compact array, the 5th literally pushed their adversaries down the hill; they then retook the guns, and limbering them to the horses which had followed their advance, drew them off in safety."

Wellington, in a general order, held up the conduct of those who took part at El Bodon before the whole army, bestowing on one and all a signal honour, such as, perhaps, no other British leader ever conferred. This is what Wellington said:

The Commander of the Forces is desirous of drawing the attention of the army to the conduct of the Second Battalion 5th and 77th Regiments, and the 21st Portuguese Regiment, and Major Arentschild's Portuguese Artillery, under the command of the Hon. Major-General Colville; and of the 11th Light Dragoons and 1st Hussars, under Major-General V. Alten, in the affair with the enemy on the 20th ultimo. These troops were attacked by between thirty and forty squadrons of cavalry, with six pieces of cannon, supported by a division consisting of fourteen battalions of infantry with cannon.

The Portuguese artillerymen were cut down at their guns before they quitted them, but the Second Battalion 5th Regiment attacked the cavalry which had taken the guns, and retook them. At the same time the 77th Regiment were attacked in front by another body of cavalry, upon which body they advanced and repulsed them.

✶✶✶✶✶✶

The troops retired with the same determined spirit, and in the same good order with which they had maintained their post; the Second Battalion 5th Regiment and 77th in one square, and the Portuguese regiment in another. The enemy's cavalry charged three faces of the square of the British infantry, but were beaten off; and, finding from their repeated fruitless efforts that these brave troops were not to be broken, they were contented with following them at a distance, and with firing upon them with their artillery, till the troops joined the remainder of the 3rd Division.

✶✶✶✶✶✶

The Commander of the Forces has been particular in stating the details of this action in the general orders, as, in his opinion, it affords a memorable example of what can be effected by steadiness, discipline, and confidence. It is impossible that any troops can at any time be exposed to the attack of numbers relatively greater than those which attacked the troops under Major-General Colville and Major-General V. Alten, and the Commander of the Forces recommends the conduct of these troops to the particular attention of the officers and soldiers of the army, as an example to be followed in all such circumstances.

Wellington was wounded only twice in his life; neither time seriously. He had, however, one or two rather narrow escapes. His first wound was in India, in the fighting before Seringapatam, when a bullet tore the cloth of his overalls and grazed his knee. His second wound was during the final stage of the Peninsular War, at the Battle of Orthez.

He was watching the progress of the battle—General Alava sitting on horseback near him—when a musket-ball struck the Spaniard severely on that part of the person any injury done to which is the occasion more frequently for mirth than commiseration. The duke, as was to be expected, laughed at Alava, but had not long enjoyed his joke when another ball, after hitting the guard of his own sword, glanced off, and gave him such a blow as caused him to spring from the saddle and fall to the ground. He got up, rubbed the part, laughed again, but rather more faintly, remounted, and went through the action; but for several days afterwards he was unable to ride and suffered great pain.

One of Wellington's narrow escapes was at Salamanca. While in advance, leading the night pursuit at the head of the Light Division, he overtook some French dragoons, part of Foy's rearguard. They spurred up their horses and galloped off, firing back at the British with their pistols and carbines. One bullet went through the cloak folded up on Wellington's saddle and struck him sharply on the thigh, causing some pain, but not breaking the skin. At Vittoria, again, in the middle of the battle, during the attack on the village of Arinez, a spent ball hit Wellington at the waist, but it only lodged in his sash, and then dropped to the ground.

He had on various occasions some rather narrow escapes from capture by the enemy.

At Talavera, just as the outposts of the two armies came into touch, he was nearly taken prisoner by a sudden rush of French *tirailleurs*, while on top of the ruins of a deserted building, up which he had climbed to get a view of the enemy.

It was on the afternoon of the first day of the battle, July 27.

The fighting began with a sharp preliminary skirmish near the River Alberche, some three or four miles in advance of the actual battlefield. One of the British brigades which had been pushed forward beyond the river, while the main army was taking up its position in rear, was surprised after falling back across the river by a sudden advance of the enemy through a wood nearby. Fording the river unobserved, shrouded by heavy smoke from a burning camp of huts on the farther bank, which the French had previously occupied and abandoned, the enemy stole forward and suddenly attacked the British brigade among some trees not far from the ruins of an old Spanish country-house called the Casa de Salinas. Our men were resting (a bad lookout apparently being kept), when a deadly fire of musketry was suddenly poured in on them from among the bushes in front. "Many of our men were shot dead on the ground as they lay."

There was fearful confusion for the moment, and two British battalions, as they retreated, fired wildly into each other. A third battalion was standing firm and holding the enemy back, when Wellington, who had not been far off, watching the enemy at another point, came galloping up. He flung himself from his horse and clambered to the top of the ruins of the Casa de Salinas, to get a clear lookout to the front. As he did so, with a sudden rush forward, the French skirmishers swarmed out from their cover and made directly for the Casa. Wellington was all but taken. He had to jump down in a hurry, and had just time to scramble on to his horse and dash off.

"If I had not been young and active," describes Wellington afterwards, "I must have been taken, for I had to leap from the ruins." Personally assuming charge of the disorganized soldiers, he saved the surprised brigade by his exertions, got them together, and drew all back rapidly, until the main British position, where the army had by then taken up its ground, was reached. So near, though, were the enemy's sharpshooters during the retirement, that an officer to whom Wellington was speaking was hit by three bullets, two of which struck his sword, while the third passed through his hat.

During the Battle of Fuentes de Onoro Wellington at one moment had to ride hard to escape, and was nearly cut off. Several officers of the Headquarters Staff were with him at the time, all in the midst of a regiment of French dragoons, who had dashed in on them and were galloping round them, racing to intercept them. Some even got ahead, and one Frenchman was cut down within a dozen yards of Wellington. In the skirmishing with Marmont before the Battle of Salamanca, when with the Light Dragoons at a ford, Wellington was again nearly taken by the French.

"He was in the thick of it," described later on an officer of the Rifles who was at the spot and saw it all, "and only escaped with difficulty. He crossed the ford with his straight sword drawn, and smiling. I did not see his Grace when the charge took place, but he had a most narrow escape: he had not any of his staff with him, and was quite alone, with a ravine in his rear."

More than one officer, indeed, in letters expressed the anxiety for Wellington's safety that not a few felt, on account of Wellington's constant venturesomeness and habit of riding about in advance unattended by any escort. One British general, as a fact, was actually captured by the French through his doing that very thing. It was Sir Edward Paget, at the time also the next senior British officer in Spain to Wellington himself. The misadventure occurred during the retreat from Burgos in the autumn of 1812. While the British divisions, with the enemy in pursuit, were making their way through a dense forest near Ciudad Rodrigo, General Paget, riding by himself between two of the divisions to ascertain why one was lagging behind, got trapped in a by-path by a patrol of French dragoons, who disarmed and carried him off prisoner in the midst of his own army, not a quarter of a mile from his own command.

The capture was considered so valuable by the enemy that, although Wellington at once offered to release in exchange any of the many French generals in our hands, Napoleon flatly refused to entertain the proposal, and kept General Paget a prisoner in France to the end of the war. The misfortune to his so highly-valued colleague did not, however, seem to make much difference to Wellington in the matter of his own exposures of himself to a similar accident. He ran grave risks on more than one subsequent occasion, notably in the warfare among the Pyrenean passes.

9

With the Men Who Took the Eagle at Barrosa

Barrosa sent to England the first of Napoleon's Eagles won on the battlefield by the British Army. In memory of the taking of that fine trophy, and the brilliantly distinguished part that its captors bore in the famous fight, one of the regiments of the present-day British Army displays proudly as its badge the device of a French Eagle standard, the Eagle having a laurel-wreath round its neck and standing on a tablet inscribed with the figure "8."

The corps in Wellington's army is represented nowadays by the First Battalion of the Royal Irish Fusiliers. At the time it was known as the Second Battalion of the 87th Foot, "The Prince of Wales's Irish Regiment"—a battalion enrolled in 1804 while Napoleon's army for the invasion of England was threatening our shores from the Camp of Boulogne. Kilkenny lads for the most part were the "Prince's Irish," as everybody called the corps when first raised; dare-devil young fellows and a wild lot to discipline and hold in hand, from all accounts. How they could fight, Barrosa proved.

That battle—it took place on March 5th, 1811—was the outcome of a daring attempt to compel the French to raise the siege of Cadiz. The idea of it originated with the veteran officer at the head of the British division of 6,000 men then assisting the Spaniards to defend the last refuge of Spanish National Independence, Lieut.-General Graham. He became Sir Thomas Graham, G.C.B; was Wellington's right-hand man in the Vittoria campaign; and later on was granted a peerage as Lord Lynedoch.

No more gallant officer ever held a King of England's commission. Few ever had so eventful a career. Fighting the French was to Graham as his life's blood. He went through the war in the spirit of an old-time Crusader:—to slay Frenchmen. He lived for that; and he had done so constantly for eighteen years before the day of Barrosa; ever since the breaking out of the French Revolution—to him the incarnation of evil—wherever and whenever opportunity offered.

A Scottish laird, noted for his sporting tastes and as a bold cross-country rider and keen cricketer—he played in the first cricket match ever played in Scotland—also a Whig Member of Parliament, a horrible outrage had impelled Graham, at the age of forty-four, suddenly to take up soldiering. Chance had flung him into the midst of the horrors of the French Revolution in 1792. His wife, the beautiful Mrs. Graham of Gainsborough's picture, stricken down with consumption, had died on the Riviera, and Graham was bearing her remains in the coffin homeward to Scotland across France, when at one place he came into collision with a tumultuous mob. He was stopped by a drunken crowd of recruits and National Guards, who swarmed round and set on him, vociferating that he was smuggling arms for the aristocrats in the coffin.

The frenzied ruffians broke the coffin open, and Graham, after resisting desperately to prevent the foul outrage, was overpowered and arrested. He was only released after the wretches had satisfied their brutal curiosity. Thenceforward it became the one duty of Graham's life to shoot down Jacobins. Whether they called themselves Bonapartists or anything else made no difference to him. After laying his wife's remains to rest in his family vault in Scotland he went off to the front, first as a volunteer with the British troops fighting at Toulon. Next, returning home, Graham spent every penny he could get together in raising a regiment, the "Perthshire Volunteers," which became the 90th Foot, and is now the Second Battalion Scottish Rifles. Of it he was appointed Colonel, and from that day onward, whether with the British Army, or independently, serving with the Austrians at one time, with Suvarroff's Russians at another, wherever there was fighting against the French, Graham was in the thick of it: in Italy, at Malta, at Minorca, in Egypt, in the Tyrol, lastly in Portugal and Spain. And all through no French bullet or bayonet seemed able to harm him. In 1811, at Barrosa, he was in his sixty-first year, and a British lieut.-general.

General Graham after planning his *coup* and arranging preliminaries with the Spanish authorities, transported 5,000 of the British troops in garrison with him at Cadiz round by sea to Gibraltar Bay, where he was joined by 8,000 Spanish regulars of the so-called "Army

The Victor of Barrosa: General Graham,
Lord Lynedoch, G.C.B.

of Andalusia," one of the patriotic organizations carrying on a desultory warfare in the field against the French. He unfortunately now assented to the senior Spanish general, Don Manuel La Peña, assuming the chief command, thinking by so doing to incite his allies to act energetically, and also to conciliate Spanish pride, as the Spanish contingent was the larger. In the result the concession wrecked the British leader's plans; and La Peña, after mismanaging everything, in the end held aloof from his ally on the battlefield, leaving Graham to fight at Barrosa, a few miles to the south of Cadiz and close to the French besieging lines, single-handed with his own men only.

La Peña's blundering gave the French besiegers timely warning and enabled them to concentrate and meet the danger that threatened them with a bold counterstroke. Keeping in concealment to the last they delivered a fierce surprise attack which meant disaster for the allies had not Graham's personal coolness and daring generalship—"a daring old man, of a ready temper for battle," is how Napier speaks of Graham on that morning—coupled with the heroic pluck and dash of his British troops, saved the day and turned imminent peril to a glorious victory for England.

The Spanish general, on the very morning of the battle, while the whereabouts of the enemy were still unknown, although it was certain that the French could not be far off and every measure of precaution was imperative, in spite of Graham's strenuous remonstrances, prematurely abandoned Barrosa ridge, an all-important covering position for the allied army. Graham had to obey, and the British contingent, which was formed in two brigades and comprised the rear portion of the allied army, had to quit the ridge. As they were following in rear of the Spanish troops, in accordance with La Peña's depositions, the enemy made their attack.

General Graham and his men were making their way through a wood farther on when the French, all unexpectedly, came sallying forth from their hiding-place in the forest of Chiclana, some two miles off. They moved out in two dense masses of infantry: one of which pushed forward at once to seize and occupy the abandoned position of Barrosa, while the other pressed on across an intervening stretch of open plain to surprise and take in flank the British corps while traversing the wood.

Marshal Victor, the French commander at that moment in charge of the siege operations against Cadiz, had been watching the movements of the Spanish General. He had marked La Peña's clumsy manoeuvring and the abandonment of the all-important Barrosa ridge. That decided him to strike at once. Sending one of the three brigades he had available, to hold in check the Spanish troops in advance as they straggled forward at some distance from the British, Marshal Victor formed up his two strongest brigades under cover along the outskirts of Chiclana forest towards Barrosa. Seeing Graham's redcoats trapped and entangled, as they looked, as they were tramping through the wood, he sent his main attack against them, sanguine of achieving an easy success over an enemy caught in so perilously awkward a situation. He did not know General Graham.

At the moment that the first of the French moved out and the alarm was given, the two British brigades were toiling along, winding their way amidst the trees in a lengthy, strung-out column along the rough and narrow road, a sandy cart-track through the wood.

It was between twelve and one o'clock. Graham and a couple of staff-officers had dismounted by the roadside to snatch a hasty meal while the soldiers were marching by, when a peasant came running up with the news. He had seen, said the man, French soldiers advancing from Chiclana. They were making towards where the general then was. Graham got on horseback instantly and galloped off to see for himself.

He took in the state of affairs at the first glance. The danger was indeed grave and imminent. The enemy were in force and coming on fast. What had to be done was to get the two British brigades clear of the wood and fronted to their threatened flank, in position to stem the onrush of the French. But to carry the evolution out needed time.

Graham's promptness and readiness of resource enabled the difficulty to be met. Two of his battalions were made up of picked troops: two composite battalions, formed from the light or skirmisher companies, which at that period used to be attached to every battalion of the line. The companies had been temporarily detached from their battalions and combined to form light skirmisher battalions for independent fighting.

At that moment one of these battalions was in rear of the main column. It had not long come down from Barrosa ridge, which it was the last to leave. A sturdy old soldier, the veteran Colonel Browne of the 28th, was in charge of it.

Colonel Browne, according to one account, had caught sight of the French when they first emerged from Chiclana forest and sent word to Graham. His messenger reached the general just as Graham got to the edge of the wood and discovered the enemy for himself. Graham sent Browne's orderly back with the laconic order—"Fight!" The officer galloped back shouting the answer out as he neared the colonel.

"What? What did the general say?" called Browne, to make quite sure.

"Fight!" answered the messenger, reining up his horse close by the colonel "Just fight!"

"Right!" was the gallant Browne's short response, and he prepared forthwith to turn back and recover the ridge.

Before he could do so General Graham himself, following the messenger, came cantering up. The general had already sent directions to his two brigadiers, Dilkes and Wheatley, in charge of the column in the wood, to form rapidly to the flank and hasten to the outskirts of the wood. "It's a bad business," said Graham to Colonel Browne on hearing that some Spanish battalions he supposed to be still on the ridge had also come down from it. "It's a bad business; you must turn round and attack!"

Graham had already sent word as well to Colonel Barnard of the 95th, in charge of his other light battalion, and marching near the head of the leading brigade, to lead out his men and attack on that side to hold in check the French column crossing the plain.

By these measures, improvised on the spur of the moment, Graham trusted to gain the time he required for the troops in the wood to get clear and take up their new front. The two light battalions were to sacrifice themselves, if it came to that, for the rest of the army. Heroically did they obey what Napier calls "Graham's Spartan order" and do their duty.

Colonel Browne, first of all, led his men up the steep ascent towards the ridge. He rode ahead of them, so it is told, singing a verse of an old sea-song—"*Come cheer up, my lads, 'tis to glory we steer!*" His gallant "light-bobs" climbed the bare hill-side under a hot fire from the French artillery, with, for their only cover, a few sparse bushes. As they neared the summit a blaze of musketry from the leading French infantry, who had already reached the ridge on their side, beat on them with murderous effect. It struck down—killed or wounded—more than 200 officers and men, out of some 530 all told; but the rest doggedly closed up and went on, until a second musketry discharge shot down half a hundred more.

The survivors threw themselves flat on the ground, and from behind what bushes there were nearby continued the fight. They managed, in spite of the odds, to hold the enemy back.

A moment later the gallant Barnard led his men out into the plain, and they, too, were quickly in hot action, aided by Graham's artillery, ten 6-pounder field-guns, admirably handled by Captain Duncan. Barnard's light battalion had to fall back in the end, but they stubbornly disputed every foot of the ground.

In that manner vitally important breathing-space was gained, while Graham's main body re-formed and deployed. These were by then ready to take their part, and now came the turn and opportunity of the 87th.

The "Prince's Irish" were with Graham's second brigade, led by Colonel Wheatley, forming the left of the British battle-line, whose task was to beat back the French troops advancing across the plain. At that moment the French were coming on at the charging step, with drums beating and shouting *"En avant!" "Vive l'Empereur!"* as they pushed back Barnard's skirmishers in their front. Graham sent forward his other brigade, forming the right wing of his line, under General Dilkes, to relieve Browne's heroes and storm Barrosa ridge.

So the general battle opened.

Wheatley's men went at the enemy in two lines, firing rapid volleys as they advanced. The 87th were in the centre of the leading line. Ahead of all the heroic old General rode into the fight, his cocked hat in hand waving them on. Two bullets cut through the breast of Graham's coat; fortunately, they came sideways, and did not harm the fine old warrior. "Now, my lads, there they are!" shouted Graham to the men nearest him, as they closed on the enemy. "Spare your powder; give them steel!"

The 87th did so, and, dashing at the enemy, charged right into them.

Rushing forward impetuously, with the war-cry of the old Irish clans from among whom the regiment had been raised, "Faugh-a-Ballagh!" (Clear the way!), they smashed through and routed the first French line, sending it back in confusion on the second. Then they went full tilt at the second French line. In front of that was the First Battalion of Napoleon's 8th of the Line, with their "golden-wreathed" Eagle standard proudly displayed.

Ensign Edward Keogh, of the 87th, caught sight of the Eagle first of all, borne gallantly in the centre of its line on high above the fray. "See that Eagle, sergeant," he called to Sergeant Masterson, a non-commissioned officer of his company. Dashing instantly into the thick of the group of Frenchmen round the Eagle, sword in hand, the heroic lad cut his way through with Masterson and four or five privates close behind him, until he got close up to the French ensign, or *porte-aiglé*. At once he closed with the Frenchman, and crossed swords, with his left hand making a grab at the Eagle pole. Keogh got hold of it and tried to pull it away, but he could not wrench it free before the brave ensign went down with half a dozen musket-bullets and two bayonet-stabs in his body.

According to French accounts, Porte-Aiglé Guillemin, as the Eagle-bearer of the 8th was named, fell dead at the same moment as Ensign Keogh, shot through the head by one of the British privates. Other Frenchmen rushed up then to rescue the Eagle, and formed round it hastily. One of the British privates who had seized hold of the staff as Keogh fell was slashed to death, and once more the French recovered it. But they were not to keep it unchallenged. A close and desperately furious tussle followed. Seven French officers and sub-officers—the records of the regiment state—fell dead in gallantly defending the Eagle. An eighth, Lieutenant Gazan, clung to the pole desperately with both hands, regardless of wounds that nearly hacked him to pieces. Finally, the Eagle was torn from his grasp by Sergeant Masterson, who remained at the end the sole unwounded survivor of the attacking British party. Gazan "survived miraculously," we are told, and lived to be decorated by Napoleon for his devoted courage. Sergeant Masterson carried the Eagle off and kept it.

On the other hand, as described by Major Hugh Gough, who was in command of the 87th at Barrosa, "Ensign Keogh was killed in the act of grasping at it, and the French officer who held it was run through by Sergeant Masterson in the midst of our officers and men. The sergeant," adds Major Gough, "never let it out of his hand until he delivered it to me, and afterwards carried it for the rest of the day between our colours."

In a letter to his wife after the battle the major gives this description of the Eagle.

It is brass, well gilt; the wreath is pure gold. The Eagle is on a pole, something stronger, but very similar, to the pole of a sergeant's halberd. It is much heavier than the colours of a regiment, and from the weight being all at the top is very unwieldy.

"The French," says the major, in relating his own experiences, "waited until we came within about twenty-five paces of them before they broke, and as they were in column when they did they could not get away. It was therefore a scene of most dreadful carnage.... As, of course, I was in front of the regiment, therefore in the middle of them, I could not, confused and flying as they were, cut down one, although I might have twenty, they seemed so confounded and so frightened. They made, while we were amongst them (about a quarter of an hour), little or no opposition.

"We would have taken or destroyed the whole regiment," continues Major Gough, "but at this moment the 47th French Regiment came down on our right, and General Graham, who was during the whole of the action in the midst of it, pointed them out and begged I would call off my men. I will not say 'Halt!' as we were in the midst of the French. With the greatest difficulty, by almost cutting them down, I got the right wing collected, with which we charged the 47th, but, after firing until we came to within about fifty paces of them, they (for us fortunately) broke and fled. Had they done their duty, fatigued as my men were at the moment, they must have cut us to pieces. We were therefore, after they broke, unable to follow them, but took the howitzer attached to them."

A second Eagle, according to another officer of the 87th—the Eagle of the French 47th—was taken by the regiment. It was not, however, kept. "The man who had charge of it was obliged to throw it away from excessive fatigue and a wound. We had been under arms thirty-two hours and sixteen on the march before the action began."

Two days after the battle, describes another officer, "we marched into the Isla (Cadiz), and from between the colours presented the Eagle to our gallant commander, amidst crowds of delighted spectators." The golden-wreathed Eagle trophy was afterwards publicly paraded in London and deposited with special ceremony in the Chapel Royal of Whitehall, whence, in later years, with other trophies, it was transferred to the chapel of Chelsea Hospital, finally to be stolen from there in April, 1852, the year in which Wellington died.

One of the leaves from the Eagle wreath, which was of pure gold, fell from it during the *mêlée*, and was picked up on the spot after the fight. It is now in the possession of a member of the Gough family, in Ireland, preserved as a treasured relic. The wreath had been presented to Napoleon's 8th of the Line—with other wreaths presented at the same time to a number of other French regiments—by the City of Paris as a reward for distinguished service at the Battle of Friedland some two years before.

Two of the six cannon captured at Barrosa were taken by the 87th, in addition to the Eagle. "We took two howitzers and the wreathed Eagle in the charge," writes an officer, "a glory never before achieved by any regiment in the world. All the other regiments"—he goes on to say—"had their Eagles screwed on, in order to take them off when hard-pushed, but Bonaparte ordered the 8th (1,600 grenadiers) to nail theirs on, as he said it was impossible to take it: but, thank God, a Roscommon man took it, one of my volunteers, Masterson. I am happy to say he was promoted to the rank of sergeant-major on the field of battle."

This may be added of Sergeant Masterson. For taking the Eagle he was not only promoted to sergeant-major, but also, later on, was awarded an ensign's commission.[1] One of the most modest of men, he was at a dinner-party in London after the war, when somebody, who did not know Ensign Masterson by sight, speaking to him of Barrosa and the taking of the Eagle, expressed wonder and admiration of the feat done by "a sergeant of your regiment." "The sergeant," was Masterson's reply, "merely did his duty. He only did what any of his comrades would have done, had he had the opportunity. It was only the Fortune of War. He succeeded by Providence in what cost the poor ensign his life!"

Wrote General Graham, immediately after Barrosa, to old Sir John Doyle, the Colonel of the 87th. "Your regiment has covered itself with glory. Recommend it and its commander, Gough, to their illustrious patron, the Prince Regent; too much cannot be done for it." In response the Prince Regent conferred on the 87th the title of the "Prince of Wales's Own Irish Regiment" as a distinction, since abbreviated and altered to "Royal Irish Fusiliers." "An Eagle with a wreath of Laurel" was further appointed by the prince as a regimental badge, a similar Eagle being embroidered in gold on the regimental colour.

A representation of the Barrosa Eagle and wreath also was granted as a special augmentation to the family arms of the officer who commanded the 87th in the battle, Major Hugh C. Gough—he was promoted to Lieut.-Colonel for Barrosa, the first instance in the British

---

1. The name was for long a family name in the regiment, through a long line of Mastersons, the direct descendants of the captor of the Barrosa Eagle. One of the Mastersons now wears the V.C., won by a splendid act of courage in South Africa at Wagon Hill—Lieutenant (later Colonel) J. E. L. Masterson. He was in the Devonshire Regiment at the time.

Army of brevet rank being conferred on an officer for the conduct of a regiment in action—on his being raised to the peerage as Viscount Gough, while Commander-in-Chief in India at the close of the first Sikh War. It figures as one of the crests of the Gough family and the heraldic blazon is set forth in these words: "a dexter arm embowed, in facings of the 87th Regiment (gules faced *vert*), the hand grasping the colour of the said regiment displayed, and a representation of a French Eagle reversed and depressed, the staff broken, proper in an *Escroll* above the word 'Barrosa.'"

Colonel Wheatley's other regiments, as they closed on the enemy, caught the 87th up and the whole brigade in a resistless onset hurled back the French second line, driving Laval and all his troops, broken and in disorder, off the plain. "There was one peculiarity about this sanguinary struggle," records one of the French officers in the middle of the fighting, "and that was that when, as happened in many cases, the English had broken their weapons, instead of using the hangers, or swords, they carried at their sides, they went on fighting with their fists!"

"The Aiglers," became the *sobriquet* of the 87th after Barrosa throughout Wellington's army. It has stuck to the corps ever since in after days, in the form of the "Aigle-Takers"; although our "uptodate" recruits, it is said, rather prefer to call themselves the "Bird-Catchers."

The contest in that part of the field from the first crossing of the bayonets to the end lasted little more than a quarter of an hour.

Elsewhere, in the other part of the battlefield, the men of Dilke's Brigade, sent to retake Barrosa ridge, had also practically finished their work in no less dashing style and no less successfully. Graham's right brigade, advancing up the hill at the double against the French on Barrosa ridge, stormed it and carried the crest line after a stubborn contest at the point of the bayonet; driving the French there back and down the hill on the farther side; with, left behind them, many dead and wounded, and prisoners, among these the French commander on the hill, General Ruffin.

> His horse, wounded by bullets, ran away with him among the advancing British and flung him off on the top of their bayonets.

The 28th, the celebrated "Slashers," now the 1st Gloucestershires, was one of the regiments which stormed Barrosa ridge. They were on the left of their brigade and moved up without firing a shot, advancing to deal with a French regiment on the right of the ridge, Napoleon's 54th of the Line. One of their officers says this, describing how the "Slashers" took their part at Barrosa:

> We had formed line under cover of the 95th and then advanced to meet their right wing which was coming down in close column—a great advantage. Here the coolness of Colonel Belson was conspicuous: he moved us up without firing a shot close to their right battalion which had just then begun to deploy. The colonel then gave orders to fire by platoons from centre to flanks, and aim low: 'Fire at their legs and spoil their dancing!' This was kept up for a short time with dreadful effect. The action being now general all along the line we twice attempted to charge. But the enemy, being double our strength (some of our flank companies being away), only retired a little on each occasion. Finally giving three cheers, we charged a third time and succeeded: the enemy now gave way and fled in every direction.[2]

The French fell back at all points along the ridge, retreating here and there more slowly, until the whole gave way *en masse*. "With loud and murmuring sounds," as another officer of the 28th puts it, "Ruffin's division and Rousseau's chosen grenadiers rolled with a whirling motion down into the valley below, leaving their two brave generals mortally wounded on the hill, which was left in the possession of their bloodstained conquerors."

In honour of their share in the day's work the Gloucestershire Regiment in our present army wears displayed on the helmet-plate beneath the old regimental badge of the Royal Cypher the name "Barrosa."

The last shots on the battlefield were fired within eighty minutes of the opening advance of the French. By that time Victor was in full retreat, leaving in Graham's hands 500 prisoners, two of his brigadiers (one dying from his wounds), the Eagle of the 8th, and six guns.

The British, it should be added, had had throughout to fight singlehanded. The 8,000 Spaniards who had joined hands with Graham

---

2. It was to this same regiment that an ensign who behaved so pluckily at the Pass of Maya, a battle in the Pyrenees, belonged. The regimental colour-bearer had been shot down, but the boy sprang forward and carried it on, exclaiming: "The 'Slashers' shall never want a man to display their colours to the enemy!" He, too, was hit, but he went on. One bullet that struck him in the chest was stopped over the heart by a tightly-folded handkerchief, thirteen folds of which it penetrated.

at Tarifa held aloof during the battle. Their general, indeed, did not fire a single shot to help the British. General La Peña, although "not a quarter of hour's ride from the field," and with the din of the firing in his ears, simply halted his men and left Graham to make what fight he could. The English, he said, would be beaten: it was useless for him to take any part. In the result he did not move a corporal's guard to the assistance of Graham.

The stirring incidents of Barrosa fight took the fancy of people at home in England at once—the 87th indeed had the rare honour of being toasted by the Lord Mayor of London at a Guildhall banquet—and the battle was for a long time one of the most popular of our soldier deeds of arms. Especially popular was the feat of the taking of the golden-wreathed Eagle. Everybody almost who could string verses together, as it would seem, tried his hand at so commemorating Barrosa. Two of the best of the "poems" which found their way into the newspapers were these. Ran the opening lines of one:

> *At Barrosa, her praises Fame still further adds;*
> *There they proved themselves truly 'the tight Irish lads,'*
> *With their sprigs of shillelagh and shamrock so green!*
>
> *To meet the French column with transport they stept,*
> *Soon found out the place where their Eagles were kept,*
> *With their sprigs of shillelagh and shamrock so green!*
>
> *One bird was full-grown, fledg'd with fame and renown;*
> *Oh! that was their work, and they soon knocked it down,*
> *With their sprigs of shillelagh and shamrock so green!*

A second set of verses, by Tom Dibdin, brother of the better-remembered Charles, the celebrated naval songster, ran after this fashion:

> *General Graham*
> *The theme of my song would a Milton delight,*
> *And it merits a singer like Braham;*
> *Were a King to turn poet, he never could write*
> *On a worthier subject than Graham!*
>
> *They tell us that eagles can stare at the sun,*
> *Whose beams nor annoy nor dismay 'em;*
> *But French Eagles fly, and French Game Chickens run,*
> *From the glory of General Graham!*
>
> *His men on slight suppers had marched a whole night*

(For their toil grateful Britain repay 'em!),
And just sat down to eat when the French came in sight—
What a breakfast for General Graham!

'They never can beat us, we're posted too high,'
Said the foe, when they heard us huzza 'em;
'Well, maybe we can't, but allow us try!'
Cried the soldiers of General Graham!

Full tilt at the boys, led by bold Major Gough,
Determined to cut, hack, and slay 'em;
A French leader came on, but his napper flew off
On a furlough from General Graham!

And many brave foes, whether leading or led,
Found, while sinking where Fate chose to lay 'em,
That as well as a heart it required a head
To cope with the soldiers of Graham!

Tho' by thickets entangled, our boys firmly stood,
And those who had tried to waylay 'em,
While hallooing ere they were out of the wood,
Were silenced by General Graham!

To mention each hero whose laurels lay claim
To applause, had I power to display 'em,
'Twould fill every leaf in the records of Fame
To inscribe the brave comrades of Graham!

Paddy Shannon, a bugler boy, was to the regiment the hero of the day, next after Sergeant Masterson; the lad who sounded the charge at Barrosa. Of him there is a story told that may fitly serve to round off our present narrative.

A pet of the corps was Paddy Shannon, in those days a smart bugler lad, always a favourite with the officers. Paddy remained that to the last; even when, in after-times, the poor fellow had taken too kindly to his whisky drams. Indeed, as to that Paddy Shannon has a story of his own. The canteen wrecked the poor fellow. There were always, particularly after Barrosa we are told, "free drinks" for Paddy Shannon at the canteen, in memory of what he had done, but his comrades unfortunately used to take Paddy there so much that the drink-habit grew on him, to his undoing. Then followed the downfall, and at last, when his colonel's patience had become exhausted, Paddy Shannon found himself sent to the halberds—to be publicly flogged as a drunkard.

How he made his first appearance there, and what happened, is told by one of the officers of the 87th. Major Gough, who led the regiment at Barrosa, was colonel in command on the occasion. It was in 1815, four years after Barrosa.

The regiment was paraded, the proceedings read, and Paddy tied up. The signal was given for the drummers to begin, when Paddy Shannon exclaimed:
'Listen now, Sir Hugh. Do you mean to say you're going to flog me? Just recollect who it was sounded the charge at Barrosa, when you took the only French Eagle ever taken. Wasn't it Paddy Shannon? Little I thought that day it would come to this; and the regiment so proud of that same Eagle on their colours.'
'Take him down!' said Sir Hugh; and Paddy escaped unpunished. A very short time, however, elapsed before Paddy again found himself in similar circumstances.
'Go on!' said the colonel.
'Don't be in a hurry,' ejaculated Paddy; 'I've a few words to say, Sir Hugh.'
'The Eagle won't save you this time, sir!'
'Is it the Eagle, indeed? Then I wasn't going to say anything about that same, though you are so proud of it! But I was just going to ask if it wasn't Paddy Shannon who, when the breach of Tarifa was stormed by 22,000 French, and only the 87th to defend it, if it wasn't Paddy Shannon who struck up "*Garry Owen to Glory, boys*," and you, Sir Hugh, have got the same two towers and the breach between them upon your coat-of-arms in testimony thereof!'
'Take him down!' said the colonel, and Paddy again got off unscathed. Paddy, however, had a long list of services to get through and a good deal of whisky, and ere another two months he was again tied up, the sentence read, and an assurance from Sir Hugh Gough given that nothing this time should again make him relent. Paddy tried the Eagle—it was no use. He appealed to Sir Hugh's family pride and the breach of Tarifa—also without avail.
'And is it me,' he at last broke out, 'that you are going to flog? I ask you, Sir Hugh Gough, before the whole regiment, who know it well, if it wasn't Paddy Shannon who picked up the

French field marshal's staff at the Battle of Vittoria that the Duke of Wellington sent to the Prince Regent, and for which he got that letter that will be long remembered, and that made him a field-marshal into the bargain? The Prince Regent said, "You've sent me the staff of a field-marshal of France; I return you that of a field-marshal of England!" Wasn't it Paddy Shannon that took it? Paddy Shannon, who never got rap or recompense, or ribbon or star, or coat-of-arms, or mark of distinction, except the flogging you are going to give him!'

'Take him down!' was all the colonel could say, and again Paddy was forgiven.

At that point the tale may close.

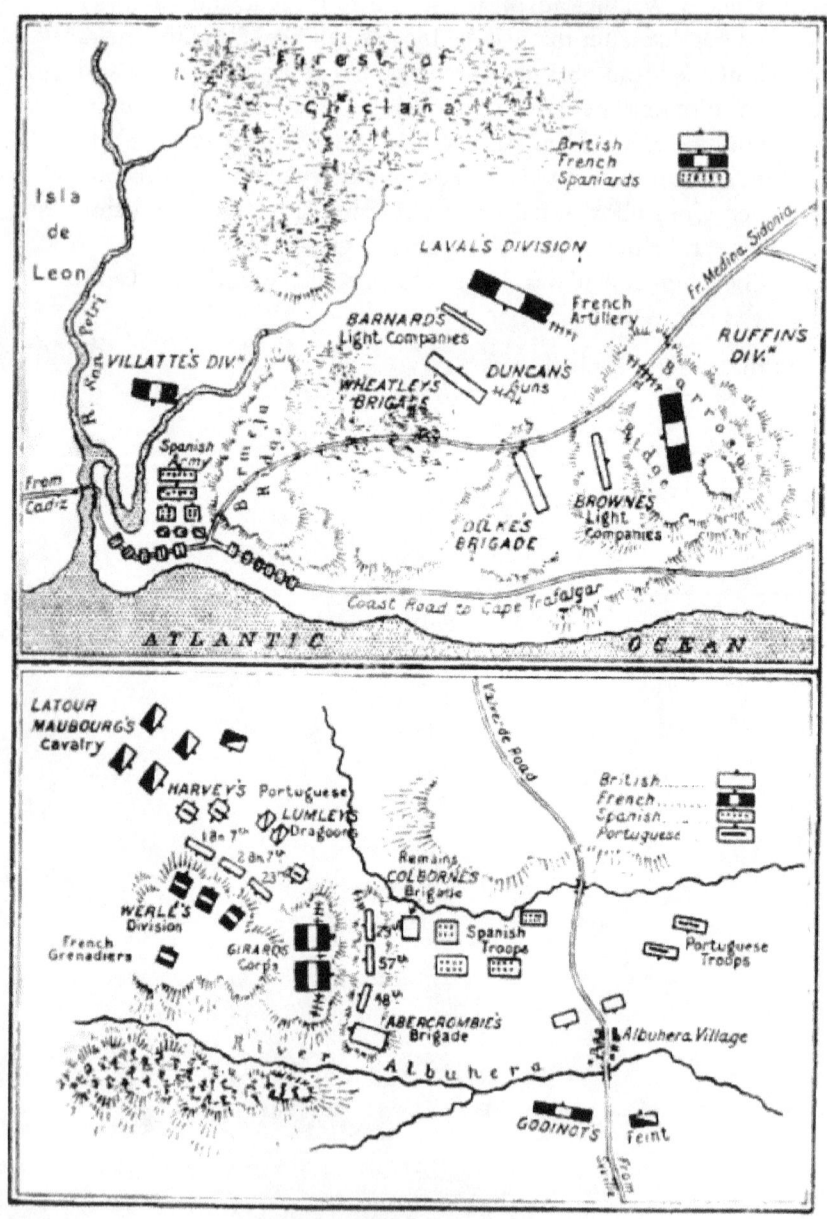

The Battle of Barrosa: March 5, 1811
The Battle of Albuhera: May 16, 1811

10

On the Day of the "Die Hards": Heroic Albuhera

Albuhera is a name to conjure with among British soldiers. Tell it to the men of the Royal Fusiliers, the "City of London Regiment,"— though no very great number of our modern-time Londoners, perhaps, amid the bustling rush of everyday commercial life, have time to remember that. Tell it to the Worcesters, the old 29th, the "Firms"; to the Gloucesters, the old 28th, the "Slashers"; to the onetime 31st, the East Surreys, the "Young Buffs." Tell it to the "Old Buffs"—the City's Trained Band Regiment of former-day renown—the Berkshires, and the old First Battalion of the 48th, now the Northamptons, even if, with the name, for two of these three regiments maybe, something of soreness is recalled, remembering how certain British infantry colours hang now as spoils of war in the Chapel of Les Invalides in Paris, and yet another Albuhera trophy flag of ours is in the crypt beside Napoleon's tomb. Tell it, if you want a hearty welcome, to those who represent in our army of today the old 23rd Royal Welsh Fusiliers:

The Welshman's bold battalion that the sun of Albuhera
Lit to such a field of glory, and to such a field of death.

And, above all, tell it to the "Die Hards"—the old 57th, the Middlesex Regiment of these times. Five hundred and seventy of them, of all ranks, went into action that morning; ten officers and 150 men, with hardly a cartridge left among them, came through the day. Of the others:

Even as they fought in files they lay,
Like the mower's grass at close of day,

When his work is o'er on the levelled plain—
Such was the fall of the foremost slain.

The King's Colour of the "Die Hards" had its staff smashed in two, and seventeen bullet-holes through the silk of the flag according to one account; thirty according to another. The Regimental Colour had twenty-one bullet-holes through it. Ensign Jackson had nine bullet-holes in his clothes and four wounds in his body. As every 16th of May comes, year by year, the officers of the regiment pass round at mess a silver cup filled with wine—the "Albuhera Cup," used only on that night of all the year—and in solemn silence drink from it in turn—"To the memory of those who fought and fell at Albuhera !"

Hardly another British battle can compare with Albuhera for the grim and terrible tragedy that marked its opening phase. The foremost brigade of British infantry was annihilated within seven minutes of firing its first shot. Three of our battalions—the 1st Buffs, the 2nd 48th, and the 2nd 66th—within that time were, literally indeed, smashed out of existence. Sent forward to assist and reinforce the weakening ranks of Zayas' bravely-resisting Spanish battalions, they were surprised by 1,200 Polish lancers, hussars, and dragoons, who swept down on them in the middle of a blinding squall of mist and sleet. Caught in the open, while extended in line, and without a moment's opportunity to attempt a rallying square, they were ridden down and slaughtered wholesale.

A moment before the three battalions were firing hotly at less than sixty yards' range into a French infantry column, and cheering exultantly as the enemy showed signs of being on the verge of giving way. The order was about to be given, indeed, to charge in on the French with the bayonet. Then, just as the hailstorm burst over the field, amid a wild turmoil of horse-hoofs and furious shoutings the cavalry charged down on them.

Four regiments of horse, 1,200 cavalry, rode over them at full gallop:—the Lancers of the Vistula, the 2nd Hussars, the 10th Hussars, the 20th Dragoons.

According to a British private soldier, the cavalry had been seen earlier, but had been mistaken for Spanish horse.

> Favoured by a tremendous shower of rain and hail, which had fallen early in the action, those lancers passed the river unobserved. On the storm abating they were seen in front, within musket-shot of our lines, and reports were made that they were

French—but not credited. From their being allowed to move thus quietly about, they evidently perceived that they were taken for friends, and kept in a compact body, waiting an opportunity to pounce on us. At length, while our divisions were detached, they advanced in squadrons at full gallop, shouting in Spanish, '*Vivan los Ingleses!*' '*Vivan los amigos de España!*' and the next moment they were in our ranks, which were so completely surprised that whole companies were destroyed without firing one shot!

The hapless three battalions were in the middle of a massacre. The Polish lancers gave no quarter. They took no prisoners. The wounded British infantrymen were stabbed to death as they lay on the ground with the long eighteen-foot spears of the ferocious troopers from the Vistula. The British survivors—it is the fact—after the battle solemnly took oath to one another never for the rest of the war to give quarter to Napoleon's Poles.

Fearful were the scenes of bloody horror in that awful welter of blows and carnage. Our men fought their very hardest, resisting heroically with their bayonets; but in vain—the odds were hopeless.

This is what one of the officers of the ill-fated 66th, Captain John Clarke, went through. He was in the midst of the murderous chaos.

A crowd of Polish Lancers and *chasseurs à cheval* swept along the rear of the brigade. Our men now ran into groups of six or eight, to do the best they could. The officers snatched up muskets and joined them, determined to sell their lives clearly. Quarter was not given. Poor Colonel Waller, of the quartermaster-general's staff, was cut down close to me He held up his hands asking for mercy, but the ruffian cut his fingers off. My ensign, Hay, was run through the lungs by a lance which came out at his back. He fell, but got up again. The lancer delivered another thrust, the lance striking Hay's breastbone. Down he went, and the Pole rolled over in the mud beside him. In the *mêlée*, when mixed up with lancers, *chasseurs à cheval* and French infantry, I came into collision with a lancer, and, being knocked over, was taken prisoner.

Captain Clarke was being hastened off the field when the unexpected arrival on the spot of the 3rd Dragoon Guards gave him a chance, and he escaped.

One of the colours of the 66th was saved, as Captain Clarke tells also. The officer bearing it, a lieutenant, who had hastily snatched it from the hands of the dead ensign, had got through the tumult somehow and managed to make his way to safety; to where, at some little way off, Cole's Fusilier Brigade was formed up.

Captain Clarke, too, made his escape there.

When I got close to the 7th Regiment they knelt to receive calvary, and I threw myself down to avoid their fire. I got up, and passing through the regiment, met Lieutenant Anderson carrying a colour. He said: 'I thought, my dear fellow, you must have been riddled; it was only presence of mind saved you.' I went a few paces to the rear and fell exhausted.

The 66th had sixteen officers and 310 men killed, wounded and missing; among the killed being Major Benning, commanding the regiment, and the two officers carrying the colours, Ensigns Walker and Colter. They went into action 400 strong, and next morning only fifty-three bayonets mustered on parade.

The regimental colour of the 66th is now at Les Invalides, hanging in the Chapel of St. Louis, where the flag can be identified without much difficulty. It is of blue silk, with a red St. George's Cross on it, and bordered white. In the centre is a shield, embroidered in silk and surrounded with roses and thistles, surmounted with a crown in gold and silver thread, and bearing the inscription, boldly lettered: "*LXVI. REGT.*"

The Buffs were on the outermost flank of the brigade. They were swooped down on first of all and caught in the full blast of the Polish tornado as it burst across the field. For sheer, downright heroism, nothing surely can excel the behaviour of the ensigns of the Buff's at Albuhera, in the midst of that tumultuous and terrifying *mêlée*.

Within the first minute the command of one of the companies—the captain being wounded and taken prisoner—devolved upon Ensign Edward Thomas, a boy-ensign only fifteen years of age. The trampling horsemen were surging round him, but fearless and quite calm, the boy only thought of his men. "Rally on me, men!" the brave lad shouted to those of his broken-up company nearest him. Ensign Thomas was carrying the regimental colour, and he stood there holding it on high for the soldiers to form round. They had, though, little chance of doing that; and the next instant a swarm of savage Poles were round the lad and upon him.

One of their officers called to the boy-ensign to give up his flag.

"Never! Never! except with my life!" came back the defiant British answer. The lancers dashed in instantly, and the splendid young hero was stabbed to death on the spot. The colour was captured, but was recovered later on. In the dim of that evening a sergeant and a private of the 57th sought out and found the body of Ensign Thomas. Crying bitterly the while, as we are told, those two rough men, they buried their boy-leader in a shallow grave that they dug with their bayonets. The two men were the only survivors of a company which had gone into action sixty-three strong.

The King's Colour of the Buffs were carried that morning by Ensign Walsh, an Irish lad, from King's County, just sixteen years of age. The men of the colour-party whose duty it had been to protect the flag had fallen in its defence, and the Ensign, running to where half a dozen of the Buffs were fighting with their bayonets, back to back, in a rallying group, was made at and chased by eight or ten Polish lancers and hussars, who darted furiously after him to seize his flag. Ensign Walsh was surrounded and wounded and knocked down, still clinging to his flag. Before he could be made a prisoner, or the colour be wrested from his hands, another officer of the Buffs rushed through and got to him.

He was Lieutenant Matthew Latham. Latham seized the colour-pole from the nearly-stunned boy-ensign's hands, and with his sword tried desperately to keep the ring of enemies off. Surrounded by the swarm of frenzied assailants, slashing or thrusting at him in their eagerness to carry off the trophy, Lieutenant Latham, in spite of them all, clung with despairing tenacity to his precious charge. He was shouted at to drop the flag and yield, but he refused. "I will give it up only with my life!" he called back in the faces of his crowding enemies. He was covered with wounds already, but, stubbornly defending himself with his sword, the magnificent fellow did his utmost to keep them all at bay. The honour of his regiment was in his hands. Matthew Latham was not going to surrender his colours to any enemy.

A French hussar seized the staff of the colour. Standing up in his stirrups he aimed a fierce cut at the head of the brave lieutenant. The blow failed to strike Latham down; but it mutilated him cruelly, shearing away one side of his face and nose. Even then, although a mass of blood from his injuries as he was, and reeling, well-nigh stunned by the hussar's blow, Latham's dauntless resolution did not weaken. Recovering himself, with desperate and amazing vigour he still fought on. A mob of assailants was swarming about him, grabbing at the flag, jostling round as they furiously strove to tear the colour from his hands. Lieutenant Latham kept them off until a second sabre-slash cut his left arm and the hand in which he held the colour clean off. But still the British lieutenant's indomitable spirit was not conquered. Maimed and horribly mutilated as he was, he let go his sword, and seizing the colour-staff with his right hand, made his last effort to hold on to the flag.

That was all he could do. A moment after he was thrown over to the ground, and trampled on by horse-hoofs, and pierced with innumerable lance-thrusts. But the very number of his enemies impeded their efforts to destroy him. Before they could make an end of the brave fellow, just as they were about to finish Latham off, half a dozen British dragoons came plunging through to the place, and the French troopers, foiled and baffled at the last moment, turned off in haste to gallop away elsewhere.

Lieutenant Latham was still alive; he was just conscious, and in that extreme moment he thought only of his flag. Exerting what little strength remained to him, he managed to rip away the silk of the colour from the staff and to drag it underneath his body; then he became unconscious from loss of blood.

When, later in the battle, the Fusilier Brigade made its forlorn-hope advance over the ground there, to turn at the last moment the fortunes of the day, Sergeant Gough, of the 7th Royal Fusiliers, found the King's Colour of the Buffs underneath the body of Lieutenant Latham, who was lying stretched over it and apparently dead. The colour was restored to the Buffs that afternoon, the sergeant being rewarded in due course with a commission.

As the battle was ending, Lieutenant Latham recovered consciousness, and, reviving somewhat, crawled down to a brook nearby. There he was found by an ambulance-party trying to quench his thirst. He was carried to a Portuguese house in the neighbourhood, where his wounds were dressed and the stump of his arm was amputated. Extraordinary as it may seem, Lieutenant Latham recovered and did duty with his regiment for some years.

Ensign Walsh was dragged away a prisoner. He escaped that night and told his surviving brother-officers what he had seen of Latham's marvellous heroism. The officers of the Buffs as soon as possible afterwards subscribed 100 guineas and presented Latham with a gold medal, bearing in relief a representation of the saving of the colour, with underneath the inscription: "I will surrender it only with my life."

A captain's commission was awarded Latham by the Duke of York, with a pension of £170 for his wounds. At the close of the war the Prince Regent, to whom Latham was presented, made himself responsible for the cost of an expensive operation by a leading surgeon of the day of special reputation "for repairing mutilations of the face in a wonderful manner."

Writes one of the officers of the Buffs in a letter home after the battle:

> I shall endeavour to give you some facts respecting the First Battalion of the Buffs. Captain Burke is killed; Captain Cameron was shot in the neck, wounded in the breast with a pike, and is a prisoner; Captain Marley was wounded twice in the body with a pike, badly; Captain Stevens was shot in the arm, was a prisoner, and made his escape; Lieutenant Woods had his leg shot off, also part of his nose and cheek; Lieutenant Juxon is wounded in the thigh with a pike; Lieutenant Hooper shot through the shoulder; Lieutenant Houghton has received a severe sabre-cut in the hand and through the skull; Lieutenant Herbert is dead; Ensigns Chadwick and Thomas are also dead; Lieutenants O'Donnell and Terlow, with Ensign Walsh, were wounded and made prisoners—they have since escaped. Twenty-four officers and 750 rank and file were actually engaged; out of that number there only remained to draw rations on the following day five officers and 134 men. I was stabbed with a pike in the breast, in the back, and elsewhere by a Polander, and the enemy's cavalry galloped over me.

"Our colours," the officer proudly records also, "were taken and retaken three times, and they are now in our possession fixed on two halberds."

The Fourth Battalion of Colborne's Brigade—the 31st—escaped with lighter losses. They were on the inner flank of the brigade, coming up last. They had not yet deployed in line, being still in column when the French cavalry charged. The 31st, under Major L'Estrange, were able to form square and keep the Polish lancers at bay, holding their ground with desperate courage until help from elsewhere got to the spot.

After being beaten off by the 31st, the Poles made a galloping sweep across the rear of the Spanish line on the right of the battlefield. In their hurried rush past some of them came upon General

Beresford, the British commander-in-chief, who had just come to the place to help in rallying the Spaniards.³ The staff, general and all, had to draw their swords and fight for their lives. One desperately bold Polish lancer rode at Beresford himself. "He knocked over one of the escort with the butt of his lance, overset another man and horse, and gave employment to the entire headquarters before he could be despatched," so a British officer writes, adding:

> Some of the Portuguese declared afterwards that the man seemed possessed by an evil spirit, and that when he fell at last he literally bit the ground.

The lancer, indeed, got through to and attacked Beresford himself; but the burly Irishman, a tall man of Herculean proportions, proved more than his match. The general parried the lance-thrust, which just missed him, and then, the length of the weapon allowing Beresford to get within its point, the general closed with the Pole and grappled him. Letting his sword go, to sling from his wrist, Beresford gripped the Pole by the collar of his uniform, and by sheer muscular strength dragged him out of his saddle and hurled him to the ground, where the general's orderly at length finished the lancer off.

The 57th went forward into the battle to retrieve the fortunes of the fight, coming up within a few minutes of the hideous catastrophe that had shattered Colborne's Brigade out of existence. They had about a mile to go, and were hastened forward at a rapid pace, advancing in open column of companies, right in front.

With the 29th and the Second Battalion of the 48th they formed the Third Brigade in Wellington's Second Division, which was serving that day with Beresford's army. Major-General Houghton was their brigadier.

As the brigade got the order to go forward, describes one of the officers, the commander of the Second Division, Major-General the Hon. William Stewart, "rode up, and, after a few energetic words, said: 'Now is the time—let us give three cheers!' This was instantly done with heart and soul; every cap was in the air. We immediately advanced up the hill under a sharp fire from the enemy's light troops, which we did not condescend to return." The men pressed forward to the front, passing through the intervals of Zayas' broken division of

---

3. He was a major-general in the British Army, Sir William Carr Beresford, holding the rank also of marshal in the Portuguese Army, which he had reorganized, and now commanded, under Wellington's supreme authority.

Spanish infantry, now nearly at its last gasp.

If at Albuhera one portion of the Spanish contingent behaved badly, others did their duty manfully. The division under General Zayas, on the extreme right of the allied line of battle, wheeled back hastily, amid all the excitement of the first critical moment when Soult's sweeping flank attack opened, threatening to take Beresford's position end-on and roll up its strung-out detachments, overwhelmed in detail and crushed under the avalanche-like onrush of the massed French columns—in the face of that alarming onset Zayas' men not only stood their ground unshaken, but held back the French advance sufficiency long for the two nearest British brigades to be brought forward to the point of danger.

Zayas' Spaniards kept their post in spite of the appalling spectacle before their eyes of the disaster to Colborne's battalions close by them; and a further disastrous misadventure in their own line. As the French came charging at them, an artillery tumbril blew up with a tremendous explosion in the midst of the Spanish soldiers, causing widespread confusion and considerable loss of life. The headmost of the French dashed through instantly at the gap thus made. The greater number of Zayas' men, however, still stood firm, and the others rallied bravely after the momentary panic that followed the explosion. They offered a strenuous resistance with devoted courage for some time, but were being gradually borne back step by step before the solid mass of French battalions, forging their way on as though to burst a passage through by sheer weight of numbers, when Hoghton's men arrived to their relief.

Added to that, Zayas and his men—they were made up of two battalions of the old "Irish Regiment" of Spain, originally recruited from Jacobite refugees after the Boyne, and known in the Spanish service as the "*Regimiento de Irlanda,*" and two of the King of Spain's former Royal Guard—had suffered losses from British bullets. Hoghton's leading battalion as it came up had to beat off a charge of the Polish lancers as they swept round in rear of the Spanish line, and in firing on the horsemen some of the British bullets shot many of the Spaniards in the back. Out of some 2,000 men in Zayas' Spanish division more than 600 had fallen before Hoghton's Brigade could get to their assistance.

The other Spaniards on the field, it is notorious, did not behave well. They gave way after offering a weak resistance, and, in the result, as they were falling back in disorder, came in for rough treatment at our hands. The Polish lancers got in among them and did deadly execution, and, at the same time, as an officer of the 29th tells, Hoghton's men had to shoot many of them down in self-defence. The Spanish fugitives, according to him, in their panic came rushing back on the 29th "in utter confusion, mixed up with the Polish lancers and others, thrusting and cutting without mercy." To beat off the Poles the regiment had to open fire on friends and foes alike.

> Many of the Spaniards threw themselves on the ground, others attempted to get through our line; but this could not be permitted, because we being in line on the slope of a bare green hill, and such a rush of friends and foes coming down on us, any opening made to let the former pass would have admitted the enemy also. We had no alternative left but, in self-defence, to fire on both.

That saved the British at any rate. "The lancers brought up and made the best of their way to their own lines, and the Spaniards were permitted to pass to the rear."

The hard-hit battalions of Zayas were recalled as the advancing British reached their position. The brave fellows proved themselves game to the last. "When we arrived near the retreating Spaniards and formed our line to advance through them," says one of the 48th, "a very noble-looking young Spaniard rode up to me and begged me, with a sort of proud anxiety, to take notice that his countrymen were ordered to retire, not running away."

The 29th at the head of the brigade, with the 57th following them, and the 48th in rear, halted on the crest of the sloping ridge along which the Spaniards of Zayas had been posted. As the British did so a fiery blast of musketry and cannon-balls beat fiercely on them from the nearest of the French columns in front. The enemy were barely fifty yards off, but they were beyond reach of a bayonet-attack for the time. A narrow but steep-sided gully intervened, extending for practically the length of the ridge. The 29th halted first and deployed swiftly, flinging its companies forward into line. A moment after the 57th and then the 48th joined them. All stood lined up and confronted the heads of the French columns immediately opposite. Three battalions, 1,800 British linesmen, faced and held in check 7,000 French infantry; nineteen battalions.

This was the scene in front as two of our officers saw it. "Just as our line had entirely cleared the Spaniards," says one, "the smoke of battle was for a moment blown aside by the slackening of the fire, and gave to our view the French grenadier caps, their glittering arms, and the whole aspect of their frowning masses. It was a grand, but momentary, sight: a heavy atmosphere of smoke enveloped us, and few objects could be discerned at all—none distinctly." Describes the other officer:

> We found the enemy in masses or columns of grand divisions, with light troops and artillery in the intervals. From the waving and rising of the ground on which some of them stood, their rear ranks in places could fire over the front, and some guns fired over the heads of a column. Notwithstanding this formidable array, our line went close up to the enemy without even a piece of artillery to support us—at least, near us there were none.

Not a bullet in reply came from the British line until every man had formed up in his place. The gallant Brigadier waited until his line was completely dressed all along its length. Not a musket went off in answer to the French fire until after that. A few moments before Hoghton gave the word to begin he rode over to Colonel Inglis of the 57th, who, on horseback of course, was in front of the right-wing companies of his regiment, rebuking them sternly for having opened fire without orders, while coming into position, on the Polish lancers in front of the 29th. Colonel Inglis dressed his line with stiff, old-fashioned formality, shoulder to shoulder. Without paying the smallest heed to the hot fire from the French, he made the whole regiment stand stock-still with ordered arms.

As he was doing that Colonel Inglis's horse went down, shot dead. "Colonel Inglis," describes an officer of the 57th, "close to and immediately in front of the colours, was dressing the line on the centre. He had finished with the right wing, and, having turned to the left, was coolly scanning the men as they formed, when a shot brought his charger to the ground, leaving his master erect on his feet. At that critical moment I observed his unchanged countenance, and that while he extricated his feet from the stirrups he never once turned his eyes from the line he was continuing to perfect, and not until that was completed did he cast a glance on the remains of his noble steed."

On General Hoghton coming to him, the colonel drew the brigadier's attention to the steadiness of the 57th. Hoghton told Colonel Inglis that the brigade was not to open fire until he gave the signal with his hat. He rode away and made the signal immediately afterwards. Giving a quick final glance along the line of his brigade, Hoghton took off his cocked hat and held it up at arm's length.

At once the opening British volley crashed out, and the terrific duel of the Third Brigade at Albuhera began.

Within five minutes the gallant Hoghton himself fell—shot dead. Colonel Inglis, as senior officer, thereupon took charge of the brigade, remaining at the head of his own men, mounted on a second charger, at his post a little in advance of the colours of the 57th, at the centre of the line.

With furious rapidity the musketry on both sides flashed across the short intervening space as the three British battalions strove their hardest to beat down the French fire; their two-deep line, from one end to the other, just equalling the heads of the French columns. The furious fusillade smote into the enemy hard and heavily as the combat raged with unabating ferocity for the first half-hour.

"A most overwhelming fire of artillery and small arms was opened on us, which was vigorously returned," says an officer of the 29th. "There we unflinchingly stood and there we fell, our ranks at some places swept away by sections."

"At intervals," relates another officer who was there, "a shriek or a groan told that men were falling around me, but it was not always that the tumult of the contest suffered me to catch individual sounds. The constant 'feeling to the centre' and the gradual diminution of our front more truly bespoke the havoc of death. We were the whole time progressively advancing upon and shaking the enemy. As we moved slowly, but ever a little in advance, our own killed and wounded lay behind us; we arrived among those of the Spaniards who had fallen in the first onset, then among those of the enemy. At last we were only twenty yards from their front."

Our men had no artillery near them to lend assistance. Cleeve's Hanoverian battery of the King's German Legion, which had gone forward with Colborne's Brigade, had been put out of action in the disaster, most of the gunners being slaughtered beside their guns by the Polish lancers. One of the survivors, a Hanoverian officer, came near the 29th with the remnant of men and guns.

> After some time an officer of artillery brought up two or three guns, but could find no one to give him orders, all the superior officers being killed. In the end he was bidden not to wait for

orders, and so he began.

The French across the gully meanwhile were fighting with no less bravery and determination, although they could make no headway in the face of the British fire. The army corps commander on the spot, General Girard, one of Napoleon's *aides-de-camp* and special favourites, a young officer and a keen and gallant soldier, exerted himself to the utmost; but in vain. His massive columns were held fast, blocked by their own numbers and unable to advance against the incessant hail of English bullets from the stubborn red-coated line. The French soldiers blazed away as fast as they could load and fire; in their hot haste "dispensing with the use of the ramrod—the cartridge fitting rather loosely, they dropped it in, and giving the butt a quick knock on the ground, depended on that for sending it home."

Their eagerness to load quickly in this way caused many cartridges to stick midway in the musket barrels, and not a few French soldiers, we are told, were maimed or killed as they fought by their own weapons bursting. Their sharpshooters at the same time, posted in the intervals between the regiments, kept at their murderous work, "and even in the thickest of the fight managed to pick off almost all our field-officers on the ground." There was no cover; the ground was "a surface smooth as a billiard-table," and the Frenchmen crept forward, "stretching along the earth like some deadly reptile," until they reached the very edge of the gully, to fire from there, each sharpshooter "using his cap as a rest for his fusil." From their bullets fell, among others, General Hoghton, with Colonels Duckworth of the 48th and White of the 29th.

Among the "Die Hards," in the hottest of the fighting Major Scott and Captain Fawcett were shot down; the first-named being killed outright, the second mortally wounded. Major Spring was severely wounded. Captains Termyn and Kisby were mortally wounded; Captains Shadforth, M'Gibbon, and Stainforth severely wounded; Captain Hely less severely. Lieutenant Sheridan was mortally wounded; Lieutenants Evatt, Baxter, M'Lachlan, Macfarlane, Hughes, Dix, Patterson, M'Dougall, Myers, and Ensigns Torrens, Veitch, and Jackson were all severely wounded.

Captain Ralph Fawcett, a young man only twenty-three years of age, on receiving his mortal wound, indifferent to his own agony, told the men who picked him up to place him on a small hillock close at hand. From there, until death ended his sufferings, he continued to command his company, calling to the men every now and again not to waste their ammunition and fire low. Ensign Torrens, carrying the King's Colour, was severely wounded, and the flag dropped to the ground. Ensign Jackson, who was carrying the regimental colour, at once told a sergeant to pick it up; and, handing him in exchange the regimental colour, took the King's Colour himself. He had already been wounded three times, but had gallantly remained at his post. A fourth wound compelled him to withdraw to the rear to have the injury attended to, leaving the flag in Ensign Veitch's charge. Immediately his wounds were tied up Jackson hurried back. But Veitch, although in the interval he too had been wounded, declined to hand the flag back. The stubborn boy refused to give up the King's Colour, and in spite of his wound kept hold of it to the end.

Colonel Inglis fell severely wounded: a grape-shot struck him below the neck and lodged in his back against the shoulder-blade. He declined all offers to carry him to the rear, telling the men who ran to pick him up to leave him where he had fallen, in front of the Colours of the Regiment. Then it was that the heroic chief gave utterance to those spirit-stirring words no soldier can hear unmoved. "Die Hard, men! Die Hard!" he called to the regiment as he lay propped up on the ground, the French bullets cutting up the turf all about him. He kept on calling out "Die Hard, 57th!" at intervals to the end of the fight, still lying where he had fallen. That is the origin of a famous and splendid *sobriquet* the like of which no other regiment in any army can boast of.

"He lay on the ground," says one of his officers in a letter, "close to the regiment, refusing all offers to be carried to the rear, and determined to share the fate of his 'Die Hards,' whom he continued to cheer to steadiness and exertion, and who, encouraged by the voice of their brave commander, continued to close in on their tattered and staff-broken colours, as their comrades fell in the line in which he had formed them."[4]

---

4. Colonel Inglis had served, boy and man, ever since he first joined the 57th as an ensign years before: in the American War of Independence, and also on active service in Flanders and in the West Indies. The grape-shot that struck him down, a ball 4 inches in circumference, and weighing a quarter of a pound, could not be removed by the surgeons until two days afterwards, at Olivenza, Colonel Inglis having had to pass the first night in the open on the field of battle. He recovered, and did further distinguished service in the Battles of the Pyrenees as major-general under Wellington, finally as Sir William Inglis, K.C.B., enjoying many years of honour in retirement at home. "No better or braver man existed," it was publicly stated of him at his death in 1836. His remains rest in Canterbury Cathedral.

"Most nobly," to use the words of the regimental historian, Captain Woollright, "did all ranks respond to his exhortations. Though their comrades fell with horrible wounds on every side, though their leaders were down and all hope of success seemed gone, undauntedly they maintained the fight, closing in on their torn and broken colours as they bit their cartridges and plied their ramrods, grimly determined to die hard; and the line of the 57th, though torn and decimated by the murderous fire directed on it, remained and stood unflinchingly on the crest of the hill, where on the following day were to be seen their dead 'lying as they fought in ranks' and 'with every wound in front.'" These were the words of General Beresford in his Albuhera dispatch: "It was observed that our dead, particularly the 57th Regiment, were lying as they fought in ranks and every wound was in front."

The set-to between the 1,800 British against 7,000 French continued without cessation for an hour and a half. "We continued to maintain this unprecedented conflict with unabated energy. The enemy, notwithstanding his superiority of numbers, had not gained an inch of ground, but, on the contrary, we were gaining on him." So says one officer in the thick of the fight. "So destructive was the fire of the enemy," says another, one of the 57th, "that in a short time the few survivors must have slept in peace with their fallen brothers."

"Our line," describes the officer of the 29th who has been quoted, "at length became so reduced that it resembled a chain of skirmishers in extended order."

One of the ensigns of the 29th was young Richard Vance, another of the brave boys of Albuhera day, a lad who had only seven months joined. "Seeing the terrible losses of the regiment, and fearing lest the regimental colour of which he had charge might fall into the enemy's hands by his death, he tore it from the pole. He was killed just after, and when the battle closed the colour was found concealed in the breast of his coat and the standard-pole near his body." Ensign Vance's sword-knot is one of the treasures of the Museum of the Royal United Service Institution in Whitehall.

Soult had at that moment the fate of Albuhera in the hollow of his hand. The marshal had victory, complete and overwhelming, within his grasp. He had but to say two words. At his side was the leader of his cavalry, Latour Maubourg, a bold and energetic officer; one of Napoleon's ablest cavalry commanders, fuming and fretting with impatience and using bad language beneath his breath. Soult had only to give one order. His lips had but to utter two words: "*Maubourg—*

The Albuhera Flag of the "Die-Hards"

Donnez!" Only that was needed to let loose ten regiments of cavalry and trample out of being the attenuated remnant of the British line, freeing Girard's columns for a fresh sweep forward.

Nothing could have stopped Maubourg. His troopers were fresh and spoiling for fight. Three thousand horsemen, twenty-six squadrons, ten regiments of dragoons, hussars, and *chasseurs*; not counting the four regiments of Polish lancers and the hussars and dragoons of the earlier charge, in form again now, and eager for more work. "*Maubourg—Donnez!*" was all that Soult had to say, and the French squadrons would spring forward amidst the shot-shattered files of the thin red line with the resistless shock of a thunderbolt. But the words were not spoken. Soult hesitated. He held back from excess of caution and his golden opportunity passed.

He had begun the battle, explained the marshal to Napoleon, understanding that only 20,000 British and Portuguese troops were in front of him, to withstand his army of 24,000. To his surprise, said Soult, he learned from prisoners brought in by the hussars after the Polish charge that 13,000 Spaniards had reinforced Beresford in the course of the past night, and, in addition, a new British brigade had come in from Badajoz during the early morning. On hearing that he refrained from sending forward his 5,600 reserved infantry of Werlé's Division and would not let Maubourg charge. So the marshal put his case in exculpation.

Soult's caution proved the turning-point of the day's fortunes. Immediately afterwards the battle entered on its final phase, and Albuhera was lost for Napoleon and France.

The coming on the scene of the Fusilier Brigade, part of Sir Lowry Cole's Fourth Division, with General Abercrombie's Brigade of the Second Division, saved the situation for England at the last moment.

The fusiliers had been on the battlefield since nine o'clock, posted in rear of the British second line, as Beresford had originally fronted his army. The general had held Cole back out of action, keeping his troops to serve as a countercheck to Maubourg's mass of squadrons, in sight on the French right, and Werlé's reserve battalions visible farther off. Cole, from where he was, had marked with growing anxiety the heavy fighting on the ridge, as well as he could make it out in the misty weather and "thick smoke on the hill owing to the concentrated and incessant fire of musketry and artillery," and had sent an *aide-de-camp*, Major Roverea, a Swiss officer serving under Wellington, to ask Beresford's leave to support Hoghton's hard-pressed troops. Roverea, however, did not come back, a French sharpshooter's bullet in the head having knocked him over while on his way, and Sir Lowry, looking for his return with increased impatience, got no answer.

It came, however, to the same thing. Beresford had no intention of letting Cole move from that part of the field. He, too, was gravely disquieted at the way the situation with the Third Brigade seemed to be shaping, as seen from some way off, but proposed to use other troops for Hoghton's relief: two of his Portuguese brigades. He had already sent them directions to hasten to the aid of the troops on the ridge, but the order had not been received, the *aide-de-camp* carrying the message having met Major Roverea's fate and been shot on the way. Beresford, besides that, tried to send some of the Spaniards, and himself rode over to one of their brigades, that of Carlos de España. All his exhortations, however, failed to move the troops there. They were mostly demoralized regiments which had done badly early in the forenoon.

In a fury Beresford caught hold of one of the Spanish ensigns and hauled him forward with his flag for some yards. But not a man of the regiment followed, and the wretched ensign then ran back to his comrades. The general seized hold, too, of a Spanish colonel by his epaulettes and tried to drag him to the front; but again to no purpose.

Providentially, elsewhere, one of Beresford's staff-officers, the deputy quartermaster-general, Colonel Henry Hardinge, a young man of twenty-five, but with considerable war experience, took action on his own initiative. Colonel Hardinge had been on the ridge among the "Die Hards." According to one story he first went down to Beresford and found him on the point of giving orders for a retreat. Hardinge said to him, "Sir, you have a Peerage on one hand and a Court Martial on the other!"

Beresford, after a pause, said slowly—"I will try for the Peerage." He then countermanded the retreat, and Hardinge rode to Cole. So it has been told.

According to Hardinge's own letters he went hurrying down from the ridge direct to Cole, whose troops were the nearest, "expressly for the purpose for causing the Fourth Division to move up to the attack of the enemy's column." So Hardinge himself puts it.

He came up to Sir Lowry "with his sword drawn, having had on the way to collect a few men to drive off a party of French skirmishers who were working round one flank, and had got within twenty paces."

When he left the Third Brigade, says Colonel Hardinge, its situation was "desperate."

Some of the soldiers in the ranks were calling to their sergeants and wounded comrades to empty their pouches to supply them with ammunition. The 29th, 57th, and 48th Regiments, were almost exterminated. My former regiment, the 57th, had scarcely any officers left. Every commanding officer was at this time either killed or wounded: Sir William Stewart, the general of the division twice wounded—Hoghton, the general of the brigade, killed; and it was evident that the whole brigade was in such a crippled and exhausted state that it could not be expected to hold the position much longer. In this desperate state of things, not admitting of delay, but requiring an instant remedy, I rode to Sir Lowry Cole to propose to him to attack the enemy's column with his division.

He rode up to General Cole, with his drawn sword in his hand, "though it was unusual for a staff-officer," and, describing the impossibility of Hoghton's men holding out, strenuously urged an immediate advance. Cole replied that General Beresford had instructed him on no account to stir from where he was. But Colonel Hardinge was not to be rebuffed.

I earnestly represented that this order had been given four hours before, under a very different state of things, and that the gain or loss of the battle depended on the immediate advance of his division. . . . I spoke as eye-witness:—I was the deputy quarter master-general of the Portuguese army, and as such my responsibility and authority were pledged for the accuracy of my report and the necessity of the movement I proposed.

While Hardinge was still speaking, Colonel Rooke of the adjutant-general's department came up. He also had been on the ridge. General Cole turned to him with "Hardinge is pressing me to attack the enemy's column." Colonel Rooke in response confirmed the critical state of things on the hill, and joined with Hardinge in urging an immediate advance. Sir Lowry Cole assented. It was a very grave responsibility that he was incurring; he was disobeying the commander-in-chief's explicit orders:—but he would take the risk. Writing afterwards to Colonel Hardinge, Sir Lowry said:

The credit of originating the movement rests with you, the

credit of having incurred the responsibility rests with me.

"After that, as soon as Cole's troops were in motion," says Colonel Hardinge, "I went to Abercrombie's Brigade, which was in rear of Hoghton's left, and authorized him to deploy and move past Hoghton's men."

Cole's men began their advance: the First and Second Battalions of the 7th Royal Fusiliers on the left, the 23rd Welsh Fusiliers on the right; together with Harvey's Portuguese Brigade, also under the orders of the Commander of the Fourth Division.

They moved forward, heading to strike diagonally at the French flank; deployed into a line of bayonets a mile long, three British and five Portuguese battalions abreast. The flank battalions moved in square, supported by three regiments of British dragoons and a horse-artillery battery. They had about half a mile to go, over the same open ground where Colborne's Brigade had been destroyed, being exposed all the time to Maubourg's cavalry. It was, as General Cole himself put it, "a most difficult and hazardous movement to accomplish." The three invincible battalions on the hill, all that was left of them, were meanwhile ever magnificently keeping the enemy at bay. "There was no yielding," remarks Colonel Hardinge with pride, "or any other perceptible change indicating a crisis."

Soult realized his position and the peril to himself as the Fusilier Brigade came on. He saw what the coming blow foreboded for his army. To ward it off four of Maubourg's regiments at once charged out on Harvey's Portuguese, while Werlé's infantry were pushed to the front rapidly to beat back the Fusiliers.

The dragoons were dealt with rolling volleys from the battalion in square on that flank, and sent flying back in disorder with many empty saddles. Werlé's division of nine battalions, making three regiments, were confronted by the fusiliers as they came down the slope. Each of the three British battalions in line engaged the French regiment opposite—one battalion against three massed in regimental columns. The dense formation of the French—each column had a front of only 120 men, who were all that could use their muskets to fire, the sixteen ranks behind being useless for the purpose—could not cope with the superiority of the fire of the wider-fronted and overlapping British line, two deep, every man of whom was shooting his hardest.

Sir Lowry headed the attack in person. The fusiliers were led by their brigadier, Sir William Myers, a young officer twenty-five years of age, but a first-rate and brilliant soldier. "It will be a glorious day for the fusiliers," were his words when the order was given to go forward. His horse was shot under him within the first few minutes as they were beginning to ascend the hill. Myers led on the brigade on foot, at the head of his regiment, the First Battalion of the Royal Fusiliers, until a second horse was brought up; then, a little way farther, a bullet struck him in the hip, passing upwards into his body, and inflicting a mortal wound. The heroic officer kept in the saddle undauntedly all the time, though suffering excruciating pain. He continued to call out words of encouragement to his men until he fainted, being lifted from his horse just in time to prevent his falling to the ground. He died next day.

"We moved steadily towards the enemy, and very soon commenced firing," describes an officer of the Royal Fusiliers, Sir Edward Blakeney, the lieut.-colonel of the Second Battalion.

> The men behaved most gloriously, never losing their ranks, and closing to the centre as casualties occurred. From the quantities of smoke, I could perceive very little but what was immediately in my front. The First Battalion closed with the right column of the French, and I moved on and closed with the second column, the 23rd with the left column. This appeared to me to be the position of the three battalions when the French faced about, at about thirty or forty yards from us. Our firing was most incessant, and we kept following the enemy until we reached the second hill and the position they had previously occupied. During the closest part of the action I saw the French officers endeavouring to deploy their columns, but all to no purpose, for as soon as a third of a company got out, they immediately ran back to be covered by the front of the column. Our loss was, of course, most severe, but the battalions never for an instant ceased advancing under artillery firing grape the whole time.

A sergeant of the First Battalion also—Cooper—gives his impressions in these words:

> We began to ascend the slope with panting breath, while the roll and thunder of the furious battle increased. Under this tremendous fire of the enemy our thin line staggers; men are knocked about like skittles, but not a step backwards is taken. Here our colonel and all the field-officers of the brigade fell,

either killed or wounded, but no confusion ensued. The orders were: 'Close up! Close in! Fire away! Forward!' We are close up to the enemy's column; they break and rush down the other side of the hill in the greatest mob-like confusion.

A comrade of his, tells Cooper also, as they were beginning the fight, called out: "Where's Arthur?" He meant Wellington.

The answer was given: "I don't know—I don't see him!"

Rejoined the first private: "Aw wish he wur here!"

"So did I," comments Sergeant Cooper.

The fight along the hill-slope lasted for some twenty minutes. Then came the end, the final scene, in his brilliant description of which Napier is at his best.

> The Fusilier Battalion, struck by the iron tempest, reeled and staggered like sinking ships; but suddenly and sternly recovering, they closed on their terrible enemies, and then was seen with what a strength and majesty the British soldier fights. In vain did Soult with voice and gesture animate his Frenchmen; in vain did the hardiest veterans break from the crowded columns and sacrifice their lives to gain time for the mass to open out on such a fair field; in vain did the mass itself bear up, and, fiercely striving, fire indiscriminately upon friends and foes, while the horsemen, hovering on the flank, threatened to charge the advancing line.
>
> Nothing could stop that astonishing infantry. No sudden burst of undisciplined valour, no nervous enthusiasm, weakened the stability of their order; their flashing eyes were bent on the dark columns in their front; their measured tread shook the ground; their dreadful volleys swept away the head of every formation; their deafening shouts overpowered the dissonant cries that broke from all parts of the tumultuous crowd as, slowly and with a horrid carnage, it was pushed by the incessant vigour of the attack to the farthest edge of the hill. In vain did the French reserves mix with the struggling multitude to sustain the fight; their efforts only increased the irremediable confusion, and the mighty mass, breaking off like a loosened cliff, went headlong down the steep.

"The fusiliers," according to Colonel Hardinge, who was watching them, "exceeded anything that the word *gallantry* can convey!"

Game to the last, the small remnants of the "Die Hards," as the fusiliers made their final conquering advance, tried to join them and take part. There were just 160 of them left, officers and men. Beresford, who had just ridden up to the spot, saw them and had them stopped. "The wreck of the 57th," in the words again of one of the officers of the regiment, "cheered on by their prostrate and almost exhausted chief, was on the point of joining in the charge when Marshal Beresford exclaimed: 'Stop them! Stop the 57th! It would be a sin to let them go on!' And when the remnant of the 'Die Hards' retired they carried with them their colours, shot to ribbons, but unpolluted by a moment's grasp of a foeman's hand."

Two French grenadier battalions, Soult's last reserves, were brought up in a forlorn-hope attempt to stem the final rush of the victorious British. They were overwhelmed in an instant, and sent flying with the loss of 370 men out of 1,000.

The sight of Werlé's whole division in wild flight was too much for the nerves of Girard's men, overwrought already by the havoc in their ranks during their own sanguinary struggle with the Third Brigade. Abercrombie's regiments came at them at the same instant, round the left flank of the Third Brigade, and followed up a furious volley with a bayonet-charge. Girard's battalions, beaten at last, gave way. Turning their backs on their antagonists, the survivors of Hoghton's heroic three battalions, they streamed off, broken up and in hopeless confusion, and flung themselves in among Werlé's mob of fugitives. All rushed off in headlong rout, battalions mixed up in utter disorder; nor did they stop running until they had got back to the position whence Soult had set out in the early morning. Latour Maubourg's cavalry, still a menacing array of squadrons, covered the flight of the infantry, supported by the forty guns of Soult's artillery, all massed in one great battery on the farther ridge. Beresford's troops were too much exhausted and reduced in numbers to attempt to press their advantage home.

So closed the most fiercely contested and, for the numbers engaged, most sanguinary of British infantry battles. It lasted from nine in the morning until between two and three in the afternoon, and had been fought, by most of the British Army at any rate, on empty stomachs. The alarm had been given at seven o'clock, just as our men were about to begin their breakfasts. "We had scarcely time to get a little tea and a morsel of biscuit," our officer of the 29th relates, "when the alarm was given: 'Stand to your arms—the French are advancing!' We accordingly got under arms instantly, leaving tents and baggage to be disposed of as the quartermaster and batmen best could,"

Under stress of the unexpectedly early alarm General Hoghton of the Third Brigade turned out, we are told, in an old green frock-coat he had hastily put on. He had no opportunity of changing it until after the firing had begun, and the Third Brigade had advanced to the ridge. His servant then overtook him and ran up, carrying the brigadier's red uniform coat, which Hoghton donned while on horseback, in sight of both armies.

Fearful, indeed, was the cost of Albuhera in human life to victors and vanquished alike. Beresford returned his losses at 4,100 British, out of a total of 10,000; 400 Portuguese of Harvey's Brigade, fallen while taking their part in the advance of the fusiliers; and 1,500 Spaniards, mostly the men of Zayas' gallant division. Soult stated his casualties to the Ministry of War in Paris as, in round numbers, 6,000 men.

Of the British, the three battalions of the Fusilier Brigade in that one charge lost more than half their strength in killed and wounded; over 50 *per cent.*: 1,045 men out of 2,015 who started for the attack. General Cole was wounded; also Colonel Wade, his adjutant-general, and all his *aides-de-camp*. All three colonels of the fusiliers fell: Brigadier Myers, mortally wounded; Colonel Sir Edward Blakeney, also of the Royal Fusiliers; and Colonel Ellis, of the 23rd, severely wounded. The two battalions of the 7th Fusiliers lost 705 officers and men. Their colour-poles were shattered to splinters by bullets, and their colours torn to strips of tattered silk. The single battalion of the Royal Welsh Fusiliers lost 332 officers and men.

One company, Captain Stainforth's, was brought out of action by a corporal, Thomas Robinson. The colours of the 23rd, too, were shot to rags. One of them, the King's Colour of the regiment, was borne throughout by a boy of seventeen, Ensign Bevis Hall. He got through the battle without a scratch until the last moment. As the fight closed, when the French were in flight, while in the act of waving his flag on high, amid the triumphantly cheering soldiers, a last shot, fired by some retreating Frenchman, turning back to let off one more cartridge, struck the gallant lad between the eyes and he fell dead.

Colborne's ill-fated First Brigade of the Second Division lost in killed and wounded seven-tenths of its officers and men: 1,400 out of 2,000, all told. Of the 400 whom the Poles and hussars made prisoners, most escaped during the night in the confusion among the French after the battle. They got back to the British lines, to be dubbed by their comrades in one regiment for the rest of their service "The Resurrection Men."

Hoghton's invincible Third Brigade lost five-eighths of its strength: 1,044 out of 1,650 of all ranks. General Stewart was wounded twice; Brigadier Hoghton and General Duckworth, of the 48th, were killed; Colonel White, of the 29th, was mortally wounded; Colonel Inglis, of the 57th, severely wounded. Every field-officer of the three battalions fell, either killed or wounded. At the end what remained of the Third Brigade was commanded by a Captain, Cimitière, of the 48th; a Frenchman, curiously—a French Royalist refugee from the Terror, who had taken service against the murderers of his King. At roll-call on the evening of the battle only two captains, three subalterns, and 96 men of the whole battalion of the 29th answered to their names—324 officers and men were lying on the field, killed or wounded.

The casualties of the 48th numbered 422, killed or wounded. The 57th, out of 30 officers and 570 men under arms that morning, had left at nightfall, capable of duty, 10 officers and 150 men. The adjutant, Lieutenant Way, fourteenth in seniority on the list of officers, brought the regiment out of the battle. According to regimental tradition, the whole of the rations issued to No. 2 Company were drawn by a drummer boy, who carried them away in his hat. Their colours, at the following regimental inspection, were officially returned by the inspecting-general as being "too much disfigured to be reported on." The tattered state of the flags may account for the discrepancy between the statements as to the numbers of bullet-holes in the King's Colour: seventeen by one account, thirty by another. Twenty-one distinct shot-holes were counted in the regimental colour.

As a special reward in honour of the heroism displayed at Albuhera, a sergeant in each battalion of Hoghton's and Cole's Brigades was awarded a commission by the Prince Regent.

The scanty remains of the battalions of Colville's and Hoghton's Brigades numbered so few that, within a few days of the battle, the survivors of the six battalions were collected together and formed into a single "provisional battalion," until drafts could arrive from England to reconstitute the different corps. The Buffs made up one company, the 66th another, the 29th and 48th two companies, the 57th two companies, the 31st four companies—all being placed under the command of the senior officer left, Major L'Estrange, of the 31st.

For their share at Albuhera our present-day "Die Hards," the Middlesex Regiment, bears for honourable distinction a silver wreath of laurel as a badge, similar to the decoration specially granted to the heroic regiments of the Minden Charge. They wear, as well, the name

"Albuhera" inscribed on helmet and waist-belt plates.[5]

In Marshal Soult's total of 6,000 casualties were included three of his Divisional Generals. Over 3,000 of killed and wounded fell among the men of the massed columns, who fought the Third Brigade on the ridge; Werlé's Division of 5,600 lost 1,800 in the fight with the Fusiliers. In that shape did the solid French columns pay the penalty for their dense formation. "Our men," says a British officer, "died in rows; the French lay in heaps and mounds, being so massed. They did not dare to deploy, as they afterwards told us, from a dread of our cavalry, having supposed that we would not have ventured to act in such an open country without a great superiority in that description of force." Soult sent his captured standards to Paris. He only carried off, however, one of the British cannon, a 5½-inch howitzer, which was afterwards recaptured, dismounted by a shot, on the ramparts of San Sebastian. It was identified by the number it bore stamped on it, "No. 388."

A drenching downpour of rain closed the day for the wearied British soldiers on that bare and bloodstained hillside. So many were our wounded that "there were not enough unwounded men left to pick them up." It was impossible to do anything for "the mounds of French wounded, some of whom could not be got at for two days."

That night's bivouac on the battlefield of Albuhera was, from all accounts, one of the most trying experiences that Wellington's men went through in the whole war. We get one brief glimpse of it from a private soldier who was there. "Our situation," he says, "if possible, was more gloomy and uncomfortable than any yet experienced. No provision of liquor was to be had, and the surrounding country so wild and depopulated as to bid defiance to all attempts to better our state even by marauding. The only means of rest, if such it could be called, was sitting on our knapsacks in the mud, into which many occasionally dropped, overcome by sleep and fatigue. The ghastly lines of

---

5. Forty-three years later, in the stress of the Battle of Inkerman, the hard-hit remnant of the 57th were lying down on the Home Ridge, and a fresh Russian column was advancing to push back the handful of wearied infantry and capture some guns in rear. Captain Stanley, who was in command, saw that the situation was desperate. Springing up, he turned to his men and shouted, "'Die Hards,' remember Albuhera!" The effect was electrical. The men sprang to their feet, and with a cheer followed their bold leader into the midst of the Russians, driving them back, after a furious hand-to-hand fight. The gallant Stanley fell, having, it is said, slain ten of the enemy with his own sword. His place was taken by Captain Inglis, son of the colonel at Albuhera.

dead were faintly visible through the gloom, while the deep snoring of those lying about, or who still maintained their balance on their seats, nearly drowned the calls of the sentinels and the moanings of the mutilated soldiers. From about midnight the howling of wolves was heard in the direction of the river: they had probably left their dens in the adjacent wood to feast on this scene of carnage. Their howlings seemed at times as if answered by the calls and croaking of the birds of prey which kept hovering about."

Wellington, at the very moment that Albuhera was being fought, was hastening as fast as he could to the assistance of Beresford, galloping sixty miles a day. He was on his way from the north, beyond the Tagus, after having driven Masséna across the Portuguese frontier. He had heard that Soult had started from Seville to force Beresford out of the siege-lines before Badajoz, and rescue the garrison, pressing on with 24,000 picked troops as fast as his men could get over the ground.

Sending off at once Picton's infantry of the "Fighting Third "Division and the Seventh Division, by forced marches of twenty miles a day, Wellington followed as soon as possible, and, passing the two divisions on the way, in four days from leaving his headquarters on the Coa had arrived at Elvas, not far from Badajoz. He learned on reaching Elvas that Beresford had already raised his camp before Badajoz, and was barring Soult's approach at Albuhera, twelve miles to the south of the fortress, astride of the Badajoz to Seville road. He was just too late for the battle. As he was on the point of starting for Albuhera Colonel Arbuthnot reached Elvas from the field with the news of Soult's defeat and retirement.

Wellington passed this judgment on the conduct of the soldiers at Albuhera in his next dispatch to England, after having had Beresford's report before him and having learned the details of the fighting:

> I think this action one of the most glorious and honourable to the character of the troops of any that has been fought during the war.[6]

---

6. In the autumn of 1811 three privates of the 57th—O'Harran, Royston, and Haines—were sentenced to death for marauding near Elvas. Wellington went out of his way to pardon them. "The conduct of the 57th Regiment in the Battle of Albuhera," says the Judge advocate-general, Mr. Larpent, "rendered the commander-in-chief anxious to pardon the men, that the regiment might avoid the disgrace of a public execution."

Marshal Soult is credited with having said this of the British Army at Albuhera:

> There is no beating these troops, in spite of their generals! I always thought them bad soldiers, but I am sure of it now. I turned their right and penetrated their centre, they were completely beaten; the day was mine; yet they did not know it, and would not run!"

And Soult really meant what he said. He went so far as to claim credit in the dispatch he sent to Paris with his flag-trophies, for "*une victoire signalèe.*" The claim, however, was disallowed by the War Minister, who had seen the *London Gazette*, brought over by a Folkestone smuggler who supplied Napoleon regularly with English newspapers, containing Wellington's and Beresford's dispatches. The marshal, however, scored in the long run. When Soult in later years became War Minister under Louis Philippe, he promptly placed the name "Albuhera" as a battle-honour on the colours of a number of regiments. In doing that no doubt he was justified, as far as concerned the soldiers. Soult's regiments at Albuhera, whatever the fortune of the battle, Girard's brave fellows in particular, had fought nobly under fire with coolness, and endurance, and signal gallantry, officers and men alike. They did their duty, and the descendants of those regiments in the French Army of today for that reason are entitled rightly and fairly to commemorate the battle.

11

"Daddy Hill" on the War-Path: the Daybreak Surprise at Arroyo

"Daddy Hill" was the soldiers' name for the most popular general in Wellington's army. Every officer and man under his orders had for General Hill a strong feeling of personal regard and attachment that was unique in the service. Others of their leaders no doubt they liked personally and trusted; some they tolerated for their capacity as leaders before the enemy; some, on the other hand, they hated absolutely, as hard tyrants.

With "Daddy Hill" it was quite otherwise at all times. An officer of Hill's Division—the Second Division—writing in after years, lets us into the secret of why all regarded Hill with such devoted affection.

> The great foundation of all his popularity with the troops was his sterling personal worth and his heroic spirit; but his popularity was increased and strengthened as soon as he was seen. He was the very picture of an English country gentleman. To those soldiers who came from the rural districts of Old England he represented *home*: his fresh complexion, his placid face, kind eyes, kind voice, the total absence of all parade, or noise in his habits, delighted them. The displeasure of Rowland Hill was worse to them than the loudest anger of other generals.
> When they saw anxiety in his face that all should be right, they doubly wished it themselves; and when they saw his countenance bright with the expression that all was right, why, they were glad for him as well as for themselves.... Also his kind attention to all the wants and comforts of his men, his visits to the sick in hospital, his vigilant protection of the poor country-

people, his just severity to marauders, his generous and humane treatment of such prisoners and wounded as at times fell into his hands—all consistent actings of a virtuous and noble spirit—made for him a place in the hearts of the soldiery; and wherever the few survivors of that army may now be scattered, in their hearts assuredly his name and image are dearly cherished still.

"Daddy Hill" made the *coup* which won him a knighthood and the ribbon of the Bath, and planted his feet on the ladder leading to a peerage, and in the end to the Horse Guards as Commander-in-Chief of the British Army, as successor to the Duke of Wellington himself. It was in the autumn of 1811, at the time of Wellington's blockade of the barrier-fortress of Ciudad Rodrigo, on the borders of Spain and Portugal, in October of the year.

At the end of the third week of October, the Second Division, posted at that time in cantonments on the Portuguese side of the frontier, with its headquarters at the fortified town of Portalegre, to the south of Ciudad Rodrigo, to serve as a covering force, was ordered to take the field. A formidable French division of 6,000 men had made its appearance in the Province of Estremadura, in the mountainous country to the south-east of the district where Hill's men were quartered, between the Tagus and the Guadiana.

The French had been sent north of the Tagus by Marshal Soult, then occupying Andalusia and besieging Cadiz, to act as a flying column and co-operate with another force to the eastward against an incursion of Spanish guerillas, then threatening Soult's line of communications with Madrid. They were picked regiments, *troupes d'élite*, and their leader was an officer of exceptional distinction, and one of Napoleon's favourites—the General Girard who made the attack at Albuhera. Girard drove back the guerillas and pushed on as far as Caçeres, a town some fifty miles from Merida, where he had crossed the Tagus, his base of operations. He was at Caçeres when news of his movements reached Wellington. Hill's Division was at once told off to beat Girard back.

Hill himself had already had news of Girard's raid. He realized that it offered an excellent opportunity of cutting Girard off from Merida by a rapid dash. Immediately Wellington's order to move reached him he was off. He had carefully laid his plans beforehand. He could count on sufficient troops not only to make Girard pay dearly for his venturesome move, but also possibly to overwhelm and capture bodily his whole division. Hill had on the spot nearly 10,000 men, of whom a third were British, while most of the remainder were British-trained Portuguese of trustworthy quality. Swiftness and secrecy, as Hill thoroughly recognized, were the great essentials for success.

On the morning of October 21 the chief commissary of the Second Division received orders to provision the troops at once with ten days' bread and a fortnight's beef, and, at the same time, the commanding officer of every regiment was directed to be ready to take the field in light marching order within twenty-four hours. Before the afternoon of the 22nd Hill's troops had all come in from their cantonments and were assembling at the starting-point, with the commissariat "beef" ready to accompany the marching column in the shape of droves of oxen.

They started off at three o'clock on the morning of the 23rd, and began by making a thirty miles' march across the steep and rugged Sierra de San Mamed in a furious gale of wind and pouring rain. That also brought them over the Spanish frontier.

In order to mislead the many French spies there were about, Hill first of all went off for six miles due south towards Badajoz. Then, when beyond observation from Portalegre, he turned sharply off due east in the direction of Cáceres, where, according to latest intelligence, Girard still was.

Crossing the Spanish frontier near the small town of Codeceira, a halt was called, and the troops did their best to shelter themselves for the night against the terrible weather under roughly extemporized huts of boughs and leaves. The rain kept on steadily all night in a soaking downpour, and officers and men had to sit or lie round spluttering, half-extinguished fires, some, at times, "trying to warm a little wine in the lid of a camp-kettle," others crouched huddling together for warmth; not a few, we are told, "cursing the French for bringing them out in such weather."

They were off again by seven next morning, and had a long six hours' march to the ancient Spanish city of Albuquerque, midway between the Tagus and the Guadiana. On the following day they covered another twenty miles, finally getting to their halting-place, Alisada, an hour before midnight. During the last part of the march the roads were so rough that "the guns of the artillery had to be dismounted from their carriages and borne up steep places by the men."

Immediately they halted at Alisada orders were sent round for the men to prepare their rations as quickly as possible and be ready to move on as soon as a hasty meal could be eaten. Beef, not half an hour killed, had to be put in the camp-kettles as it was, and even then the soup could not be got ready until within a few minutes before the bugles were sounding the "Assembly."

"The bullocks on which we were to dine," says an officer, "were running and jumping about us, but in less than an hour they were amusing us with more interesting leaps in our camp-kettles." He adds that "the soup, just off the fire, having been placed before us at the same time that the bugle called us to arms, we were compelled to dispatch it in a state little colder than boiling lead."

The hasty start from Alisada was the result of news that Hill's Spanish cavalry had just brought in. The enemy, they reported, had moved from Caçeres and were at Malpartida—within striking distance of the British at Alisada. General Hill proposed to make for them forthwith.

The troops hastened forward, as before, under pitiless incessant rain for the whole of that day and the succeeding night. They forded the River Salor, a difficult task for the infantry, wading across slippery rocks, the water breast-high in places, so that the men had to hold up their *cartouche*-boxes and bullet-pouches, and then pressed on at the best speed the weather and rough cross-country mountain roads would let them. On the way a brief halt was made in anticipation of an early battle, at which muskets were inspected and flints seen to. That done, all went on, ploughing their way all night through mud and water, or tripping and stumbling over deep ruts and rocky boulders. "The men were so worn out by the morning that they were only kept on their feet by the prospect of battle."

But all their exertions proved in vain. To their intense chagrin they learned, as they were drawing near to Malpartida, that the enemy had given them the slip. The cavalry brought in word that Girard, warned by some "*Afrancescados*," local Spanish officials who had taken service under the French, had withdrawn just two hours before the horsemen got the news. The enemy had gone along the Torremocha road, it was stated, apparently retreating towards Merida again.

All Hill could do on that news was to halt the men and let them rest awhile. The soldiers were dead-beat, and had outstripped most of the commissariat bullocks, their rations. He had to halt for nearly twenty-four hours until the men had been fed and were ready to resume the march. He had again by that time intelligence of the enemy's whereabouts. It was rather vague, but would suffice. Apparently Girard, as far as Hill could learn, had only heard some vague rumour about his move, and was falling back at a leisurely pace. All the French apparently knew was that a hostile force, of the strength and actual position of which they were unaware, had crossed the frontier from Portugal towards Caçeres.

The twenty-four hours' rest set Hill's men in trim again. Once more the indefatigable general was on the war-path. If he could not cut Girard off, at least he might overtake him and bring him to battle. Another rapid march would probably serve that purpose.

The troops set off soon after daybreak on the 27th. They recrossed the River Salor at another ford, making for the small town of Torremocha. The French, Hill thought, might be halting there; if they had had no further news about him since quitting Malpartida. So far the wild and barren districts Hill had been traversing seemed practically uninhabited.

During that forenoon as they marched along the officers of one of the regiments, the 92nd Highlanders, contrived, as we are told, to get up a hare-hunt. A mounted officer by chance put up a hare and some of the greyhounds, which many of the officers in Spain at that time used to keep, went after it and killed it. Officers in other regiments took up the idea, and as the coursing seemed to enliven the men, hares also proving plentiful, they too let their dogs go. "We continued the sport, and so beguiled the time that many of the men thought we had marched only half the distance that we really had."

Towards midday, as they were toiling through the rough and steep pass of Trasquillon, Hill at last, and suddenly, got on the direct track of the enemy. A message was brought in that Girard had left Torremocha for Arroyo dos Molinos, a small place on the farther side of the Sierra de Montanches. The French, Hill was given to understand, were still totally unaware of his move.

Arroyo dos Molinos was thirty miles off from where the British then were, and two difficult mountain-ranges intervened. Hill, however, made up his mind to make for Arroyo at once, trusting to good fortune that Girard might be delaying his next move.

The march forward was stopped, and the whole British force, comprising two infantry brigades and a cavalry brigade with ten or a dozen guns, turned off quickly in the new direction. The nearest route to Arroyo led across the wildest country, while the weather was on that day, if possible, even more trying than before. Torrents of rain drenched the soldiers afresh; a biting wind blew in fierce gusts that chilled them to the bones. For most of the way they had to scramble along goat-tracks, now toiling through narrow ravines, now floundering in thick mud. But all were intent on bringing the enemy to battle, and they got over the ground even faster than before.

By nightfall they had reached Alcuescar, a small town some three miles from Arroyo dos Molinos. And the enemy were still there. So Hill, to his complete satisfaction, now heard.

Girard had contented himself on that day with a twelve miles' march as against the twenty-eight miles that Hill's men had covered. The French, it was reported, were sheltering from the weather at Arroyo, and were likely to stop there for at least that night. They were all unaware still, it appeared certain, of Hill's approach, in spite of a warning Girard had privately had that the hostile troops from across the frontier previously reported had left Malpartida. Not a cavalry *vedette* of the French was out on that side of Arroyo; not a reconnoitring patrol had been on the move towards Alcuescar, although Girard had with him three dragoon regiments. No precautions whatever, apparently, had been taken against a surprise.

The game at the critical moment was being played into Hill's hands. He decided to deliver a surprise attack at daybreak next morning.

Every precaution possible was taken to keep the presence of the British a secret. A range of high ground, rugged and difficult to traverse, which stretched at right angles across the road between Alcuescar and Arroyo, facilitated matters. No military detail was omitted to ensure that the surprise should be complete. The light companies of the regiments were thrown forward as outlying pickets all round Alcuescar and formed a close cordon of sentries in order to prevent any of the natives from carrying information or alarming the enemy. The cavalry, artillery, and infantry bivouacked in the neighbouring fields, with the strictest orders, regardless of the damp and cold, not to strike a flint, not to light a single fire lest any flickering or reflection in the sky might rouse suspicion amongst the French that a hostile force was near.

The wind blew furiously; the rain fell in torrents; and the soldiers, some in the open, lying down wrapped up in their soaked blankets, others crouching behind walls and hedges to try and obtain cover from the chill wind that raged all through the night, went through the roughest of the experiences that they had had, "but their patience and firmness and implicit confidence in their leader sustained them." They passed the cruelly inhospitable night without a murmur, contenting themselves with the expectation that morning would recompense them for everything.

The soldiers seemed only concerned to keep their muskets and powder as dry as possible.

The unsuspecting French remained meanwhile asleep in snug billets, for the most part among the cottages and houses of Arroyo.

At two in the morning "the orderly sergeants went round and whispered the order to turn out." A few minutes later all fell in and formed up silently in the dark in their last column of march. Then, between half-past two and three o'clock, without note of bugle or tap of drum, the troops moved forward.

The wind and rain beat furiously in their faces as, practically blindfold in the darkness, they set out to feel their way cautiously and very slowly across the intervening ridge between Arroyo and Alcuescar, keeping in the track of a rough country road. It took them four hours to get over two and a half miles. During the last hour the lights of French watch-fires on the outskirts of the village were caught a glimpse of now and again between the squalls. That kept up their spirits: the enemy had not yet moved away. Another halt became now necessary for the final dispositions for the attack to be made.

The distance between the two armies in the morning," says one of the regimental officers, "was about three miles. To march this short way occupied us fully four hours, the narrow and broken state of the road having caused the files of the column to open out to an unusual extent. It was nearly seven o'clock before the whole of the troops had defiled from the mountains and formed by brigades in close column of companies under cover of a small height about half a mile from Arroyo.

The troops moved off from their muster-ground formed in one column, the two infantry brigades leading, and the cavalry and guns bringing up the rear. In advance went General Howard's Brigade, the First Battalion of the 50th leading, with the 71st Light Infantry and the 92nd Highlanders, and a company of the 60th. After them came Wilson's Brigade, the First Battalion of the 28th, the Second Battalion of the 34th, with the 39th, another company of the 60th, and some Portuguese and Spaniards. The cavalry followed, Long's Brigade, the 2nd Hanoverian Hussars of the King's German Legion, the 9th and

13th Light Dragoons, and some Spanish mounted corps. In that order they moved forward until they halted within half a mile of Arroyo.

An idea of the ground around Arroyo had been given to General Hill late on the evening before by an officer of the 60th, a Captain Blaquière, who had been scouting in that direction, and had coolly entered the town, evading French questioners. He knew the country, having been in the neighbourhood a short time previously on special Intelligence Department service. The immediate approach on that side was over moderately open ground, sparsely covered with cork-trees. Beyond lay the town, at the foot of a steep outlying ridge from the Sierra de Montanches, which stretched across at the back of Arroyo to the north and east, in the form of a crescent, half enclosing the place with steep rocky heights.

For troops to escape on that side, to climb up anywhere between the two horns of the crescent, was believed to be practically impossible. Hill satisfied himself that the enemy to all intents were held fast, caught in a trap. Three roads led from Arroyo in the direction of the French line of retreat towards Merida. The most important of these, the road that the enemy when attacked would inevitably select, Hill proposed to bar by means of an intercepting brigade and his cavalry, pushed ahead into position, if possible, before the first shot was fired.

This is how one of the officers with Howard's Brigade describes the scene just before the attack opened:

> "Although on arriving before the village it was approaching that period of the morning when daylight should appear, yet it was nearly dark at the time we halted, after our long and weary march. Heavy black clouds were rolling along the sides of the Sierra, which, enveloped in a gloomy and almost impenetrable mist, seemed, as it were, to frown upon the forest underneath. Every now and then the wind, with a fierce and angry howl, swept across the plain, its hollow and melancholy gusts in like manner echoing even beyond the far-off mountains; but after the tempestuous night we passed since leaving the village and cheerless bivouac (for we had orders to light no fires) of Alcuescar, we were by this time pretty well inured to drenching weather, and prepared to encounter the very worst the elements might have in store.
>
> We stood in our position cold and shivering, wondering what was to come next, and looking almost as black as the dismal

squall that menaced us, when, the matter we had on hand soon beginning to wear a business-like appearance, the whole current of our ideas assumed another aspect: we forgot the pelting of the storm, with all its dire accompaniments, and with one exciting impulse (an impulse which before the enemy ever has that effect with British soldiers) were filled with life and animation.

The weather cleared up a little for a short while after seven o'clock, after which, again, just as daylight came on, another violent rain-squall burst over the scene, accompanied by a thick mist.

Hill at that moment gave the order for all to advance. Under cover of the new storm he would come to close quarters and do the work.

Swiftly the regiments of Howard's Brigade, with three guns, moved along the road and over the plain directly towards Arroyo, in quarter-column, bayonets ready. The Second Brigade, under General Wilson—designed as the intercepting force—also with three guns, started in a direction towards the farther horn of the mountain-crescent overlooking the town. The cavalry set off to skirt the town and post themselves across the principal road towards Merida, beyond Arroyo.

The enemy did not discover their approach until the very last moment. The British had got within 200 yards of the outskirts of the town before any of the French sentries saw them. The rain-squall beat straight in the faces of the French, and the mist served to blind them to the very last.

The headmost of the attacking British, indeed, as it befell, gave the first alarm themselves. The Light Company of the 71st, led by Lieutenant and Adjutant Law, as they went forward, stumbled on a French picket near a small chapel: "a dismounted picket of the enemy's cavalry with their horses near them, seated round a fire composed of the chapel-doors and window-frames piled up in heaps." The Frenchmen were sitting huddled together under shelter of some trees, with their backs to the driving rain, and consequently their faces away from the approaching British. Our men bounded in among them before they could get on their feet and seized hold of most of them. Two or three, however, managed to break away, and, leaving their horses, rushed off into the town, yelling out at the top of their voices.

After that further concealment for the oncoming British force was no longer possible, nor necessary.

General Hill, "inspired, as was every brave man he commanded, with the enthusiasm of the moment," gave the word to set on. "The usual calmness of his demeanour," describes an eyewitness, "rendered even more than commonly striking by the precautions he had taken for silence, became suddenly converted into an animation that cheered and almost amused everybody. It seemed kindled in an instant. He drew his sword, gave a loud hurrah, spurred his horse, and led the charge on the astonished ranks of the French then forming without a thought that he was so close at hand."

Why that was so, why the French let themselves be trapped unawares, is inexplicable.

At the moment that the refugees from the surprised picket ran in among them, Girard's men had been up for three hours. They had cooked and eaten their breakfasts unaware that several thousand enemies were within half a mile of them. Some of them had already started towards Merida, and the others at the moment of the attack were falling in on parade to leave Arroyo and follow with the baggage, for, as they anticipated, an ordinary day's march.

> One brigade of Girard's Division had marched at four o'clock by the road of Medellin, but Dombrouski's Brigade and the cavalry of Briche were still in the place, and the horses of the rearguard, unbridled, were tied to trees. The infantry were gathering on the Medellin road outside the village, and Girard was in a house waiting for his horse, when two British officers galloped into the street, and in an instant all was confusion. Hastily the cavalry bridled their horses and the infantry ran to their alarm-posts, but a tempest raged, and a thick mist rolled down the craggy mountain, a terrific shout was heard amidst the clatter of the elements, and with the driving storm the 71st and the 92nd Regiments came charging down.

(Thus Napier describes the loosing of the bolt).

The Light Company of the 71st who had captured the French picket doubled off to the left of the town, through an olive grove, and came upon the enemy on that side just after they got the alarm. "In the lurid glare of fires which the rain had but partially extinguished," as one of our officers describes, "officers and soldiers both of cavalry and infantry, whose voices and footsteps were distinctly heard, and whose movements were illumined by the aforesaid glare, were running wildly in all directions. They had no time to 'forge their weapons for the fight.' Confusion reigned where all a little before was wrapped in gloom and stillness. Some were calling for their horses, others seeking for their knapsacks, while consternation and dismay were pictured on every countenance. In trying to make their escape, and scarcely aroused from their dreams and reveries, instead of keeping to the main street, they levanted, some by the back premises, and many more by different loopholes, which the straggling nature of the place afforded."

At a sharp run, in disciplined silence for the moment, the 92nd swept on, making swiftly for the entrance to the village. Not a voice was raised, not a shot went off, as the eager Highlanders doubled forward. They reached the first of the houses and rushed past up the main street, making no sound except the trampling of their feet. As they went they intercepted on all sides and took prisoners a number of the enemy, running together in confusion, startled and dazed at the sudden apparition of a British regiment in their midst. The next moment, as the Highlanders were about to make a dash for the market-place, all of a sudden a piercing skreel from the bagpipes shrilled wildly forth. It was quite impromptu and entirely contrary to orders.

"Gie 'em 'Johnny Cope,' lads!" exclaimed one of the pipers, with a sense of the humour of the situation, to his comrades as they ran forward. The next moment, without orders given, sounded out the stirring notes of "Hech, Johnny Cope, are ye waukin' yet!" in a re-echoing outburst of mountain music which utterly scared the French on every side. A roar of cheering responded to the pipes, as, with tumultuous shouting now, the 92nd went hustling on through Arroyo. What groups of Frenchmen strove here and there to face them and hastily offer resistance were swept away like straws before the wind. Those of the French who tried to make a stand were pounced down on and seized, or shot down, or bayoneted on the spot.

Close in rear of the Highlanders, following fast, came on the 50th, disarming and gathering in the prisoners taken, "mopping them up as it were."

One of Girard's principal officers fell into the hands of the Highlanders in the village street: General Bron, the commander of the French cavalry. He was intercepted on the doorstep of the house in which he had had his quarters, just as he had come out and was about to mount his horse. A sergeant of the 92nd seized hold of the French general as he got one leg across the saddle, pulled him back, shoved him into the road, and then, prodding him behind with the point of his halberd, bundled the luckless cavalry officer along up the street among the foremost of the Highlanders until General Bron could be handed over among the other captives.

The 71st on their side were clearing the side streets and outskirts of Arroyo with equal rapidity. They, in like manner, drove before them to the farther end of the village "the French rearguard of dragoons and chasseurs, many hanging on to their horses after mounting bareback, not having had time even to saddle, yet fighting and struggling hard as they were thrust forward."

The colonel of the French 34th was among the captives of the 71st. He had lodged in the main street, and had run outside the house on hearing the shrill din of the bagpipes of the 92nd. An orderly was standing at the door with his charger, and the colonel scrambled on to it and galloped off to rally his men outside the village. As he got there he met Colonel Cadogan of the 71st. The two colonels crossed swords and slashed at each other. The Frenchman missed his first cut and his second was parried. He in turn parried Cadogan's first cut, but with his second smote Cadogan over the head—fortunately doing him little harm, as the British colonel's head-dress saved him. Before the Frenchman could make a third stroke a couple of Cadogan's men sprang at him and disarmed him and made him a prisoner.

Prince d'Arenberg, the colonel of the 27th Chasseurs, a nephew of Josephine by marriage, was another officer whom the 71st got hold of. The bagpipes of the 92nd gave him, too, the alarm. The prince ran out of his lodgings in the *padre's* house with his cloak hastily wrapped round him, mounted his horse at the door, and scurried off to his men quartered on the outskirts of Arroyo. "He was endeavouring to make his escape," according to one of our officers, "when Corporal Doherty of the 71st, perceiving his manoeuvre, charged with his bayonet, and stopped the prince in his career. Muffled up in a large green cloak, which almost extinguished him (he was a very little personage), he was but indifferently prepared for an encounter with the stalwart Irishman, who suddenly reining back the Frenchman's horse, the force of the bit, which was very powerful, threw the animal upon his haunches, the rider at the same time falling upon the pavement.

Doherty, at once perceiving the advantage of his own position, resolved to profit by it; and, presenting his weapon, he called out to the Prince for his surrender, The latter, prostrate on the ground, and therefore, in no condition for a contest, sung out '*Peccavi!*' when, throwing the ample folds of his cloak aside, he exposed the honours and decorations by which his breast was covered, which he thought would protect him—and he judged rightly—from being transfixed by the corporal's bayonet. Making signs to him to rise, Doherty marched him in a prisoner to Captain Clements of the 71st, into whose charge he was delivered."

General Girard himself, indeed, had the narrowest of escapes from being taken. He was at breakfast in the *alcalde's* house in the market-place, when all of a sudden he heard the first notes of the bagpipes. Catching up his hat, the French commander-in-chief sprang hastily from the table and ran to the front door. His charger had been ordered round, but had not yet come. General Girard turned and ran through the kitchen to the back-door and across the yard to the stables, where at that moment the horse was being brought out. Flinging himself into the saddle, he spurred off down a side lane and got clear in the confusion to the far end of the village.

There the French were already rallying on a battalion of the 40th of the Line, which had begun falling in there as baggage-guard for the day's march a moment or two before the British came on the scene. In and about Arroyo, when the firing opened, Girard had a brigade of some 4,000 troops all told: the six battalions of the 34th and 40th of the Line, two cavalry regiments (one of dragoons, one of chasseurs), and a battery of artillery. The other brigade of his division had marched for Merida between five and six o'clock, and was too far off by then to be recalled to help.

The French were granted a momentary respite in the street beyond the market-place. There some of the 34th of the Line, getting into order hastily before the Highlanders reached the spot, made a brave effort to keep the assailants off with musketry. But the 92nd were not to be balked by French bullets. They roughly broke through the enemy with the bayonet and drove the 34th out of Arroyo.

In the breathing-space that the 34th obtained for him, Girard, directing operations personally, packed off his baggage-train along the road, and formed the 40th into square just beyond Arroyo. To them, as a second square, he added what companies of the 34th were able to reach him, as they came running up on being bundled out of the place by the Highlanders.

The two squares closed up and set themselves to try and stem the rush and gain time for the baggage-train to make good its escape.

But by then the 71st had been able to get round outside Arroyo, having done their part no less successfully than the Highlanders. The 71st promptly lined up along some vineyard walls and garden hedges along the road, and began a sharp and telling fire on the two French squares. These replied by pushing out skirmishers, who pluckily engaged the 71st, and for the time held them back.

The 92nd had halted at the exit from the village street, to re-form ranks after their rush, and get into column of sections. The ground immediately in front of them was restricted, and the cross-fire from the 71st and the French skirmishers, as these fought each other, prevented the Highlanders from pushing through between. The 92nd had to stand there for some minutes, by order of Hill himself, without firing or replying to the enemy, whose skirmishers opened a brisk fusillade on them also. The men bore it patiently while a message was sent to the 71st to cease firing for a moment. That, after a short while, the 71st did, which gave the 92nd a chance again.

The Highlanders went forward quickly to clear the narrow way and deploy beyond on more open ground, where they could face the squares and charge them. An opportunity, however, was denied them. As the Gordons were coming through the three guns with Howard's column opened fire on the squares with grape and case. The first discharge settled the combat near the village. Without waiting for a second, both squares forthwith turned away, and, forming column, went off at the double along the highway, Girard's route towards Merida. Their skirmishers followed in rear to cover the retreat. The road they took led along the foot of the mountain-range, and close beneath the eastern horn of the crescent of precipitous slopes at the back of Arroyo, the point to which Hill had sent forward his other troops in order to bar the way.

Girard's entire force was cut off and overtaken within an hour. The French cavalry in advance of the retreating column was headed off by Hill's Spanish Horse, charged smartly and roughly, forced apart from the infantry in rear, and then finally driven off in disorder. The French guns and baggage were swooped down on and captured *en bloc*. The hapless 34th and 40th, comprising the enemy's main column, were cornered and compelled to break up and disperse in a last-hope effort at escape by trying to climb up the steep mountain-side.

"Girard," says Napier, "an intrepid officer, although wounded, still kept his infantry together, retreating by the Truxillo road; but the right column of the allies was in possession of that line, the cavalry and artillery were close upon his flank, and the left column followed fast; his men fell by fifties, and his situation was desperate, yet he would not surrender, and giving the word to disperse, endeavoured to scale the almost inaccessible rocks of the *Sierra*."

It was Wilson's men of the Second Brigade who brought about the final catastrophe. They, while the surprise of the French in the village was taking place, had been marching round at their fastest to intercept the enemy's retreat where, as has been said, the mountain-range curved round to the road farther on. The final blow fell on the French General a mile and a half beyond Arroyo. His cavalry had been sent flying just before, and his guns had been rushed and taken by the British 13th Light Dragoons. The infantry resisted stubbornly and bravely to the last, doggedly doing their utmost to hold together and keep back the incessant attacks of the 71st and 92nd, who with the 50th were hotly pelting after them, close behind. The sudden appearance of Wilson's men on his flank and to his front wrecked Girard's last chance. After that *sauve qui peut* was the order for one and all.

The break-up came about, as it happened, in quite a dramatic way. The rain-storm ceased suddenly and the thick mist lifted, disclosing Wilson's men to the ill-fated French general within 600 yards of him, rapidly nearing the vital point of passage. At the sight the French at once began running hard, general and staff and soldiers on foot. Wilson's men saw them, and began running also. In advance of the British hastened on the light companies of the 28th, 34th, and 39th, the regiments of Wilson's Brigade. The light companies reached the road exactly at the place where the steep mountain-side overhung it, and boldly dashed at the headmost of the French as they were about to pass. They caught Girard, so to speak, by the throat.

They were but few in numbers compared with the massed ranks of the enemy in column, and a counter-charge on them there and then must inevitably have annihilated them before the nearest British battalion could come to the rescue. But it was not attempted.

Girard's nerve seemed suddenly to fail him. He was on horseback, and close by the point at which the light companies made their daring dash. Instead of smashing his assailants the French general threw up the sponge.

He shouted to his men not to stop to fight, but to leave the road at once and climb up the rocks of the Sierra above. The general himself and his staff set the example. Turning their horses loose, they ran off towards a place nearby, where the mountain-side sloped down less steeply than elsewhere, to scramble up on foot. The nearest soldiers, together with the Eagle-escorts of the two regiments, were told to follow and keep close to the general, and after them a number of men of the leading companies of the 40th, with some of the 34th, clambered up. So these got off, helping one another as they struggled for a foothold, and having now and then to crawl on hands and knees.

Others were able to get up the steep at one or two other points, but the rest, most of those in rear, were less favoured. They were faced by a sheer wall of rock that was insurmountable. These, penned in on either side, flung down their arms and surrendered on Wilson's troops coming up. Over 1,000 of Girard's soldiers were so taken. The prisoners were handed over to the custody of the foremost of Howard's regiments, who at that moment reached the spot.

Part of Wilson's men had already taken up the chase of the fugitives up the mountain-side; the rest, leaving the captives, immediately followed suit. The scene that ensued as the British pursuers scrambled up after the French is described by an officer who was in the thick of it all as one "of laughter rather than bloodshed."

"They clambered," says another of our officers present at "the memorable pursuit of that extraordinary day," as he calls it, "in a state of utter confusion, throwing away their arms and ammunition and knapsacks, and yielding their persons as prisoners to their pursuers at every step. In the excitement of such a chase the British, the Portuguese, and the Spaniards seemed all to forget that they had been without rest and soaked with rain and mist all the night before. They laughed, shouted, and jumped in their heavy accoutrements, or caught the scrambling horses of the fugitives, who could not ride them over the mountain, and came down mounted in triumph, till fatigue caused some to desist, and the rest, being too much scattered, were judiciously stopped on the summit of the Sierra."

One regiment of our modern British Army commemorates every year an incident of the chase at Arroyo dos Molinos—the old 34th, now known as the First Battalion of the Border Regiment. The battalion still possesses the drums and drum-major's staff captured from the 34th of the French line at Arroyo. A sergeant, Moses Simpson, took the staff, wrenching it out of the hands of the French drum-major. According to regimental tradition, some of the French officers, on tendering their swords to the British, embraced them, one officer exclaiming: "Ah, gentlemen, we are brothers: we are the 34th, both of us. You are brave men," he added, with a well-timed compliment: "The English always fight with chivalry and treat their prisoners well!" At midnight on every anniversary of Hill's surprise of Arroyo the drummers of the Border Regiment assemble and beat the drums captured from the French 34th, the youngest drummer-boy brandishing the French drum-major's staff.[1]

Brigadier Howard, some of whose men joined with Wilson's, as senior officer took over charge of the chase up the mountain-side. He carried it through, himself amongst the foremost pursuers. He led them, of course on foot, until it was impossible to go farther, as the men were almost dropping from fatigue after their protracted exertions. They had taken scores of prisoners, but were unable to catch General Girard. Howard sounded the "Halt "high up the mountain and drew his men off, making his way back with some 600 prisoners to where Hill with the other prisoners and the rest of the troops had gone into bivouac some six miles beyond Arroyo.

Near there the concluding incident of the day took place; in view of all, victors and vanquished. It was just as Howard was bringing in his men. A large party of the French 23rd Dragoons had been out reconnoitring at a distance, and having missed discovering any enemy, were returning to rejoin Girard at Arroyo, unaware of the battle and expecting to find their general in the village. They had just heard of what had happened, and, making towards Merida, were galloping across an open plain near Hill's new bivouac, when a picket of British Light Dragoons caught sight of them, and dashed off to intercept and round them up. Charging into them, after a sharp contest hand to hand, full in sight of Howard's men and the prisoners, they made them all surrender and brought them in as prisoners also. (See note below).

> *Note*:—To cheer the French up on that evening double rations of food and spirits were served out to them. The majority of the prisoners, however, did not seem to need much consolation. They astonished their captors by the nonchalant, if not actually cheerful, way in which most of them took the blow which had befallen them. It was only the fortune of war, they explained; for themselves, they had nothing to be ashamed of.

1. Years afterwards, in the Crimean War, when the French were our allies, the British 34th met the 34th of Napoleon III.'s army in the camp before Sebastopol. The British 34th at the time had in use the French drums taken at Arroyo. There was some fear, it is said, that their origin might get known to the French regiment, who were inclined to fraternize with their corresponding number in the British Army. To avoid possible awkwardness, the story goes, the colonel of our 34th had the drums white-washed over until he had obtained a new set from England, whereupon the French drums were quietly shipped back to the regimental depot in Cumberland. The colours of Wellington's 34th carried in the Peninsular War and at Arroyo are now preserved in Carlisle Cathedral.

Says an officer of the 50th on the day after the battle: "When the prisoners were marching by next day on their route to Lisbon, it was remarkable with what indifference and gaiety they went along. The dispirited countenance or clouded brow, which might naturally appear under the circumstances of their late defeat and consequent surrender, formed no part of their expression on the journey. On the contrary, the loud laugh of independence, mirth, and glee was more evident and rife among them. Though mostly young men full of health and vigour, their features bore the stamp of service in many climes; they formed withal a motley assemblage. Specimens of sundry nations were here collected: the brown Italian, the fair-complexioned German, the hardy Swiss, the muscular Swede, the light, gay-hearted Frenchman. All had abandoned, as it seemed, hopes of returning to their homes or country, and pursued their way under the motto of '*Sans souci,*' as though they were themselves the favourites of fortune, and not the vanquished party."

Another of Hill's officers, a subaltern in charge of some of the prisoners on their way to captivity, tells this story. His party, he says, had to put up for a night in a village chapel allotted them as quarters. "They took possession of it as if free and on the march on their own account, running in and singing '*Grenadiers ici! Grenadiers ici! Voltigeurs la! la! Voltigeurs la!*' the grenadiers running to the altar and chancel, and the *voltigeurs* to the gallery. In ten minutes they had made themselves quite at home, some playing cards, some singing, some dancing, some round a comrade performing Punch with great drollery behind a great-coat. The quieter men were sitting about repairing their clothes. In one place a self-elected orator was addressing some of his comrades on their capture. 'Gentlemen,' said he, 'you are not dishonoured. We have been betrayed. That spy, that Spaniard sold us.'

"'Who told you that?' called someone.

"'Sir,' replied the orator, 'you will permit me to know. I am a Parisian, and I understand war.'

The speech was much applauded with cries of 'Yes, he is right! We have been sold by that villain of a spy. We should have beaten the English in a stand-up fight !' Immediately afterwards the rations appeared, and all ran to the door, singing in chorus, '*Soupe, soupe, bonne soupe!*' But some of the sergeants and older soldiers showed their anger with mutterings and smothered oaths."

Hill did not stop his advance. The troops were off at two next morning for another forced march to beat up Girard's headquarters at Merida. They reached there at five on the afternoon of the 29th, "after a journey of fifteen hours in the rain without bite or sup on the way." Next day the troops were allowed to rest, while the French magazines and storehouses were ransacked and the supplies of corn in them loaded in wagons to be taken back and sent to Wellington's army. Then they started back for their cantonments, on their way having to ford two rivers "so deep and rapid that even the kilted regiments fared no better than those in trews." Portalegre was re-entered on November 4, the troops marching in "greeted by the loud acclamations of a grateful populace."

The news of Girard's defeat, as we are told, "electrified all the forces in the Peninsula, and even disturbed the serenity of Napoleon." The unfortunate Girard, after wandering about the mountains in great straits, at length recrossed the Guadiana and gained a place of safety with between 200 and 300 officers and men, all that came through of his battalions at Arroyo. He was placed in arrest by Marshal Soult and reported to Napoleon for punishment, but was eventually pardoned on the score of previous good service.

Hill's reward, in addition to the hearty appreciation and warm personal thanks of Wellington, was a Knighthood of the Bath.

"It would be particularly agreeable to me," wrote Wellington in reporting the victory at Arroyo to Lord Liverpool, the War Minister in England, "if some mark of favour of H.R.H. the Prince Regent were conferred upon General Hill. His services have always been meritorious, and very distinguished in this country, and he is beloved by the whole army.... In recommending him, as I do most anxiously, I really feel that there is no officer to whom an act of grace and favour would be received by the army with more satisfaction than on General Hill."

Wellington's suggestion to the War Minister, it may be added, was made against Hill's own wish. Hill's exceptional modesty made him demur to any distinction whatever being asked for or conferred on him. After the reward was announced, the investiture took place at Wellington's hands, but by Hill's request in as private a manner as possible, in the presence only of his personal Staff. This also is how Hill bore his honour: "When he was knighted," says one of Hill's *aides-de-camp*, "there was not one of us dared for nearly six months to call him ' Sir Rowland.' He was quite distressed at being called anything but 'General,' and it was only very gradually that he could be driven to bear his honour."

In reply to a request as to what heraldic supporters he would select for his arms, Hill wrote that he would "rather not have soldiers or anything like that, 'as other military officers had chosen.' A greyhound or foxhound might do, or any other animal. Indeed," he added, "he would rather leave the matter of choice to the ladies of the family—they have better taste than we have." In the end the ladies selected a red lion with a golden wreath round its neck for one supporter, and a white horse with another wreath round its neck for the other supporter.

12

One of the Very Bravest: Ensign Dyas of the Forlorn-Hope

"One of the greatest heroes of the Peninsular War," is what Ensign Joseph Dyas of the 51st Light Infantry (Sir John Moore's old corps, a regiment in the Seventh Division before Badajoz) has been called. It was in June, 1811, during the second of three sieges of Badajoz, at the close of the preliminary attack on the Fort San Christoval, an outlying work of considerable strength, situated across the Guadiana, on the right bank of the river opposite the main fortress.

The bombardment of Badajoz had lasted a week, by which time the guns on the ramparts of San Christoval had been practically silenced, and a breach made in the walls, which, it was specially reported, was "practicable." The report was made to Wellington at noon on June 6, and orders were issued forthwith that the fort should be stormed at nine o'clock that night.

The storming-party, as told off, consisted of 100 men, under the command of Major Macintosh of the 85th Foot. Ensign Dyas volunteered to lead the Forlorn-Hope—six men, all volunteers like himself for the perilous duty of leading the way in advance of the stormers. The French garrison they were to face numbered between 150 and 200 men.

They set off from the besieging lines on the stroke of the hour, an officer of the Royal Engineers accompanying Dyas. The two were the only persons there who knew the exact whereabouts of the bastion in which the breach had been made. Nobody else among the assailants, even the commanding officer, Major Macintosh, had, as it would seem, been informed on a point of such vital importance. At once misfortunes began.

As they got to the edge of the moat round the fort, Lieutenant Forster, the engineer officer, fell mortally wounded by the fire that the French, who were on the alert and had quickly discovered their approach, opened hotly on them from the parapet. Ensign Dyas, though, did not hesitate. Leading on his little party of half a dozen, so far unscathed, he boldly jumped down into the moat, a drop of twelve feet sheer down. Then, quickly running along at the foot of the curtain—the line of rampart-wall connecting one bastion with the next—he made his way to where the breach was. Apparently the French did not see the little group, but Dyas and his men found it impossible to get up the breach.

The enemy, as it happened, after the final bombardment had cleared away the debris of fallen stone and brickwork shattered by the cannonade, and had thus exposed seven feet of perpendicular wall, besides blocking up the gap on the slope of broken rampart above, with pointed beams of timber, chained together, and an impassable barricade of carts and damaged garrison vehicles, all interlocked and inextricably jammed together.

The storming-party, however, who had ladders with them, did not arrive. They had also got into the moat; but, in their ignorance of where the breach really was, had stopped short, in front of another bastion, only partially damaged by the bombardment, which they mistook for the real breach. All the time, before they reached the ditch even, they had been under fire from the enemy. Nearly half of the hundred had already fallen, but with the aid of the ladders they had brought the survivors made a brave effort to mount to the ramparts.

The ladders, though, proved to be too short at the place where they were trying, and, "while the soldiers were endeavouring to place them upright, they were cut off almost to a man." The French from above kept up a furious fusillade on the luckless storming-party, flinging down on their heads shells that burst with cruel effect among the dwindling band. After a quarter of an hour's vain attempt to get a footing on the ramparts, Major Macintosh, with the handful of survivors, mostly wounded, found themselves compelled to draw off, and with difficulty at length regained the British lines.

Almost immediately after the stormers had gone Ensign Dyas, having waited at the breach in vain for their arrival, came running back to the spot where they had been foiled to bring them on. Now first he saw what had happened. He found the fatal place "occupied only by dead and wounded." Even then, though, the brave leader of the

Forlorn-Hope would not retire, hoping against hope that reinforcements of fresh men would arrive. But none came, and he too had to withdraw. He only quitted the ditch, however, when "he heard the enemy entering it by the sally-port." The forlorn-hope scrambled out after that and made their way to the British lines—to find themselves given up for dead.

None of the survivors of the stormers, it would appear, had been able to give any account of Ensign Dyas.

"Indeed," as an officer puts it, "how could they? The storming-party had never seen the Forlorn-Hope from the moment they descended the ditch! As is common in such cases, there were many who said, each one, that he believed that he, individually, was the last living man in the ditch; and it was the generally received opinion that Dyas had fallen. Major Macintosh, in company with a few friends, was sitting in his tent, talking over the failure of the attack, and regretting, amongst others, the loss of his officer, when to his amazement Dyas entered the tent, not only alive but unhurt !"

There was, however, more in store for the brave ensign.

Wellington promptly decided that a second attempt to storm San Christoval must be made: the capture of the outwork being all important for the furtherance of the main attack on Badajoz. But it required three days more of pounding at the walls before it was considered advisable to attempt the new assault. The British siege-battery guns, unequal to their work before, proved quite incapable of doing expeditious work. "The brass guns," relates an officer, "were inadequate to the task they had to perform, and after being a short time at work became so hot as to be useless. The artillerymen were occupied for several hours throwing buckets of water over their barrels, in order the sooner to render them fit for work."

The officer adds this:

> The touch-holes of several of the cannon melted away, and became so large that they were unserviceable; others were rendered useless by being plugged up with the enemy's shot; and by ten o'clock each morning our line of batteries presented a very disorganized appearance: sand-bags, gabions, and fascines knocked here and there, guns flung off their carriages, and carriages beaten down under their guns. The boarded platforms of the batteries, damp with the blood of our artillerymen, or the headless trunks of our devoted engineers, bore testimony to

the murderous fire opposed to us, but nevertheless every-thing went on with alacrity and spirit; the damage done to the embrasures was speedily repaired, and many a fine fellow lost his life endeavouring to vie with the men of the engineers in braving dangers, unknown to any but those who have been placed in a similar situation.

Ensign Dyas, during the interval on the second day of the renewed bombardment, found a fresh opportunity of showing the stuff he was made of. The tale is thus told by a brother-officer present in front of Fort San Christoval:

On the night of June 8 (the one previous to the second assault), Ensign Dyas being on duty in the trenches, an order arrived to send an officer and fifteen men to a hollow spot in front of our lines, between San Christoval and the *tête du pont*, close to the Roman bridge which communicated with the Elvas gate. I know not how it happened, but Dyas was selected for this arduous duty. The object of this movement was for the purpose of observing if any, and what, communication or reinforcement would be sent to the fort. The detachment was to be recalled before day.

The night was unusually still, and every sound was distinctly heard, but nothing could be ascertained except that one piece of ordnance (a howitzer, I believe) had passed over to the fort. Day at last began to dawn, yet no order had been received for the withdrawal of the party so stationed; their situation was most critical—within point-blank shot of the fort in their rear. Dyas ordered his men to lie flat on their faces, though he every moment expected his situation would be discovered, and a rush made at him; nevertheless, unintimidated by his perilous posture, he dispatched a trusty man to the trenches, with orders to make known to the officer commanding the information he had been enabled to collect, and to know what was to be the final duty of the party.

'Now, mind,' said Dyas, ' if we are to be recalled, do you raise your cap on your forelock above the Battery No. 1. If we are to remain, you know what your duty is.'

'By G——, and plase your honour, I do; and recall or no recall, I'll be back with you in five minutes, dead or alive.' So replied the poor fellow, who, I need not add (after his speech), was an

Hibernian.

'Do as you are ordered, sir,' said Dyas; 'we have not a moment to lose.'

A few minutes (a long time under the circumstances) only elapsed before the signal agreed upon was made; and Dyas, addressing his men in a few words, told them that their safety depended on their adhering strictly to his directions. He then started them singly to different parts of the lines; and, singular as it may appear, although it was now clear daylight, not one man was hit!

While the plans for the second assault on San Christoval were being discussed, Ensign Dyas was sent for to the tent of the brigadier directing the operations against the fort. General Houston put several questions to him; amongst others one as to the real depth of the moat, about which there was a difference of opinion. Dyas gave the depth at twelve feet.

"He judged it at that," he said," from the great shock he had felt when he jumped down!" The chief engineer, Colonel Squires, dissented, remarking rather superciliously that "allowances should be made for young beginners!" Ensign Dyas did not like the remark. But he only replied that he was convinced his estimate was correct, "and," as his brother-officer tells us, "from that moment he made up his mind to head the next attack."

He volunteered for it immediately the breach was again reported practicable, waiting on General Houston and asking leave to lead the forlorn-hope again. The brigadier tried to dissuade him. "No," he said, "you have already done enough. It would be unfair that you should again bear the brunt of this business!"

But Ensign Dyas was not to be put off. "Why, general," he went on, "there seemed to be some doubts of the practicability of this business on the last night of our attack. Although I myself don't think the breach is even now practicable, I request you to allow me to lead the party."

Again the brigadier refused, and then the ensign spoke up again. "General Houston," he said, "I hope you won't refuse my request. I am determined, if you order the fort to be stormed fifty times, to lead the advance as long as I have life!"

The general was still unwilling for Ensign Dyas to run the risk, but in the end the young officer's earnestness overcame him, and he assented.

Dyas went off at once to see the officer who was to head the stormers, a Major MacGeechy. With him he arranged to prevent another mistake by their personally reconnoitring the fort together at dusk that evening, two hours before the storming-party fell in.

The pair went off secretly, and, making a detour along the bank of the river, managed to creep undiscovered by the French sentries to within a short distance of the fort. Keeping sheltered under cover of some reeds, they carefully examined the breach, which, to Major MacGeechy, appeared a practicable one. "But Dyas, better informed from experience, disagreed with his companion, and desired him to watch attentively the effect of the next salvo from our batteries. He did so, and appeared satisfied with the result: 'Because the wall,' he said to Dyas, 'gave way very freely.'

"'Yes,' replied Dyas, 'but did you observe how the stones *fell*, instead of rolling? If there was rubbish about the base, or face of it, the stone would *roll*, not *fall*.'"

The observation was not lost on Major MacGeechy; but it had been already ordered that the attack should be made that night, the order had already gone forth for the assault. Both the leader of the forlorn-hope and the commander of the storming-party, that being so, made up their minds for the trial.

Ten o'clock that night was the hour fixed, and punctually, as the cathedral clock in Badajoz struck the hour, 200 men moved out stealthily from the British lines towards the moat. Ensign Dyas led in advance of all, as before at the head of the Forlorn-Hope, twenty men. He made a circuit this time, following a sheep-path which he and Major MacGeechy had marked earlier, which guided them all to immediately in front of the breach. As they got there, however, the enemy discovered them, and instantly opened a furious fire from every musket and gun they had. Many men were struck down, but the others faced the fire firmly, and went on. Again Ensign Dyas, foremost of all, sprang boldly down into the moat, and again he landed safely on his feet.

Behind the forlorn-hope, who followed their leader nobly, the rest of the stormers were pressing on, when of a sudden the ladder-bearers in rear failed in their duty. Their defection proved disastrous. Their miscarriage wrecked the enterprise at the outset, before even the real attack had begun. "The ladders," we are told, "were entrusted to a party composed of a foreign corps in our pay, called the 'Chasseurs Britanniques.' These men, the moment they reached the glacis, glad to rid themselves of their load, flung the ladders into the ditch, instead of sliding them between the palisades. The ladders fell across and stuck fast, and being made of heavy green wood, it was next to impossible to move, much less place them upright against the breach, and almost all the storming-party were massacred in the attempt."

Yet even then the heroic soldiers of the storming-party left alive persevered, and tried their hardest to get to the breach. Several jumped down into the moat after the forlorn-hope; others lined up on the glacis and replied with their muskets to the French fusillade, and, notwithstanding their fearfully exposed situation, "their determined fire forced the enemy in front to waver."

Major MacGeechy had already fallen, pierced with bullets, and the other officers of the storming-party were also speedily shot down. Within five minutes Ensign Dyas and some twenty-five men were all that remained of the 200 who had mustered for the night's work. Ensign Dyas himself, indeed, was wounded. "He was struck by a pellet in the forehead"—by one of the small bullets, stuck round small wooden cylinders, each three inches long, which the French later used with such deadly effect in the breach at Badajoz as musket projectiles, the wood splintering as it left the muzzle, and the pellets scattering like miniature shrapnel. He "fell on his face, but, undaunted by this, he sprang up and rallied his remaining followers."

Wounded as he was, Dyas succeeded in getting hold of one of the ladders, and placed it against the breach, or where the breach should have been. The ladder was speedily mounted, but upon arriving at the top, instead of the breach, there was found a stone wall which the French had built during the previous night. The wall "completely cut off all communication between the ditch and the bastion, so that when the men reached the top of the wall they were, in effect, as far from the breach as if they had been in their own batteries."

All the time the enemy on the ramparts were blazing away incessantly at them, flinging flaring port-fires down to give light to aim by, scoffingly defying them and rolling down on them barrels of powder and bursting grenades and shells.

Dyas persevered, but at length the heroic Ensign had to give up and own himself baffled the second time. He could finally only tell those left alive round him to shift for themselves. Nineteen men, fifteen of them wounded, were all that made good their escape to the British lines!

Ensign Dyas himself, as before, was the last man to quit the moat.

He got back on the glacis again by making use of one of the abandoned ladders which hung over from the glacis, projecting across the palisades into the moat. Dyas sprang up this, and so reached the glacis, where, to avoid the French bullets, he flung himself down flat among the heap of dead and wounded there. As he dropped the enemy on the ramparts fired a volley at him, after which, seeing him go down, they shouted in triumph: "*Il est tué, en voila le dernier!*"

The brave fellow, though, was untouched by the last bullets, and, seeing that his only chance of escape was to lie quiet, he waited, stretched out and motionless. He remained so for a few minutes; then he seized his opportunity. Realizing that the French, from the silence, thought all was over, and had ceased to point their muskets at the spot, he sprang to his feet, and ran until he safely reached the nearest British batteries.

This is how the story of Ensign Dyas ends: the after-career of this truly heroic officer. In these days there would have been for him the V.C. for certain, and promotion and a brevet as well, and the whole Empire would have rung with his name. Practically, Dyas got nothing at all. Wellington mentioned him in dispatches, and recommended him strongly to the notice of the War Office, but his name and services were overlooked there. He had no interest to help him with the Home Authorities in Pall Mall, and he was too modest a fellow to press himself forward. Three years later he fought at Waterloo with his regiment as one of the subalterns, a lieutenant just half-way up the list, having got that step by seniority, in his turn in the ordinary way. And ten years after Badajoz Dyas was still a subaltern. After that, quite by accident, his case came before the Duke of York, then Commander-in-Chief of the Army, and he was gazetted to a captaincy in a local corps in Ceylon.

It was not very much, not very generous for such a fellow, but it was all he got. And even then Dyas was unable to avail himself of it. "The number of campaigns he had served in had materially injured his health, and he was obliged to retire on the half-pay of his company."

Where and when he died, or in what circumstances, is unknown. Joseph Dyas, the bravest of the brave, the ensign hero of the second Siege of Badajoz, went to his grave uncared for, unhonoured, and unremembered by his country. R.I.P.

These verses were written about Dyas by someone unknown some time after Waterloo:

I know a man of whom 'tis truly said
He bravely twice a storming-party led,
And volunteer'd both times. Now here's the rub:
The gallant fellow still remains a Sub.!

13

On Badajoz Night: How Picton's Men Stormed the Castle

The storming of Badajoz stands by itself as a surpassing feat of arms in the annals of the British Army. More gallant and daring deeds were never done by our soldiers than on that terrific night of 1812—just 100 years ago last April, (as at time of first publication). The annals of European warfare hardly record incidents more terrible than those of that spring-night's tragedy in Spain. The taking of the fortress by hand-to-hand fight was a matter of grim necessity. Badajoz barred Wellington's way; it had to be captured; it could in no circumstances be left with its powerful garrison on one side; there was no other means of getting past.

On the afternoon of April 6, 1812, after a three weeks' siege, Wellington decided to snatch the fortress from the enemy that night with the pick of the British Army—18,000 men,—attacking the fortress on three sides at once.

Picton, Wellington's fiercest fighter, with his own command, the ever-renowned "Fighting Third" Division, was to carry the castle by escalade, a great fort at the north-east angle of Badajoz. Two divisions, the Fourth Division and the Light Division, were to storm the main breach, which had been battered in on the south-east side of the ramparts. The Fifth Division was at the same time to assault the fortress on its western side.

Ten at night was the hour fixed for the attack, which was to be delivered simultaneously at all points.

All were in the highest spirits and full of eager anticipation, and also full of the calmest confidence in the issue. "The soldiers heard the orders for the assault and proceeded to clean their appointments as if a parade only was intended." After that, as evening came on and the gathering darkness shut out distant objects, the regiments fell in and formed up; "the roll was called in an under-voice—the forlorn-hope stepped out—the storming-party was told off." These at once moved down to the first parallel and silently in the dark all took their places and then stood fast.

But the enemy on their side were on the alert and well prepared. The fine old soldier in command at Badajoz, the French General Philippon, "well aware that an assault might be expected, had employed every resource that skill and ingenuity could devise to render the attempt a failure." He had just sufficient time, and his men did their work thoroughly. The three breaches in the ramparts battered in by the British cannon were effectively insulated. The debris of masonry was removed; retrenchments formed; the broken-down parapets repaired by means of sand-bags, casks filled with earth, and woolpacks. Kegs of powder and hand-grenades were laid along in trenches cut in the ditch below, in front of the breaches, as well as rows of huge 14-inch bombshells, all linked together by quick-match and embedded in the ground, ready to explode.

Solid beams set round closely with sharp sword-blades bristled like grim hedges of gleaming steel across the top of the breaches: planks stuck over with ugly iron spikes were planted on the sloping surfaces wherever daring men might climb up, tilted and arranged to upset and roll over the moment a foot trod on them. Plugs of wood, studded with buck-shot and slugs, were served round to every soldier, for discharging with deadly spreading effect on masses of men at close quarters.

Ten o'clock was Wellington's appointed hour, but the wary Philippon had planned to forestall his antagonist in time. Just before ten a blazing carcass, or fireball, shot up of a sudden from the citadel ramparts, shedding a vivid glare of light widely round and showing up, clear as in the daytime, the edge of the ditches, with, arrayed on the glacis, the serried ranks of British redcoats standing there in long, close-ranged lines, awaiting the word to go forward. The light of the fireball flickered out, and darkness, blacker than ever as it seemed, closed again over the scene. A surprise was now out of the question. The forlorn-hope parties moved out quite near to the brink of the ditch, with, close at their heels, the ladder-men and the stormers, and, in rear, the columns of the regiments.

Engraving of the batteries before Badajoz

At that moment the deep bell of the Cathedral of St. John struck ten; the most perfect silence reigned around, and except the softened footsteps of the storming-parties, as they fell upon the turf with military precision, not a movement was audible. A terrible suspense, a horrible stillness, darkness, a compression of breathing, the dull and ill-defined outline of the town, the knowledge that similar and simultaneous movements were making on other points, the certainty that two or three minutes would probably involve the forlorn-hope in ruin or make it the beacon-light to conquest—all these made the heart throb quicker and long for the bursting of the storm, when victory would crown daring with success, or hope and life should end together.

On went the storming-parties—one solitary musket was discharged beside the breach—but none answered it.... The ditch was gained, the ladders were lowered, on rushed the forlorn-hope, with the storming-party close behind them. The divisions were now on the brink of a sheer descent, when a gun boomed from the parapet. The earth trembled—a mine was fired, an explosion, and an infernal hissing from lighted fuses succeeded, and, like the rising of a curtain on the stage, the hellish glare that suddenly burst out round the breaches, the French lining the ramparts in crowds, and the English descending the ditch, were exposed as distinctly visible to each other as if the hour were noontide!"

Picton's men, fronting the Citadel, or "Castle" of Badajoz, by chance made their attack first of all. The blazing fireball so unexpectedly sent up had disclosed them standing close up by the glacis. As its flaring light fell on the columns of the Third Division, Picton—standing near the stormers with their scaling-ladders and iron crowbars ready, with Kempt, one of Picton's brigadiers, and his staff close beside him—instantly gave the order to set on. In his great bull voice Picton shouted almost with a roar: "They've seen us! It's no use waiting! Forward!"

Major Burgoyne of the Royal Engineers and Lieutenant Macarthy of the 50th led the way; and all surged forward, moving on in silence for a few paces amid the black darkness that again came on. Now it was again the enemy's turn. As though well aware of what was taking place, the castle garrison opened fire: lighting up the scene momentarily, at first with a fresh outburst of fireballs from the ramparts, then by a shattering discharge of cannon which belched forth with the suddenness of a thunderclap, the guns double-shotted with grape and canister. The *feu d'enfer* was added to quickly by volleys of musketry fired off in rapid succession. Every French soldier on the castle ramparts had by him some two, some three, muskets ready loaded in advance to beat back the opening onrush.

But Picton's men were not to be lightly checked or shaken off. Without slackening their pace a moment, the forlorn-hope and escalading-parties pressed forward, regardless of the balls and bullets. Keeping together until the outwork fortifications were close before them, the men in advance replied to the French fire with a cheer, and ran up with their ladders to the outer palisades. As they came on, handgrenades were showered on their heads; to which several of the stormers answered by shooting back at the men on the wall.

Brigadier Kempt fell wounded. He was struck down among the first and was carried to the rear. Then Picton himself and Lieutenant Macarthy ran forward together. Laying hold of a palisade, Macarthy shouted: "Down with the palings !" and the crowbar-men setting to instantly, a gap through was speedily made. Picton at once led in with a rush of stormers close after him; and the rest of the palisades at all points were smashed through, or sent crashing to the ground.

Rushing over and through the wreckage, the jostling throng quickly reached the foot of the wall, to find confronting them a sheer face of smooth solid stone and brick, "a sheer cliff of masonry," which rose from eighteen to twenty feet overhead. Under a furious fusillade from the enemy above, several long scaling-ladders were quickly reared against the wall, and a swarm of gallant fellows scrambled up them, hustling and shoving one another in their endeavours to be the first to reach the ramparts. But the enemy on the walls were as brave men and as determined. As fast as the tops of the ladders were clapped against the parapets they were flung roughly back. Again and again they were set up; as many times they were shoved off; and the men, clustered like bees on them, were hurled back, to fall crashing on the heads of the men below, or to the ground, amidst an infernal ceaseless din from every side—shot and shouts, oaths and cursing, and frenzied French yells and cries of exultation.

Showers of heavy stones, logs of wood and bursting shells rolled off the parapet, while from the flanks musketry was plied with

THE MAN WHO STORMED THE CASTLE OF BADAJOZ
LIEUTENANT-GENERAL SIR THOMAS PICTON, G.C.B.

fearful rapidity, and in front the leading assailants were with pike and bayonet stabbed and the ladders pushed from the walls: and all this was attended with deafening shouts, the crash of breaking ladders and the shrieks of crushed soldiers answering to the sullen stroke of the falling weights.

That is Napier's description of the scene.

One ladder the defenders hauled up bodily by main force on to the rampart. Everywhere around men fell in horrible heaps; the dead, the mangled and maimed, mingled all together, but more brave fellows surged forward, instantly ready, and clamouring, one and all, to take their places.

Then, for an instant, the attack seemed to recoil. It seemed beyond possibility to keep the ladders up. Picton personally checked the first sign of shrinking back. Again his stentorian voice resounded amid the roaring turmoil, calling to his brave fellows for yet another effort. "Fighting Third! you have never been defeated!" he bellowed out. "Now's the time to win or die!"

Again the ladders, those that were left unbroken, were, as well as possible, upreared and heaved up and poised on high. Again they were swung forward to the walls. Again the intrepid soldiers crowded to them and on them and clambered up, recking nothing, as it looked, of what had gone before. But once again the strong-armed enemy along the ramparts were their match. The French sent the laden ladders rocking back; pushed them over, to fall once more in hideous crashes to the ground. The spirit, though, of Picton's soldiers was indomitable. Once more the panting heroes prepared stubbornly to make a fresh attempt. Picton, beside himself in his excitement, saw it. He raised his mighty voice yet once again to cheer them on. "If we cannot win," he shouted like a trumpet-call, "let us die up there on the walls!"

As the last words left Picton's lips, one more ladder was deftly swung aloft. It struck the wall close by an embrasure, through which a great cannon pointed and filled the gap. Somebody among the enemy on top nearby blundered; or the Frenchmen fumbled this time in getting their hold. Before they could well realize what had happened, a British officer had bounded up the ladder, and was at the top, standing on the parapet, slashing and thrusting out with his sword to right and left. He was the heroic Colonel Ridge of the 5th Northumberland Fusiliers, as gallant and bold a soldier as ever wore our King's uniform. A second ladder by good fortune at that moment had been hastily planted close by, and Ridge was quickly joined by Ensign Canch, of the grenadier company of the "Fighting Fifth."[1]

The shouting troops pressed after them, and the garrison, amazed, and in a manner surprised, were driven fighting through the double gate into the town: the castle was won. Soon a reinforcement from the French reserve came to the gate, through which both sides fired, and the enemy retired; but Ridge fell, and no man died that night with more glory—yet many died, and there was much glory.

He had made a dash along the ramparts calling out as he led the way: "Come on, my lads, let's be the first to seize the governor!" The party, composed of Ensign Canch's grenadiers and some others, all of them of the 5th, fought their way on, "exposed to a heavy fire by which numbers fell, who were soon replaced by those who followed," until near the centre of the castle. "Then," as an officer beside the colonel tells, "a column was observed which caused a momentary hesitation in our advance."

Again Colonel Ridge led on undauntedly. He called to the men: "Why hesitate? Forward!" They were his last words. A moment later a volley from the enemy smashed in among them.

Our beloved and heroic commander fell, having received a wound in the breast which immediately proved fatal. I was so near as to be in contact with him at the instant of his fall. We left a guard by his honoured remains.

There was yet another officer among the foremost stormers to win immortal fame that night.

Not very long after Colonel Ridge and Ensign Canch had reached the ramparts a third hero got there. He was the officer who was to have the honour of hauling down the Garrison Flag of Badajoz. That flag is now at Chelsea Hospital: a trophy as good as any of Napoleon's Eagles, for none was ever more bravely won. Lieutenant Macpherson of the 45th was the officer. He came up close after Ensign Canch, on the second ladder; with, at his heels, Sir Edward Pakenham, Wellington's brother-in-law, Picton's second in command in the Third

---

1. Robert Canch died in 1850, Fort-Major of Edinburgh Castle. It was claimed for him that he, not Colonel Ridge, was actually the first man to set foot on top of the walls—"the foremost to plant his foot on the ramparts of Badajoz." He hardly missed a battle throughout the war, and was granted the Peninsular War medal, with no fewer than twelve clasps.

Division.

The story of Macpherson's feat is a stirring and magnificent one.

As he got near the parapet Macpherson found the ladder was some three feet short of reaching the top. He shouted to those below to shove the ladder higher while he tried to push the ladder a little from the wall, to ease it. The men cheered, and Macpherson, giving a swing forward, was even with the battlements in a moment. An instant later he was severely wounded. Before he could get his hands off the wall to use his sword, a French soldier clapped a musket at Macpherson's body and fired. The ball struck one of the Spanish silver buttons on Macpherson's waistcoat and glanced off, but broke two ribs, 'the broken part of one being so clamped on his lungs as to stop his breath.'

He still hung on grimly, however, though he could get no farther. General Pakenham struggled to pass him, but he was badly wounded too. The ladder began to break. Pakenham gripped Macpherson by the hand. 'God bless you, my dear fellow! We shall meet again!' Both, however, after that reached the ground alive; Macpherson, by dazedly working his way down the back of the ladder. In the ditch he became insensible, until coming to he found himself being attended to by two of his own men; one supporting his head on the man's knee, while the second soldier held a cup of chocolate to his lips.

Macpherson then roused himself, and put all his strength into an effort to rise; the struggle actually forcing the broken rib back into its place, giving him instant relief.

With rare spirit the brave fellow at once went up the ladder again, to capture the French garrison flag.

Leading on a fresh party of stormers up the ladder, Lieutenant Macpherson forced his way along the walls towards the 'great tower' that topped the citadel, whence on the summit the French flag, a tricolour standard, was visible to all as it floated above the glare of the firing and the smoke of the continuous explosions all round. Macpherson quickly got to the foot of the 'great tower.' He found there a gallant French infantryman by himself. He was standing on sentry, and had remained at his post regardless of what was happening round him. Sword in hand the British lieutenant rushed on the sentry, seized hold of him, and bade him in French to point out the way to the staircase leading up to the flagstaff.

'*Je ne sais pas!*' replied the sentry, on which Macpherson, mad with excitement, lost command of himself. He slashed the French soldier across the face with his sword, angrily shouting at him: '*Vous le savez à présent!*'

The unfortunate sentry started back, dazed at the blow. Then the poor fellow dashed his musket to the ground, and, striking his breast, lifted his head up and fronted his antagonist. Pointing to his heart, the man exclaimed: '*Frappez! frappez la! Je suis Français!*'

Macpherson, we are told, was so surprised at the Frenchman's "spirited demeanour," that he called to a sergeant who was following him, and gave him explicit orders to protect the sentry's life. Then, seeing his way, he ran round to a door and up the tower stairs to the flagstaff platform. Hauling down the flag there, he stripped off and hoisted his own red uniform jacket as the British colours in its place, as the signal that the castle of Badajoz had been won.

The all-important news that the citadel was ours was sent off by Picton to Wellington at once. It was half an hour before midnight. The desperate fight to win at that point had taken all that time.

Wellington so far had not had a word from Picton. All he knew was that the second attack, the attempt to storm the great breach, was, so far, going disastrously. Nor had he had news as yet of the Fifth Division and their attempt on the farther side.

> The wounded came fast to the rear, but they could tell little how matters were progressing. At last a mounted officer rode up. He was the bearer of evil tidings: 'the attack upon the breaches had failed, the majority of the officers had fallen; the men, left without leaders to direct them, were straggling about the ditch, and unless instant assistance was sent, the assault must fail entirely!' Pale, but collected, the British general heard the disastrous communication, and issued orders to send forward a fresh brigade (Hay's) to the breaches. Half an hour passed, and another officer appeared. He came from Picton to say the castle had been escaladed, and that the Third Division was actually in the town."

How, in that terrible hour, Wellington bore himself, and how the news of Picton's success was brought to him, is told by an officer who was nearby at the moment.

"Lord Wellington," the officer relates, "was attended only by two of his *aides-de-camp*—the Prince of Orange and the Duke of Richmond (then Lord March), both young men. His lordship, on our coming up, was so intent on what was going on, that I believe that he did not observe at first that Dr. Forbes and I had joined him. Soon after our arrival, an officer came up with an unfavourable report of the assault, announcing that Colonel McLeod and several officers were killed, with heaps of men, who choked the approach to the breach! At the place where we stood, we were within hearing of the voices of the assailants and of the assailed. It was painful to notice that the voices of our countrymen had become fainter, while the French cry of '*Avancez! étrillons ces Anglais!*' became stronger. Another officer came up with a still more unfavourable report—that no progress was being made, and that he feared none could be made, for almost all the officers were killed, and none were left to lead on the men, of whom a great many had fallen.

"At this moment I cast my eyes on the countenance of Lord Wellington, lit up by the glare of the torch held by Lord March. I never shall forget it to the last moment of my existence, and I could even now sketch it. The jaw had fallen, and the face was of unusual length; while the torchlight gave his countenance a lurid aspect, but still, the expression of the face was firm. Suddenly, turning to me and putting his hand on my arm, he said:' Go over immediately to Picton, and tell him he must try if he cannot succeed on the castle.'

"I replied: My lord, I have not my horse, but I will walk as fast as I can, and I think I can find the way. I know part of the road is swampy.'

"'No, no! 'he replied. 'I beg your pardon, I thought it was Delancey.'

"I repeated my offer, saying I was sure I could find the way. But he said, 'No.'

"In this very uncomfortable state of mind Lord Wellington had remained for a few minutes, when we heard a noise; and we all instantly said it was a horseman approaching. Immediately after this a voice called out, harshly and loudly: 'Where is Lord Wellington?' We all exclaimed, 'Here! here!'

"' My lord,' exclaimed the officer, 'the castle is your own!'

"'Who brings that intelligence?' exclaimed Lord Wellington. The officer gave his name.

"'Are you certain, sir?'

"'I entered the castle with the troops; I have just left it, and General Picton is in possession.'

"'With how many men?'

"'His division.'

"It is impossible to imagine the change that this produced in the feelings of all around.

"'Return, sir, and desire General Picton to maintain his position at all hazards!'

"Having dispatched this messenger, Lord Wellington directed a second officer to proceed to the castle to repeat his orders to General Picton."

That is the story of the taking of the Citadel of Badajoz.

14

Wellington's Master-Stroke: the Thunderbolt of Salamanca

Salamanca was to Wellington himself his favourite victory. The duke looked on it as his diploma of generalship, so to speak; his masterpiece in tactics, although no doubt, to the world at large, Salamanca is eclipsed in the dazzling radiance of "king-making" Waterloo. Invited by the allied Sovereigns in Paris after Waterloo to give a display before them of how he handled an army in the presence of the enemy, Wellington chose Salamanca for repetition, in preference to all his other victories, and fought the battle "over again, with blank cartridge, as a field-day on the plain of St. Denis," under the eyes of the foremost soldiers of Europe.

In a sense, of course, Wellington's partiality was justified. The fighting at Salamanca lasted six hours, from the first shot to the end; but the battle had been practically won in less than three-quarters of an hour. It was at Salamanca that Wellington, as a French general epigrammatically put it, "defeated 40,000 men in forty minutes."

"I never saw an army receive such a beating," was Wellington's own comment on his victory at Salamanca. Six thousand prisoners were taken, including one general and 130 other officers of rank. Six thousand more of the enemy, at the lowest computation, were left dead or wounded on the field of battle. Three French generals were killed and three wounded; among these last Marshal Marmont himself, the enemy's commander-in-chief, put *hors de combat* by a bursting shell at the moment of extreme crisis for his army, while "spurring furiously to the point of danger." Marmont was carried off the field under fire, on a stretcher improvised with a soldier's great-coat and a couple of muskets thrust through the armholes to give it shape and serve

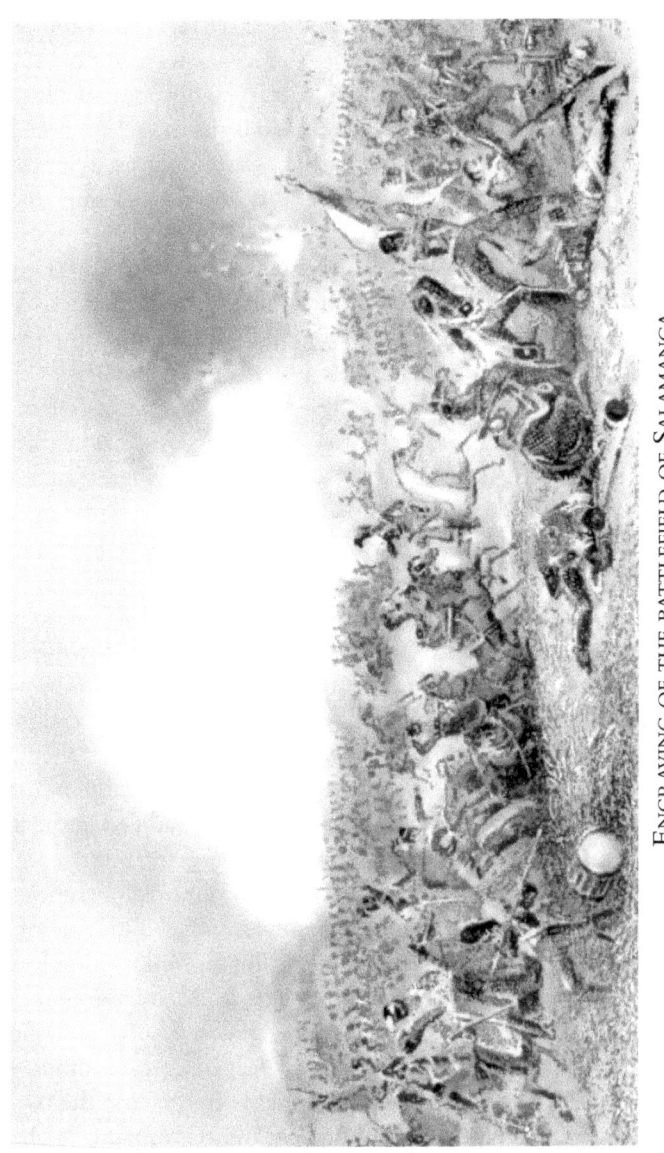

Engraving of the Battlefield of Salamanca

as handles for the bearers, by four grenadier privates. Eleven cannon and two Eagles, with six other standards, were among the trophies of the day. The Eagles are among our proudest spoils of victory now at Chelsea Hospital.

The battle was fought on Sunday, July 2, 1812; one of the "Red Sundays "of Wellington's career in war. Vimiero was fought on a Sunday, as was Fuentes de Onoro. On a Sunday afternoon Wellington issued his memorable order—"Ciudad Rodrigo must be carried by assault this evening." The Battle of Orthez was fought on a Sunday, as was that of Toulouse, the closing battle of the war. On a Sunday, too, were fought Vittoria and Waterloo.

Under arms on either side were between 50,000 and 60,000 men; the advantage of numbers, but only to a small extent, being in Wellington's favour. Less, though, than 30,000 of Wellington's men were British, his total including Portuguese and Spaniards, the best of them hardly a match for half their force of Napoleon's veterans, some of the finest specimens of whom were in the ranks of Marmont's army.

One of the most trying of experiences for Wellington's men, as they bivouacked in the open, was that night before the Battle of Salamanca. The eve of Salamanca those who fought in Spain never forgot, for the tremendous thunderstorm that burst over the camp.

"A calm and sultry evening," describes an officer, "was succeeded by a sudden clouding over of the sky and a tremendous downpour of rain. The wind rose and howled in long bitterly cold gusts, followed by peal on peal of crashing thunder." The Light Division were caught by the storm while in the act of passing a ford near Salamanca; "the lightning passed in sheets of fire over the column, playing on the points of the bayonets." The horses of the cavalry, kept ready saddled in the lines, against an expected night-attack, stampeded, "dragging out the pickets to which they were haltered, and bolting in fright in all directions."

One flash "killed many men and horses, while hundreds of the frightened animals, breaking loose and galloping wildly about, were supposed to be the enemy charging in the dark." Many horses, indeed, galloped away into the enemy's lines and were lost. The vivid flashes of lightning "wholly illuminated the plain, succeeding each other with such rapidity that a constant blaze filled the space between the two armies." The storm lasted till early morning, and then gradually abated. "By six o'clock the dusky vapour which had veiled the rising sun passed off and showed the two armies standing in the array in which they had been placed the evening before."

The two armies on the morning of the battle were drawn up on opposite ranges of hills along two sides of a wide sandy valley, sparsely covered in places with bushes and straggling copses of dwarf oak, a rough oval in general shape, some three miles from end to end, and from a mile to a mile and a half across. Wellington's troops were ranged along the hills on the northern and western sides. They were, as usual with Wellington, being kept concealed from the enemy as much as possible, posted mostly on the hill-side slopes farthest from the French; but few were visible to the enemy from the front.

"We could see," says a French general, "one English division in a small wood, a cannon-shot from the village of Calvariza, on the Salamanca road; in the distance, in rear, a small column was mounting the hill of Tejares; everything else was completely hidden from us by the range of hills which ends in the high conicle peaks called the two Arapiles. Wellington and his Staff, however, could be made out on the watch at one place on the crest of the chain of hills."

The French main position was along the eastern hills across the valley. The enemy, on their side, were not so careful about keeping themselves concealed—with results that the sequel showed. The two Arapiles were isolated peaks of bare grey rock which rose abruptly from one end of the plain at one end of the valley. They were about half a cannon-shot apart, one being held by the British and the other by the French.

Wellington on that morning was for the time being in an awkward situation. He had been outmanoeuvred by his able antagonist in a series of marches and counter-marches during the previous week, and, having been unable to bring the enemy to battle under conditions satisfactory to himself, was contemplating a withdrawal across the Spanish frontier into Portugal again. There seemed, indeed, so little prospect of an immediate battle when he confronted Marshal Marmont across the valley on the morning of July 22 that he had practically decided to retreat and draw off, under cover of the next night, along the road to the frontier-fortress of Ciudad Rodrigo, taken by storm seven months before, and now serving as the base of the British operations.

But shortly after midday a sudden and unexpected move on the French side entirely altered the state of affairs.

Wellington had passed most of the forenoon in posting his troops so as to be prepared, should the enemy give him a fair chance, to attack and force on a general battle. He had it in his mind that Marmont was getting over-confident after his successful manoeuvring of the past few days, and might well beguile himself into a false step. That, in fact, was what actually happened. Wellington was watching to see what Marmont would do next, when a blundering move on the French side—flagrant and patent at the first glance—suddenly gave him an opportunity beyond anything he had ventured to hope for.

Confident on his part that Wellington did not really want to fight, that he was only waiting a chance to slip away and get clear off under cover of night, Marmont, within sight of his enemy, rashly detached the entire division forming his left wing, with the intention of threatening Wellington's line of retreat beforehand, and forcing the British into a situation where defeat must be disaster. Opening with a brisk cannonade from some fifty guns to cover the move, Marmont marched off his left wing to seize the heights of Miranda, to the south of the valley, some two miles from the French main position. The move, as it proceeded, made an ever-widening gap between the French left wing and Marmont's centre, taking the detached division beyond reach of assistance from the main army, and exposing it to sudden attack while isolated.

How Marmont's false move was seen and taken advantage of, and its immediate consequence for the whole of the French army, forms one of the most dramatic of battle stories.

It was a little past noon. Wellington from his lookout post on the Arapile Hill, on the British side, had been watching the enemy for some time, but without being able, so far, to observe any sign of serious movement. Then he gave his telescope to an *aide-de-camp*, and, bidding him keep watch, rode down below to a farm not far off, where breakfast had been got ready for him and the staff.

The enemy's cannonade had been going on for some time, and after Wellington reached the farm their shells fell so close to the farmhouse that the breakfast dishes had to be moved behind the building. There Wellington began his meal. He would not sit down, but kept "stumping about munching," continually taking peeps towards the enemy with a staff-officer's spyglass. As he was doing so the *aide-de-camp* he had left on the Arapile came hurrying down.

"The enemy are in motion, my lord."

"Very well. Observe what they are doing," was the answer in a quiet tone.

The officer moved away a short distance, and stood taking a long look through the glass. Then he came back again, and said:

"I think they are extending to the left!"

"The devil they are!" replied Wellington hastily, with his mouth full. "Give me the glass!"

He took it, and for nearly a minute scanned the movements of the enemy with fixed attention.

"Come!" exclaimed Wellington, as he lowered the glass; "I think that'll do!" He turned abruptly to another *aide-de-camp*. "Ride off and tell Clinton and Leith to return to their former ground."

These were the generals commanding the British Fifth and Sixth Divisions, which occupied the centre of Wellington's position.

Then Wellington ordered up his horse. Closing his spyglass with a snap, he turned to his Spanish *aide- de-camp*, Colonel Alava, with the words: "*Mon cher Alava, Marmont est perdu!*" A moment later Wellington was on horseback and his staff also, all galloping off.

Wellington had fully taken in the meaning of Marmont's move. He saw his chance of falling on the detached French wing in force and overpowering it before support could reach it from the main body. Thus a third of Marmont's strength would be shorn away at a stroke, and at the same time he would smash in the French centre.

The British Third Division was by itself, apart from the rest of the army. It was lying in wait, so to speak, in a wood in rear of Wellington's right flank, completely concealed from view. From its situation there it could at short notice sweep round across the front of the detached French column in the midst of its march.

Wellington first rode off to the Fifth and Fourth Divisions nearer at hand. He gave orders to the two generals in charge, Leith and Lowry Cole, to begin their advance at once. They were to make a frontal attack on the troops opposite to them in the French line, Marmont's centre, and press the enemy hard, while Pakenham, with the Third Division, was marching round behind the hills.

Then Wellington galloped on, to appear suddenly in the midst of the Third Division, as yet at the halt and awaiting orders. The famous "Fighting Third" Division, Picton's men, was commanded temporarily by Wellington's brother-in-law, Sir Edward Pakenham, a junior Major-General, during Picton's absence, while recovering from his wound at Badajoz.

"As he rode up to Pakenham," says an officer whose regiment was nearby, "every eye was turned on him. He looked paler than usual, but was quite unruffled in his manner, and as calm as if the battle to be fought was nothing more than an ordinary assemblage of troops for a field-day."

"Ned," said Wellington, drawing rein beside Pakenham, tapping him on the shoulder, and pointing in the direction where the separated French column was on the move—"Ned, move on with the Third Division; take those heights in your front; drive everything before you!"

"I will, my lord!" was Pakenham's laconic reply. He wheeled his horse round and went to give the necessary orders to his command.

Wellington himself turned away and galloped elsewhere.

Now he rode off to where, between the Third Division and Leith's men of the Fifth, the cavalry were. They also had been halted out of direct view of the French, behind some rising ground, taking cover from the French shells which were bursting all round them and overhead as Marmont's artillery searched out the British position. The men were dismounted, and lying down holding their horses. Wellington spoke a few words to General Le Marchant, who was in charge of the heavy cavalry brigade of dragoons, bidding him to keep prepared to support the Third Division in its attack. Pakenham's success, he told Le Marchant, would depend largely on the assistance received from the cavalry. "You must be ready," said Wellington, "to take the first opportunity to attack the enemy's infantry. You will charge them then at all hazards."

With that, desiring Le Marchant to remain where he was for the present, Wellington rode back to his former post near the Arapile Hill on the British side, and, according to one story, dismounted and took a short nap. The movements he had ordered would take some little time to execute, and Marmont's detached division had not yet got sufficiently far enough on its way.

On the French side, while Wellington slept, Marmont was sitting with his staff, smoking cigars and taking it easy after their *déjeuner*, on some rising ground near the French Arapile, opposite the British General, and barely three-quarters of a mile off. "The marshal," says one of Marmont's officers, "had made up his mind that the English Army had fallen back, or, at least, that it was going to take position farther to the left behind the River Zurguen."

Except for the French cannonade and an occasional reply fire from British batteries here and there, as yet no signs of activity were visible on the British side as far as Marmont could make out.

Wellington was awakened between three and four with the news that the enemy were nearing the critical point. Within a few minutes of that the French marshal's daydream was rudely interrupted.

The two divisions of Leith and Cole showed themselves, advancing swiftly to their attack in long lines down the hill-side in front. Marmont, though, as yet, from where he was, could see nothing of Pakenham's move, owing to the high ground that intervened; nor had he, as to that, so far, the least suspicion.

Leith's men, when they got the order to go forward, had "for an hour been lying down with shot and howitzer shells either passing over us or ricocheting through the ranks." Then "the welcome news came that we were no longer to be cannonaded with impunity. It is impossible," says one of the officers of the Fifth Division, "to describe the energetic exultation with which the soldiers sprang to their feet: if ever primary impulse gained a battle that of Salamanca was won before the troops moved forward. In front of the centre of that wonderful line rode General Leith, directing its movements and regulating its advance. Occasionally every soldier was visible, the sun shining bright upon their arms, while at intervals all were enveloped in a dense cloud of dust, from whence at times issued the animated cheer of British infantry."

With the Fourth Division keeping pace steadily on their right, the intervening space between them and the enemy was crossed, and Leith's men approached the nearest part of the French position along the crest of the range of hills on Marmont's side of the battlefield. There the massed columns of Marmont's centre divisions, all formed up, stood awaiting them.

> We were now near the summit of the ridge. The men marched with the same orderly steadiness: no advance in line at a review was ever more correctly executed. The dressing was admirable, and the spaces were no sooner formed by casualties than closed up with the most perfect regularity and without the slightest deviation from the order of march. General Leith and the officers of his staff, being on horseback, first perceived the enemy, and had time to observe his formation previous to the infantry line becoming so visible as to induce him to commence firing. He was drawn up in contiguous squares, the front rank kneeling and prepared to fire when the drum beat for its commencement. All was still and quiet in these squares: not a musket was discharged until the whole opened. Nearly at the same time General Leith ordered the line to fire and charge. The roll of musketry was succeeded by that proud cheer that has become habitual to British soldiers on similar occasions. Then all was

smoke and obscurity.

In that manner the contest in the centre opened; and at the outset the French stubbornly held their ground. They were still keeping their assailants at bay, to Marmont's satisfaction as he viewed the combat from his position on the Arapile, when with startling rapidity Wellington's tactical master-stroke disclosed itself before the eyes of the marshal. Pakenham's foremost men suddenly came into view. With dramatic abruptness Marmont now discovered the deadly intention of his opponent's tactics.

The foremost troops in Pakenham's column suddenly disclosed themselves before the marshal's startled eyes, coming into view from behind the hill. It was a stunning surprise for Marmont. He saw his fate. As he looked he saw the Third Division deploy into line and form up like a wall across his left flank, and move forward swiftly. "Pakenham shot with the Third Division like a meteor across Thomières' path." Now Marshal Marmont realized the awful jeopardy in which his venturesome move had placed his whole army. He spurred off furiously towards the point of danger, but on the way dropped from the saddle, struck down by a bursting shell, which grievously wounded him in the side and shattered one arm, maiming him for life.

"It was five o'clock," tells Napier in his vivid way, "when Pakenham fell upon Thomières; and it was at a moment when that general, whose column had gained an open isolated hill, expected to see the allies in full retreat towards the Rodrigo road, closely followed by Marmont from the Arapiles. The counter-stroke was terrible! Two batteries of artillery, placed on the summit of the western heights, suddenly took his troops in flank; Pakenham's massive columns, supported by cavalry, were in front, and two-thirds of his own division, lengthened out and unconnected, were still in a wood, where they could hear, but where they could not see, the storm now bursting; from the chief to the lowest soldier all felt they were lost, and in an instant, Pakenham, the most frank and gallant of men, commenced the battle.

"As the British masses came on, forming lines while on the march, the French gunners, standing up manfully, sent out showers of grape, and a crowd of light troops poured in a fire of musketry, under cover of which the main body endeavoured to display a front. But bearing on through the skirmishers with the might of a giant, Pakenham broke the half-formed lines into fragments, and sent the whole into confusion upon the advancing supports. Only one officer remained

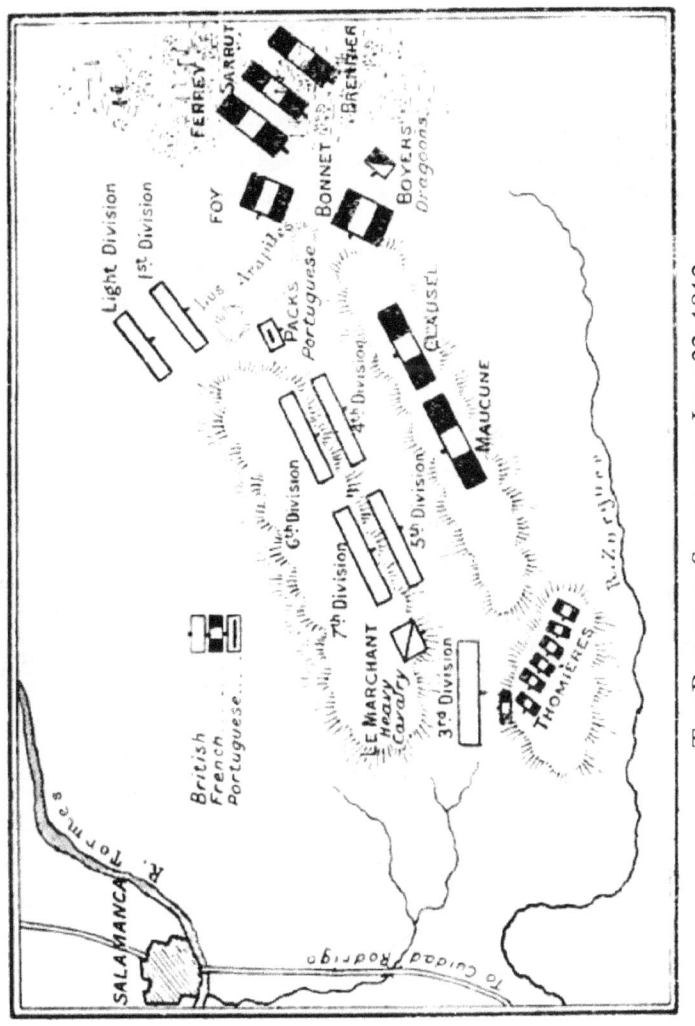

The Battle of Salamanca, July 22, 1812

by the artillery; standing alone, he fired the last gun at the distance of a few yards, but whether he lived or there died could not be seen for the smoke."

The Third Division swept forward in three lines: the first a brigade of three regiments; the old 45th, the 74th, and the 88th—known to us nowadays as battalions of the Derbyshires or Sherwood Foresters, the Highland Light Infantry, and the Connaught Rangers.

Holding their way on impetuously, the leading British soldiers rolled up the French skirmishers and quickly got footing on the nearest ridge of ground, halfway up the hill. Then came the clash. Before they could gain the top, the next moment, with the suddenness of a thunderclap, the enemy came storming at them. Before our men had well time to take breath the whole of the French division, with loud shouts and drums beating, came charging forward to meet them over the crest, blazing into them a furious burst of bullets from 5,000 muskets at less than sixty yards. It brought down within five seconds most of the British front rank all along the line, and more than half the officers.

The brigade staggered and for one instant seemed to reel under the force of the terrific discharge. Then it closed up and dashed on. "Before the smoke had altogether cleared away," describes an officer of the Connaught Rangers, "Wallace" (the veteran colonel of the Connaughts, acting as a Brigadier on that occasion), "looking full in the face of his soldiers, pointed to the French column, and leading the shattered brigade up the hill, without a moment's hesitation, brought them face to face with the foe, before the French had time to realize the terrible effect of their murderous fire."

The sharpness of the counter-move took the enemy aback.

The heroic steadiness of Wallace's gallant men astounded the French. Those in front seemed for a moment inclined to waver. Then, however, they quickly began firing again.

> A heavy discharge of musketry blazed at us; but it was unlike the former; it was irregular and ill-directed, the men acted without concert or method, and many fired in the air.... Their fire ceased, whereupon the three regiments, for the first time, cheered!

The cheers apparently surprised the enemy.

> The effect was electrical: the French were seized with a panic, and, as Wallace closed on them, our men distinctly marked their

bearing. Their *moustachioed* faces, one and all, presented the same ghastly hue, a horrid family likeness throughout; and as they stood to receive the shock they were about to be assailed with, they reeled to and fro like men intoxicated.

The French officers did all that was possible, by voice, gesture, and example, to rouse their men to a sense of their situation, but in vain. One, the colonel of the leading regiment (the 22nd), seizing a firelock, and beckoning to his men to follow, ran forward a few paces and shot Major Murphy dead at the head of the 88th. However, his career soon closed: a bullet, the first which had been fired from our ranks, pierced his head; he flung up his arms and fell forward dead to the ground.

The shot, indeed, settled the fate of the nearest Frenchmen in that part of the field.

Mad with excitement, while poor Murphy's dead body, with one foot still in the stirrup, was being dragged by his frightened horse at a wild gallop along the front of the regiment, the Connaught Rangers clamoured with a wild roar of fury to be allowed to charge. General Pakenham heard them. He called to Colonel Wallace at the top of his voice: "Let them loose!" The word was given instantly, and with a mighty rush the brigade rushed forward with levelled bayonets. They broke through the enemy and hurled their massed ranks to fragments in an instant.

The mighty phalanx, a moment before so formidable, loosened and fell in pieces before 1,500 invincible British soldiers, fighting in a line only two deep.

Sturdy old Colonel Wallace galloped in the midst of the charging throng, cheering the men on. "Push on!" he kept shouting; "push on to the muzzle!"

The shock to the French was amazing in its results. The confusion of the enemy as the charge was pressed home became so great that almost at once they became mixed pell-mell together in hopeless disorder.

That, though, was not all. The crashing overthrow of Thomières' ill-fated column involved in similar disaster, in a very few minutes more, the two French divisions of the centre. The men of Marmont's broken left wing, driven before Pakenham's onset in panic-stricken flight along the heights, flung themselves in their rout on to the flank and rear of the French division next to them, Maucune's column, which was facing Leith's attack. Maucune's ranks had already begun to weaken and yield ground under the stress of the impetuous onset of the regiments of the Fifth Division. The shattered remnants of Thomières' battalions ran for succour wildly in among their comrades. Their frantic rush broke up Maucune's already shaken battalions, and, in not many minutes, the whole mass of the men of the two divisions, huddled together in a mob of struggling fugitives, went rolling back against the next French column, the troops of Clausel's Division, who themselves were at that moment holding their own with much difficulty in the midst of a furious fight with Cole's Fourth Division. The resulting confusion was fearful. The French centre and left wing to all appearances had been hopelessly wrecked at one blow.

Nothing short of a miracle, indeed, as it looked, could save the whole French army now from overwhelming disaster. But it was too exhausting and uphill work for the British to carry the fight through without a pause. The men had got out of hand in their furious onrush. The pursuit had to be checked while the ranks closed up and the men got breath again. They halted for a brief two minutes, to re-form before making their final onset and drive the enemy over the hill.

Clausel seized at the chance and made the most of it. His men were Napoleon's veterans, inured to war on many battlefields. Their leader was a skilful soldier who knew his business. With marvellous smartness and ready presence of mind General Clausel extricated his own men and drew them back at a run for a short distance clear of the fight. Like magic he managed to restore order in his division almost instantaneously. Then, being joined by most of Maucune's men, no less quickly rallied by their able commander, Clausel's battalions turned back to meet their antagonists as they came on again with a tremendous counterattack.

The gallant Clausel turned back and took the offensive. Pakenham, whose men had been leading in the onset, was to be assailed in his turn, "opposed by a multitude who, reinforced, again rallied and turned upon us with fury."

Clausel's fight with the Third Division reopened with the utmost fierceness.

"The peals of musketry along the centre," says one of our officers, "continued without intermission; the smoke was so thick that nothing to our left was distinguishable; some men of the Fifth Division got intermingled with ours; the dry grass was set on fire by the numerous cartridge-papers that strewed the battlefield; the air was scorching; and the smoke rolling onwards in huge volumes nearly suffocated us."

In the midst of it all, just at that moment, Le Marchant with the heavy cavalry, riding through at a gallop between Pakenham's men and Leith's, arrived on the scene.

A loud cheering was heard in our rear; the brigade half turned round, supposing themselves about to be attacked by the French cavalry. The order to form in squares was already on Wallace's lips, when the next moment the foremost of our own troopers burst on his view. A few seconds passed; the trampling of horses was heard; the smoke cleared away, and the heavy brigade of Le Marchant was seen coming forward in line at a canter. 'Open right and left' was an order quickly obeyed; the line opened, the cavalry passed through the intervals.

Le Marchant came on impetuously. He rode in advance of all, flushed and angry. A sneering gibe, flung at him a moment before by his immediate chief, the commander of Wellington's Cavalry, Sir Stapleton Cotton, had stung him to the quick. Getting impatient at the changings and shiftings of position General Cotton kept ordering, Le Marchant a minute or two earlier had ridden up to him and brusquely asked in what direction Sir Stapleton wanted him to front. "To the enemy, sir!" was the curt reply, given before the whole Staff in the lofty, supercilious tone which Cotton affected at times. Le Marchant flushed up in hot resentment at the implication, but made no rejoinder, though it is said that, had he lived through the day, he would quite possibly have called his chief out for it. He rode off, and immediately gave the order to his dragoons to charge.

The thunderbolt struck just at the right moment with terrific and shattering effect. Down on the French it came, wreaking catastrophe—swift, overwhelming, irremediable. In less than twenty minutes a third of Marmont's army had ceased to exist as an organized force. Three French divisions had in that time been struck down and shattered; had been broken to fragments and annihilated.

There was:

> ..... a whirling cloud of dust moving swiftly forward, and carrying within its womb the trampling sound of a charging multitude. As it passed the left of the Third Division, Le Marchant's heavy horsemen, flanked by Anson's light cavalry, broke out at full speed, and the next instant 1,200 French infantry, formed in several lines, were trampled down with terrible clangour and

tumult. Bewildered and blinded, they cast away their arms, and ran through the openings of the British squadron, stooping and demanding quarter, while the dragoons, big men on big horses, rode onward, smiting with their long glittering swords in uncontrollable power, and the Third Division, following at speed, shouted as the French masses fell in succession before this dreadful charge.

So Napier describes the tremendous onset.

Right into the midst of the enemy swooped our heavy cavalry, 1,200 flashing British sabres, a brigade of three of the finest regiments of horsemen in the British Army—the 3rd Dragoons, the "King's Own"; the 4th Dragoons, the "Queen's Own"; the 5th Dragoon Guards. Strong-limbed young fellows all were they, and well-mounted on big-boned horses; sinewy arms wielding keen-edged blades. Lord Charles Manners, as Lieut.-Colonel, led the 3rd Dragoons; Lord Edward Somerset, the 4th Dragoons; Colonel the Hon. William Ponsonby—he fell at Waterloo—the 5th Dragoon Guards.

The nine squadrons came on in two lines. They quickened their pace as they closed on the enemy. It helped the horsemen materially that the sun was shining full in the eyes of the French, while also at the same moment a gust of wind blew the sand and dust in clouds and the smoke of the battle right into the faces of their opponents.

Startled and taken aback at what they suddenly saw coming on them, the leading French regiments hastily attempted to form in squares. But Le Marchant's galloping dragoons rode down on them too quickly. They charged straight at the French infantry; riding their hardest, racing forward with, as it were, the irresistible sweep of an avalanche; crashing into the thick of the enemy before a single square could be closed up.

A French regiment a little in advance of the rest, Napoleon's ill-fated 62nd of the Line— their Eagle of gilded brass is one of the Salamanca trophies now at Chelsea—first of all tried bravely to stand up to the trampling onrush. They had no chance to form in square. Posted in the forefront of Clausel's rallied column, they were too near, and had no time. They were, though, in a massed formation that was but little less formidable for charging horse to face. The 62nd, a regiment made up of three battalions, and upwards of 3,000 strong, stood their ground, formed up in a dense column of half-battalions. They presented six successive lines, closely massed one behind the other.

The men stood three deep, each row bristling all over with bayonets to the front and on the flanks.

As the leading horsemen reached them the front ranks opened fire. But it was ragged and ill-aimed and ineffective. The discharge might have been blank cartridge for the results it had. It did not check the British onset, not for a moment. With a wild shout the cavalry bore vigorously forward at a gallop right in among the French before they had time to draw their ramrods and reload; bursting into and through the column, rending it apart and riding it down on the spot. According to French official returns, the unlucky regiment, out of a total strength on parade that morning of 2,800 of all ranks, in three battalions, lost 20 officers and 1,100 men in killed alone. Scores flung down their arms and frantically screamed for quarter. The survivors who escaped capture afterwards were not sufficient to make up half a battalion.

The 62nd were disposed of by the horsemen in less than five minutes.

But there was no pause at that. There was no delaying to make prisoners. Triumphantly cheering, the charging squadrons at once spurred forward as before, the gallant Le Marchant showing the way, to come full tilt the next moment on a second French regiment, the 22nd. These they caught in the act of forming square. The front face of the square was already drawn up. Its men met the troopers with a hasty fire which brought down several of the dragoons and many horses. But it made little difference to their fate. The next moment the cavalry were upon them and among them. The front of the square was burst in at once, and the mass in rear made but a weak attempt at resistance. They swayed backwards, and, breaking up their ranks, fell away in utter confusion. Slashed down under the sharp blades of the dragoons, their end was the same as that of the 62nd. "The ground was strewn thickly with killed and wounded"; only broken-up groups of panic-stricken fugitives were left to be made prisoners by the British infantry, following hard after the dragoons at a run.

Again now the cavalry plunged forward.

The three regiments had by now become mixed: officers rode where they could find places; but a good front and connected body was maintained, and, though going at speed, there was still no confusion.

They raced ahead to make yet another attack on a third French regiment, apparently the 63rd of the Line, which, in turn, was doing what it could to make a stand. That regiment, too, had to undergo its fate. It was dealt with in like manner. Caught before its square was completed, the luckless French linesmen were ridden down remorselessly, attacked while wavering, their *moral* shaken at the sight of the sudden overthrow of their comrades in front. Those who stood their ground were hacked to pieces, vainly attempting resistance with their bayonets.

But there were still more of the enemy to encounter. Yet another French corps bravely essayed to confront Le Marchant's horsemen. It was the strongest body in its formation that they had met. At that point the enemy had had time to take advantage of the protection of a small copse of evergreen oak-trees and stood along the edge formed up in *colonne serrée*, courageously hoping to stem the rush. "These men reserved their fire with much coolness until the cavalry came within twenty yards." Then they poured it in on the approaching men and horses in a tremendous discharge. Many saddles were emptied; many of the dragoons came to the ground; but the greater number escaped unharmed, and unflinchingly continued their career. They succeeded in breaking up the French ranks, though only after a fiercely contested hand-to-hand fight. "The French, cut down by the troopers and trampled under the horses' feet, offered all the resistance that brave men could."

General Le Marchant was in the midst of the *mêlée*. "He fought like a private soldier," we are told, "and more than one of the enemy fell by his hand."

The splendid leader met his death almost immediately afterwards, while following hard on the heels of the now broken-up enemy.

It was in this manner that the tragic event came about:

The last charge had given the *coup de grâce* to organized resistance in that quarter of the field, and the dragoons after that let themselves go as they chased their hardest, dashing on like a pack of hounds in full cry. "The violence of the onset had thrown the brigade into disorder. The dragoons, excited by the struggle, vied with each other in the pursuit and galloped recklessly into the crowd of fugitives. The general, having dispatched his son (and *aide-de-camp*) for some fresh troops, continued among the foremost in the pursuit, with the view of guarding against any attempts of the enemy to rally, which the nature of the ground rendered far from improbable."

While so doing, in the act of breaking up a rallied half-battalion of the enemy at one point, Le Marchant met a soldier's death.

This is the story of what happened as told by one who saw Le Marchant fall:

He perceived a considerable body collecting in a wood, where they endeavoured to make a stand. Lieutenant Gregory, with part of a squadron of the 4th Dragoons, was approaching them. The general, with his usual contempt for danger, immediately headed this little band, and, waving his sword, with a few words of encouragement charged at full gallop. The French had formed a hollow square: they waited until the British cavalry almost plunged on their bayonets, and then fired. Several of the dragoons fell. Lieutenant Gregory's clothes were perforated with balls. General Le Marchant received a shot in the groin, which caused him to fall senseless from his horse, absolutely within the enemy's ranks.

The French had no sooner fired than they fled. Some of the dragoons having been joined by some men of the 9th Foot, belonging to General Leith's Division, raised their gallant commander from the ground, in the hope that he might yet be spared to lead them to future victory. Life, however, was totally extinct. The bullet, passing through the sash, had lodged deeply in a vital part, and the surgeons, on examining the wound, stated that death must have been instantaneous.

Le Marchant's body was carried from the field and placed in a stable in the rear. It was buried on the battlefield two days later, in a grove of olives close by where the general fell, enveloped in a military cloak. The army had gone forward in pursuit, and only four persons attended the funeral—Ensign Le Marchant of the Guards, the general's son and *aide-de-camp;* Major Onslow, a wounded officer of the Dragoon Guards, who read the burial service; the senior medical officer in charge of the wounded on the battlefield; and the general's body-servant. (See note below).

Note:—"Major-General Le Marchant was killed at the head of his brigade, and I have to regret the loss of a most capable officer," wrote Wellington when notifying the death in his Salamanca dispatch. His fall, indeed, deprived the army of one of its most useful and talented leaders. The British cavalry owe to Le Marchant their first initiation into the art of using their swords effectively in fight, the outcome of Le Marchant's personal experiences on the battlefield when a young captain in the campaign in Flanders: "on observing the many instances of discomfiture which our dragoons experienced in single combat with the enemy; also, on learning from the surgeons that many of the troopers' wounds had been inflicted by no other weapons than their own"; while their poor horses, "perhaps the principal victims, were often gashed about the head and neck by their riders."

General Le Marchant also it was who originally organized Sandhurst, and was the first lieutenant-governor of the college while in its earlier locale at High Wycombe. On campaign, as we are told, "the general absolutely identified himself with his brigade, in which he appeared like a parent among his children. The hardest day's march could not prevent his walking through the cantonment or bivouac to see whether the comfort of the men had been properly cared for." Said Picton, an officer by no means easily satisfied, of him in the field: "I always feel easy when Le Marchant's men are between me and the enemy; they do their duty, and can be trusted. I heartily wish the rest were like them." A *beau sabreur* in the fullest sense, his courage was on a par with his abilities.

"In one fight he charged ahead of half a dozen of his own men to rescue a party of Hanoverian horse in difficulties, met the oncoming French, and cut down two with his own hand." And on the personal side Le Marchant was one of the best of men—as true-minded and simple-hearted a man as ever wore a soldier's uniform. "His eldest son once, admiring his calm composure under a heavy fire, asked him how he had obtained such command over himself. 'I never,' was the reply, 'go into a battle without subjecting myself to a strict examination; then, having, as I humbly hope, made my peace with God, I leave the result in His hands, with perfect confidence that He will determine what is best for me.'"

For a brief interval Colonel Ponsonby, as senior surviving officer, took charge of the brigade. Then General Cotton came on the scene, galloping up at the head of his staff. Sir Stapleton had the recall sounded in order to re-form ranks, "and would have resumed the attack, but men and horses had suffered too much to do more."

The 4th King's Own made the two last charges in the cavalry combat. One was headed by Lieutenant Norcliffe, with Sergeant-Major

Major-General John Gaspard Le Marchant

Chambers, Sergeant Cattle, and some thirty men. They took summary vengeance for their general's death among the men of the last French square who had fired the fatal volley. Getting through the wood ahead of the other pursuers, they rode down the flying Frenchmen, sabring them on every side. Young Norcliffe, the gallant subaltern who led that charge, escaped with his life by the barest chance; badly wounded and unhorsed, he was left lying on the field among the dead all the following night. A second party of the 4th Queen's Own, the right squadron, led by Lord Edward Somerset, the lieut.-colonel, finished off the Heavy Cavalry Brigade's work by dashing at and capturing a battery of seven French field-guns farther on.

In that masterly style did the Heavy Brigade do its work at Salamanca. Wellington rode up as the men were re-forming. "Egad, Cotton!" he exclaimed enthusiastically as he met Sir Stapleton, "I never saw anything more splendid in my life!"

One other incident of the cavalry attack that afternoon may be added here. A British infantry officer took part on his own account in the charge, as it curiously happened, in the midst of the dragoons. He was a dashing young Scotsman, belonging to the 88th Connaught Rangers, in the Third Division, Captain William Mackie. To seek a daring adventure on his own account, Captain Mackie had slipped in among the cavalry as Le Marchant's horsemen passed through Wallace's Brigade at the outset. He was on horseback by chance, being mounted for the day to act as *aide-de-camp* to Colonel Wallace, who was doing duty, as has been said, as brigadier. No one saw Mackie go, and it was not till after the cavalry had passed through that he was missed. Then there was a hue and cry for him.

"Where's Mackie?" asked Wallace anxiously, as did others. Nobody knew. No one had seen him fall. He had been alive and unhurt among them there not a moment before. "No one could give any account of him," we are told; "but in a short lapse of time, after the cavalry had charged, he returned, covered with dust and blood, his horse tottering from fatigue, and nothing left of his sabre—but the hilt. He had joined the cavalry as soon as the fighting amongst the infantry had ceased; and those who knew the temperament of the man were not surprised at it. Wherever glory and danger were to be met, there was Mackie to be found, and nothing could daunt his daring spirit."

The British infantry of the Third and Fifth Divisions had all the time been racing after the cavalry with exultant cheers, finishing off the cavalrymen's work as fast as they came up. It was an easy task. All the fight had been scared out of the smitten Frenchmen under the stress of the fearful experience they had gone through. They now only thought of how to save themselves.

> Such as got away from the sabres of the horsemen sought safety amongst the ranks of our infantry, and, scrambling under the horses, ran to us for protection, like men who, having escaped the first shock of a shipwreck, will cling to any broken spar, no matter how little to be depended on.

So an officer amidst it all describes:

> Hundreds of beings, frightfully disfigured, in whom the human face and form were almost obliterated, black with dust, worn down with fatigue, and covered with sabre-cuts and blood, threw themselves among us for safety. Not a man was bayoneted, not one even molested or plundered, and the invincible old Third on this day surpassed themselves; for they not only defeated their terrible enemies in a fair stand-up fight, but saved them when total annihilation seemed the only thing.

The two Salamanca Eagles now in London were taken at this time. They fell as spoil to two infantry officers, who were their actual captors: one an officer of a regiment in the Third Division, the other an officer in the Fifth, part of which were following in the track of the cavalry, mixed up among Pakenham's men.

One Eagle was that of the hapless French 62nd, whose fate has been told. It fell to Lieutenant Pierce of the 44th, a regiment belonging to the Fifth Division. Pierce came on the officer carrying it, the *porte-aiglé*, or ensign, while in the act of unscrewing the Eagle from its pole, in hope of hiding it underneath his long coat and getting away with it to safety. Lieutenant Pierce sprang on the Frenchman and tussled with him. One of the soldiers from the Eagle-guard joined in the defence, and then two men of the 44th ran up to their officer's assistance. They killed the two Frenchmen, and the Eagle became a British trophy. In his enthusiasm at the taking of such a prize, Pierce emptied his pockets on the spot, and distributed what money he had on him among the men who had helped him. After that, the Eagle-pole not being found, a sergeant's halberd was got, on which the Eagle was carried for the rest of the day.

Not far off, and about the same time, Lieutenant Pratt, an officer of the 30th, doing duty with a Portuguese regiment, made prize of the second Salamanca Eagle at Chelsea, that of Napoleon's 22nd of the Line. He took it to General Pakenham, whose mounted orderly, we are told, carried the trophy wherever the General went during the next two days.

In honour of the 44th having taken an Eagle at Salamanca, the present-day Essex Regiment bears the badge of a Napoleonic Eagle on the regimental colour, and the officers wear a similar badge on their mess-jackets.

From the opening of Pakenham's attack, from the first crossing of the bayonets, it had taken just forty minutes to carry the fighting to that point. The fate of Marmont's false move had, to all intent, already sealed the fate of the day for France. Wellington had virtually "defeated 40,000 men in forty minutes."

But the battle was not yet over. A serious set-back took place in another part of the field almost immediately afterwards, which threatened to undo all that had been done. Within a very short time of the victorious charge of the Heavy Brigade a sudden and unanticipated reverse came about for the British.

To rescue what was left of the three divisions of the French left wing and centre, General Bonnet, the general in command of the wounded Marmont's place, had hastened up with his own division from the French right. Beating back with heavy loss a Portuguese brigade which bravely tried to bar his way, Bonnet rapidly drew together three fresh divisions of Marmont's reserve, which had just arrived on the field, and with them and his own division took up a new line of battle at right angles to Marmont's original position.

At that moment the Fourth Division, led by Sir Lowry Cole, were winning their way forward in a desperate contest with the enemy immediately in front of them, gradually forcing their stubborn opponents to give ground. They were stopped short in their victorious career by the coming up of Bonnet's reinforcements. The Third and Fifth Divisions soon afterwards joined hands with Cole, but the enemy, fighting at bay with furious desperation, stood fast. The Fourth Division recoiled for a short distance to re-form. They were about to attack again when the failure to make a stand of a Portuguese brigade sent forward to assist them, "gave the French artillery full liberty to turn a slaughtering fire against the flank and rear of Cole's soldiers."

The broken divisions of the enemy had rallied on Bonnet's fresh troops. They returned to the fight with them now. Veteran soldiers as they were, they had re-formed with surprising celerity. On that, being further reinforced by a brigade of dragoons, the French, all together, turned on the British in a terrific counter-attack. They came charging forward, in the words of one of our officers, "as it were with the fury of despair."

The whole of the French army (except Foy's Division at some distance away) was making practically a forlorn effort in unison.

Bonnet's reserves were all up in a line, the fugitives from the routed divisions had joined them. It was growing dark, and the great glare of light caused by the thunder of the artillery, the continued blaze of musketry, and burning grass, gave the face of the hill a terrific appearance. It was one sheet of flame. The French prolonged the battle till dark. Clausel was then in command, Bonnet having fallen wounded. His men, besmeared with blood, dust, and smoke-stains, many half-naked, and some carrying only broken weapons, came on with a fury that could not be surpassed.

That counter-attack proved a fearful time of trial and anxiety for the British.

Cole fell wounded, half his division was cut off, the remainder could scarce contain themselves. Fresh French troops kept pressing forward in compact bodies; it was manifest to all that the fortune of the battle was trembling in the balance at the eleventh hour.

What it meant for more than one of the regiments of the Fourth Division at that terrible moment can be realized from the account given by an officer—speaking for the state of things among his own men.

The French regiments came up the hill with a brisk and regular step, and their drums beating the *pas de charge*. Our men fired wildly and at random among them. The French never returned a shot, and continued their steady advance. The English fired again, but still without return; they stood their ground, however, with great courage. But men in such confusion had no chance against the perfect order of the enemy, and when the French were close upon them they wavered and gave way. The officers all advanced in a line in front, waving their swords and cheering their men to come on, but the confusion became a panic, and there was a regular *sauve qui peut*.

Cole's men, however, were British soldiers, and the lapse was but for a brief space.

In five minutes they were formed in perfect order at a short distance below, and they then re-ascended the hill most gallantly and drove the French down on the other side as quickly as they themselves had been driven before.

What the heroism of the Third Division and Le Marchant's horsemen had won elsewhere was not to be thrown away. The scale dipped heavily against us, then it rose again.

Wellington's coolness and promptitude in that most intensely critical of situations saved and decided the battle. He ordered up the Sixth Division, hitherto kept in reserve, to the support of the Fourth, "and the battle, at half-past eight o'clock at night, seemed to recommence with the same fury as at the outset."

Salamanca was saved and won a second time by the intrepidity of the Sixth Division— General Clinton's men. They threw themselves into the fight determined to win or die.

"Nothing," describes an officer of the Connaught Rangers, "could stop the intrepid valour of the Sixth Division as they advanced to carry the hill. The troops posted to arrest their advance were trampled down and destroyed at the first charge, and each reserve sent forward to extricate them suffered the same fate."

There was no stopping the Sixth Division. They stemmed and turned the tide of battle.

> The French were now fighting, not for victory, but for safety. After a frightful struggle they were driven from their last hold in confusion. A general and overwhelming charge, in which the Third Division again got round their left and outflanked them once more, carried this ill-formed mass of gallant soldiers before it like a shattered wreck borne along by the force of some mighty current of the sea.

The flashes of the musketry told to the rest of the army the progress and fortunes of the fighting. "In the darkness of the night," describes Napier, who was one of those looking on, "the fire showed from afar how the battle went. On the English side a sheet of flame was seen, sometimes advancing with an even front, sometimes pricking forth in spear-heads, now falling back in waving lines, *anon* darting upwards in one vast pyramid, the apex of which often approached, yet never gained, the actual summit of the mountain; but the French musketry, rapid as lightning, sparkled along the brow of the height with unvarying fullness, and with what destructive effects the dark gaps and changing shapes of the adverse fire showed too plainly."

To the last it was stubborn uphill work for the British, but resistlessly the Sixth Division held on their conquering way. They bore back all opposition. All that French valour and desperation might accomplish was attempted, but all in vain. Nothing could stop the intrepid valour of Clinton's men as the Sixth Division persistently made head, with unfaltering determination to storm the hill at all costs. And they did so triumphantly in the end. The French battalions who held out on the crest at the last were bayoneted and trampled down, and hurled into the darkness beyond in confusion.

It was not till after ten o'clock that night that the fighting was over. After that "the effulgent crest of the ridge became black and silent, and the whole French army vanished as it were in the darkness."

No higher tribute could have been paid to Clinton's splendid soldiers than was implied in the laconic brevity of Wellington's mention of them in his Salamanca dispatch:

> I ordered up the Sixth Division under Major-General Clinton, and the battle was soon restored to its former success.

The 11th Foot, the Devonshire Regiment, led the attack of the Sixth Division, and their magnificent heroism at Salamanca, where they won their sobriquet of the "Bloody Eleventh," is one of the treasured glories of the British Army. The Devons that morning mustered 32 officers, 30 sergeants, and 412 rank and file. At roll-call at midnight there paraded unwounded only 4 officers and 67 non-commissioned officers and men. The rest, officers and sergeants and privates, lay on the battlefield, either killed or wounded. The survivors carried the flag of one of the French battalions, a "large green standard without an Eagle," probably belonging to a foreign regiment of Napoleon's service, several of which were serving in Spain.

It was conveyed to England with the two Eagles captured in the battle by the officer who carried Wellington's dispatches—a West-Country man himself by the way—Lord Clinton. The companion regiment of the Devons at the head of the Sixth Division, fighting close beside them throughout, was the 61st, now one of the battalions of the Gloucestershire Regiment. The Gloucestershires had on parade that morning 27 officers and 420 men. After the "Cease fire" sounded, only 7 officers and 78 men were accounted for at roll-call. No fewer than 20 officers and 342 men had gone down in action, had fallen on the field either killed or wounded, Six reliefs of Ensigns and sergeants of the Gloucestershires were shot down while carrying the colours in turn, and at last the colours went through the battle borne by two privates. So few of the two regiments were left that they were amalgamated after the battle into a single "provisional battalion."

This may be added by way of epilogue to the story of the battle:

Wellington's dispatch announcing the victory of Salamanca arrived in London on August 16. It was much overdue, and had been anxiously awaited. For days past it had been looked for with restless eagerness. Letters from the front, received at the end of July, had told that the armies were in presence near Salamanca and that a decisive battle was imminent. But no further news reached England for several days. Stormy weather prevailed in the Channel, with persistent headwinds for ships coming from the south. The public anxiety was intense. It was added to in the first week in August by a curious mischance.

On August 5 a naval cutter from Ferrol, the *Sybil*, reached Plymouth with advices to the effect that the expected battle had been fought and a great victory won. The Port-Admiral, Sir Robert Calder, promptly forwarded the intelligence to London by the coast semaphore telegraph, but a sudden sea-fog stopped communication between two stations in an out-of-the-way spot on the borders of Dorset and Hampshire, just as the transmission of the message from one to the other began. The admiral unfortunately had worded his information awkwardly. The message as sent began "Wellington defeated," which two words of the message were all that had got through at the moment that the fog rolled up suddenly and stopped further communication between the stations for forty-eight hours.

The first two words were passed on from the last receiving-station to London and caused blank dismay, throwing everybody into a fever of excitement. For two days they had to wait for further news, before it was possible for the rest of the message to get through. It reached the Admiralty just as a courier from Plymouth arrived in London. The full message as telegraphed now read, "Wellington defeated the French at Salamanca with heavy loss."

The Plymouth courier brought with him a copy of a hasty note from Wellington to the Spanish titular commander-in-chief, General Castaños, giving the result of the battle, which had reached Ferrol only an hour before the *Sybil* sailed.

"On July 22," ran the note, "the French army under the command of Marshal Marmont was completely routed near Salamanca by the allied army, to which was united the Third Division of the Sixth Spanish army. The enemy lost many Eagles, almost all their baggage, and an immense quantity of military stores. Their loss in killed, wounded, and prisoners is estimated from 10,000 to 12,000 men. The routed army retreated by Alba de Tormes, and the victorious army is in close pursuit."

The news gave instant relief and sent all England into enthusiastic transports of delight, but there were no details available as to the British casualties. Not a word more came to hand for days, and again the public anxiety became intense. Nothing could be heard of the special packet known to be bringing Wellington's detailed dispatch.

Only on the 14th of the month did that reach Plymouth. The dispatch was brought on to London forthwith by its bearer, Wellington's *aide-de-camp*, Lord Clinton. He reached London on the morning of the 16th "in a chaise and four, decorated with laurel and with French Eagles and flags displayed out of the windows. A special issue of the *London Gazette* made the contents of the dispatch public, and once more London went mad with excitement. The Metropolis was illuminated for three nights, while the mail-coaches, decked out with laurel festoons and wreaths, carried the news all over the country. At every cross-road for days past people had been watching in crowds for the coaches to pass and learn the names of those who had fallen. In London, we are told, Wellington's brother, the Marquess Wellesley, "while returning from viewing the illuminations in the city, was recognized in the Strand, and the populace took out his horses and drew the carriage to Apsley House."

This may be added to round the story off: How Napoleon received the news of the disaster to his army at Salamanca has been recorded, as it curiously happens, in Wellington's own words; as he in later years told it to a friend.

"We took in Spain," said Wellington, "a dispatch which was on its way to Marmont, from the *aide-de- camp* whom he had sent to Russia to explain to Napoleon the circumstances of his defeat at Salamanca. The officer, as is well known, reached the French army at about the time when Napoleon was taking up his quarters in the *Kremlin*. As soon as the purport of his intelligence was known to Napoleon, he was confined, not under nominal arrest, but in as strict confinement as a State criminal, in the *Kremlin*. When admitted, after some delay, to

Napoleon's presence, the latter, after some silent perusal of the report, asked how many troops had the marshal.

"'Forty thousand, Sire!'

"'Well,' said Napoleon, 'a man who has one million under his charge can hardly afford much attention to what happens to forty thousand at the other side of the world.' He said nothing more at that audience, and sent the officer back to his seclusion. The latter was not, I believe, released, nor did Napoleon give an opinion on the transaction till after he had received a copy of the published report of the battle. He then sent for the officer and said:' I see by this account that the affair was a smart one and well contested. You may tell the marshal I am satisfied.'"

15

Where Sabre Conquered Bayonet: the Breaking of the Square

Three Regiments of the German Army record British victories on their colours and appointments as "battle-honours." They are the 13th Uhlans, the 73rd Fusilier Regiment, and the 10th Regiment of Field Artillery. The Uhlans, or King's Lancers, as they are also styled, bear the three names, "Peninsula," "Garcia Hernandez," "Waterloo." The Fusiliers commemorate on their flag "Peninsula" and "Waterloo," and the Artillery bear the same two "battle- honours." The Emperor William directed the inscriptions to be placed on the colours in January, 1899—a significant date, by the way, for it was just at the time in the South African War when our German cousins were looking forward every day to hear that Ladysmith had fallen—asserting the right of the regiments concerned to the "battle-honours," as representing corps of the old Hanoverian Army of George III., which, as the "King's German Legion," fought under Wellington. To some extent, no doubt, the claim is justified, and the connection can, with a little working out, be traced.

As regularly-enrolled regiments of the British Army of that day, we also have our own interest in their doings. No soldiers under Wellington did better service, and one of their exploits in particular stands by itself for as fine a feat of arms as was ever achieved on the battlefield—that is, the magnificent deed of daring done by the heavy dragoons of the King's German Legion which the name "*Garcia Hernandez*" commemorates for the Kaiser's 13th Uhlans.

It was in the pursuit after Salamanca, in following up the retreating enemy on the morning after the victory. Two regiments of horsemen of the King's German Legion, the 1st and 2nd Dragoons, armed and equipped and uniformed in red coats with blue facings, exactly as our own British dragoons, came upon the French rearguard in the act of taking post to bar the way at a place called Garcia Hernandez. They were in the forefront of a brigade made up partly of British cavalry, and led by the same General Anson who had ordered the charge of the Light Dragoons at Talavera.

In front were several squadrons of French cavalry; in rear was an infantry regiment, the 105th of the Line, its three battalions in column, with guns in the intervals. Not seeing the infantry and guns at first, owing to an intervening ridge, Anson went at the cavalry and drove them in. Their squadrons fled from his troopers, abandoning their battalions of infantry, who, in separate columns, were then seen moving up a hollow slope, hoping to gain the crest of some heights ahead before the pursuing cavalry could arrive; and the two foremost did reach higher ground and there formed squares. The squares at once opened fire on the horsemen, and for a moment checked them.

The Hanoverian Dragoons formed the advance of the pursuers, as has been said, Captain von Decken, whose squadron was foremost of all in the chase, on the spur of the moment, took the daring decision to attack the square with the one squadron he had with him on the spot. Without a moment's hesitation the daring officer gallantly charged at the square, regardless of the fierce fusillade that met him, from which men went down fast all round. "They dropped fast under fire. By twos and threes, by tens, by twenties, they fell; yet the mass, surmounting the difficulties of the ground, hurtled on the column and went clean through it."

This is how it was done:

The brave von Decken fell dead, shot among the first, struck down 100 yards from the French square. But no less heroic a brother-officer was at hand to take his place. Captain von Uslar Gleichen, the officer in command of the squadron following, dashed out instantly to the front. He put himself at the head of the first squadron, "inciting the men by voice and gesture and example." Another French volley was blazed off at them. It smote hard on the squadron, but the intrepid troopers galloped on. Bringing up their right flank, they swept forward without a check, going directly for the enemy's bayonets on two sides of the square. The two foremost ranks of the French were on the knee, with bayonets to the front, presenting a deadly double hedgerow bristling with sharp steel. In rear were the steady muskets of four standing ranks, firing fast and furiously.

But that did not daunt the sturdy Hanoverian troopers. The dragoons galloped up to the very points of the bayonets. They tried with their sword-blades, indeed, to beat aside the points and hack a pathway through. Was it possible? Again and again they made the attempt. They were still vainly trying to break in when by fortunate chance an accident gave them their opportunity. A shot fired from the kneeling ranks of the French killed a trooper's horse in the act of trying to leap the bayonets. The horse fell, and its rider with it, in the midst of the defenders, crashing down right across and on top of the bayonets. A lane into the heart of the square was thus laid open in an instant.

Immediately the rest of the first squadron seized their opportunity. The nearest dragoons pressed forward eagerly, and burst in through with a rush. The French square was broken. Instantly more dragoons dashed in after the leaders. The mass of infantry was cleft apart; their ranks were scattered and dispersed. All was over with the square at once. Within a few moments the entire battalion had been either cut down or taken prisoners.

As that took place the second squadron, led now by von Reitzenstein, came galloping by. They saw what had been done, and forthwith on their own account rode straight for the second French square. The men of that tried to meet the charge with a bold front, and fired a volley into the faces of the horsemen as they neared them. But the *moral* of the infantry had been badly shaken under the shock of the startling and horrible scene among their comrades of the first battalion they had just witnessed. Instinctively the front face of the second square swayed, and sagged, and gave back as the dragoons got to the spot. Reitzenstein offered them no chances. With a dozen men close at his back he rode into the square at full gallop. Resistance collapsed on the instant. The square broke up: four-fifths of that battalion were either sabred on the spot or threw themselves on the ground screaming for mercy.

There was yet near by a third battalion of the regiment, in square and with its numbers added to by what fugitives from the first and second squares could reach the place. But its fate was the same as that of the others. The third squadron of the dragoons, Captain Baron Marschalck leading them, joined by the left troop of Reitzenstein's squadron, dealt with the third French square with equal promptness and similar result. Riding boldly at their enemy Marschalck and his men broke in among the infantry; meeting, though, with but little real resistance. These hapless Frenchmen, too, were slashed to pieces in their turn.

Described a British officer who went over the ground after the fight:

> The contest ended in a dreadful massacre of the French infantry. They bravely tried to stand their ground, but the ponderous weight of the heavy cavalry broke down all resistance; and arms lopped off, and heads cloven to the spine, or gashed across the breast and shoulders, showed the fearful encounter that had taken place.

Some fifty men killed, and as many more wounded, was the price paid by the victors.

Napier describes the field of battle as he saw it after the combat was over:

> The track of the Germans was marked by their huge bodies. A few minutes only had the contest lasted, and above 100 had fallen—fifty-one. were killed outright. In several places man and horse had died simultaneously, and so suddenly that, falling together on their sides, they appeared yet alive: the horse's legs stretched out as in movement, the rider's feet in the stirrups, the bridle in hand, the sword raised to strike, and the large hat fastened under the chin, giving to the grim yet undistorted countenance a supernatural and terrible expression.

Another officer corroborates Napier. "I saw," he says, "a man and his horse dead, the rider still in the saddle, and they must have received their mortal wound together." And he adds this of the French:

> I observed 500 stand of muskets on their left, lying on the ground in line, as if they had been piled and knocked down, and the owners had shifted as well as they could; the muskets were not grounded to the front, but lying sideways."

"*La charge la plus audacieuse de la guerre d'Espagne,*" was how General Foy, in command of the French rearguard division, who was not 100 yards from where the last square stood, characterized the exploit. Wellington on his side, watching the attack through his telescope, wrote this in his dispatch: "I have never witnessed a more gallant charge than was made by the Heavy Brigade of the King's German Legion under Major-General von Bock, which was completely successful, and the whole body of infantry consisting of three battalions of the enemy's

First Division were made prisoners." On Wellington's recommendation, and in official recognition of the magnificent courage displayed at Garcia Hernandez, the officers of the King's German Legion were granted rank in the British Army from that time forward, a privilege hitherto jealously kept back from them by the War Office.

16

Among Officers and Men in Camp and Quarters

This to begin with is Napier's tribute to the British soldier of Wellington's time—to the men who won the day at Oporto and saved the situation at Talavera, who stormed the citadel of Badajoz, drove Marmont's troops in rout before them at Salamanca, and sealed the doom of Napoleon's armies in Spain on the field of Vittoria:

> That the British infantry soldier is more robust than the soldier of any other nation can scarcely be doubted by those who, in 1815, observed his powerful frame, distinguished amidst the united armies of Europe; and, notwithstanding his habitual excess in drinking, he sustains fatigues and wet and the extremes of cold and heat with incredible vigour. When completely disciplined—and three years are required to accomplish this—his port is lofty and his movements free, the whole world cannot produce a nobler specimen of military bearing; nor is the mind unworthy of the outward man. He does not, indeed, possess that presumptuous vivacity which would lead him to dictate to his commanders, or even to censure real errors, although he may perceive them; but he is observant and quick to comprehend his orders, full of resources under difficulties, calm and resolute in danger, and more than usually obedient and careful of his officers in moments of imminent peril.
> It has been asserted that his undeniable firmness in battle is the result of a phlegmatic constitution uninspired by moral feeling. Never was a more stupid calumny uttered! Napoleon's troops fought in bright fields, where every helmet caught some gleams

of glory; but the British soldiers conquered under the cold shade of aristocracy. No honours awaited his daring, no dispatch gave his name to the applause of his countrymen; his life of danger and hardship was uncheered by hope, his death unnoticed. Did his heart sink therefore? Did he not endure with surpassing fortitude the sorest of ills, sustain the most terrible assaults in battle unmoved, overthrow with incredible energy every opponent, and at all times prove that, while no physical military qualification was wanting, the fount of honour was also full and fresh within him?

Much of Napier's history has since been questioned, but he knew here at least what he was saying.

*****

An interesting glimpse behind the scenes is given us as an incident of the men's life on campaign by an officer of the Light Division, Colonel Leach, of the 95th Rifles. Speaking of the hardships experienced at the time of Wellington's retreat after Talavera, in 1809, to avoid being cut off by Soult, who was making a flank march from Galicia towards the Tagus Valley—in describing the encampment near Casas del Puerco near Almaraz, he tells us this:

> The time which we passed at this spot, although sufficiently monotonous, was such as one is not likely to forget. To the best of my belief, not one issue of bread was made to the troops during the fortnight, but an exceedingly coarse kind of flour, mixed with beans and chopped straw, and in very small quantities, was distributed by the commissariat. This, moistened with water, and made into a sort of pancake, was baked in a camp-kettle, and speedily devoured. The only regret was that the quantity was so very small. If any person who belonged to the troops stationed at Almaraz at that period can say that his appetite was satisfied on any day of the fourteen spent there, I can only remark that he was infinitely more fortunate than his neighbours. Now and then half a dozen antiquated goats, which the commissary had taken by surprise in the mountains, found their way into the camp-kettles. A small slice of one of these quadrupeds, without salt, a very limited allowance of bran-cake, and an unlimited quantity of spring water, constituted our chief food.

That the famishing soldiers broke away on one occasion in the midst of the hardships of their campaigning, when they found themselves unexpectedly in the midst of plenty in the shape of the semi-wild pig, with which parts of Spain swarmed, is perhaps not surprising, however reprehensible the lapse from good order and military discipline. It was during the retreat from Burgos that the outbreak occurred, when the troops had got out of hand, demoralized after the severe and disheartening trials they had undergone. "For several days past," says one officer, "we had been living on acorns, and the horses were fain to be content with leaves of trees."

"The army," describes Captain Brotherton, of the 14th Light Dragoons, relating what then took place, "was totally without rations and almost starving, owing to neglect in the commissariat department. The forest in which we bivouacked abounded in large herds of pigs, amounting to many thousands—tempting objects to a starving army. Many of these droves passed along the front of our army, as if saying, 'Come, kill me!' No wonder that volley after volley was let fly at them, laying thousands prostrate. This, of course, when so close to the enemy as we were—our *vedettes* almost touching one another—was a dreadful irregularity. Lord Wellington was roused out of his sleep, and rode immediately to the front, thinking the enemy were attacking. His indignation at finding the cause of alarm was excessive, and the consequence was that he next day issued a most severe censure."

Captain Brotherton also adds this of the scene in front of the lines on the following morning—a most extraordinary one indeed:

> As the night had been very dark when these droves of pigs rushed past the front, the men fired their volleys at random, and many in front, particularly the cavalry, suffered. I myself saw two heavy dragoons and one horse lying dead. I shall never forget the singularity of the scene at dawn of day, close to the bivouac of the 14th Light Dragoons, and near where Lord Wellington himself had bivouacked, surrounded as it was by dead pigs strewed on the ground, dead dragoons, dead horses, etc.

On another occasion of which we are told the killing was by order.

Colonel Leach, of the Light Division, tells the story of that, describing the manner in which his men obtained fresh pork after the passage of the Bridge of Arzobispo:

> As neither bread, meat, nor rations of any kind were to be had, General Craufurd ordered that any animals in the shape of cat-

tle, sheep, or pigs which could be found in the extensive woods in which we halted should forthwith be put in requisition for the troops, and never do I remember having seen orders so promptly obeyed. A most furious attack was instantly made on a large herd of pigs, which, most fortunately for us, little dreamed of the fate that awaited them, or, I presume, they would have absconded, on our first appearance, into the forest. It would be useless to attempt a description of the scene of noise and confusion which ensued. The screeches and cries of these ill-fated swine, as they met their death at the point of the bayonet, the sword, or sergeant's pike, and the rapidity with which they were cut up into junks, with their hair on, and fried on the lids of camp-kettles, or toasted at the fire on a pointed stick, to allay the cravings of hunger of some thousands of half-famished soldiers, were quite incredible, and, I must add, truly ludicrous. As neither bread, salt, nor vegetables were to be procured, it must be confessed that the repast was a singular one, although it was eaten with the greatest *goût*, and was washed down with some water from a rivulet hard by.

The foreigners in Wellington's army, the Hanoverians of the King's German Legion, it would appear, managed generally to fare much better on whatever was forthcoming by way of rations than did our men. "The helplessness of the British soldier when left to himself is proverbial," remarks an officer, contrasting the way in which the German troopers contrived to make the best of their provisions.

The 60th (Fifth Battalion) was for the most part composed of Germans, a thrifty body of soldiers, who showed how easy it was, with a very little trouble and forethought, to make a palatable meal in the field with rations. It was settled among themselves that every man of the mess should carry something; that is to say, spiced meats (such as sausages), cheese, onions, garlic, lard, pepper, salt, vinegar, mustard, sugar, coffee, etc.—in short, whatever could improve their food or make it more nourishing and conducive to health. As soon as the daily allowance of beef was issued, they set to work, and soon produced a first-rate dinner or supper, which was often improved by certain wild herbs which they knew where to look for. The English soldiers, on the other hand, rarely troubled themselves to carry any of the condiments which so much contributed to the luxury of their brethren in arms.

"Day after day," says another officer (Colonel Campbell), "they boiled their beef, just killed, in a lump in water, which they seldom contrived to make deserving of the name of soup or broth. This and their biscuit or bread was what they usually lived upon."

This amusing instance of resourcefulness also stands to the credit of the Hanoverians. The story is told by one of our officers of the Light Division. "Throughout the war," says he, "the peasantry living on the line of march were put to desperate straits to preserve their poultry. The moment a detachment marched into a village, fowls, ducks, geese, and turkeys were demanded. At length the owners of brood-hens and patriarchal ganders, as soon as the drum was heard, used to lock them up in chests and presses, where darkness ensured silence. They then would reply to inquiries with a protest that their last visitors had eaten the whole. For a time this device succeeded, but one day a shrewd old campaigner carried a live duck he had contrived to borrow into a farmhouse where it had been solemnly declared not a feathered denizen remained. He pinched the creature until loud repetitions of 'quack!' 'quack!' were extorted, and directly a simultaneous reply resounded from all the house cupboards in the room, to the utter dismay of the Spanish farmer."

For a passing glance now at Wellington's men from a different point of view:

"We had no unnecessary drilling," says one of them, "nor were we tormented with that greatest of all bores to an officer at any time, but particularly on service—uniformity of dress. The consequence was that every duty was performed with cheerfulness; the army was in the highest state of discipline, and those gentlemen who had, or fancied they had, a taste for leading the fashion, had now a fine opportunity of bringing their talents into play.

"With such latitude, it is not to be wondered at that our appearance was not quite as uniform as some general officers would approve of; but Lord Wellington was a most indulgent commander; he never harassed us with reviews or petty annoyances, which, so far from promoting discipline, or doing good in any way, has a contrary effect. A corporal's guard frequently did the duty at headquarters; and every officer who chose to purchase a horse might ride on the march. Provided we brought our men into the field well-appointed and with sixty rounds of good ammunition each, he never looked to see whether their trousers were black, blue, or grey; and as to ourselves, we might be rigged out in all the colours of the rainbow if we fancied it.

"The consequence was that scarcely any two officers were dressed alike! Some had grey-braided coats, others brown; some again liked blue; while many from choice, or perhaps necessity, stuck to the ' old red rag.' Overalls, of all things, were in vogue, and the comical appearance of a number of infantry officers loaded with leather bottoms to their pantaloons, and huge chains suspended from the side buttons, like a parcel of troopers, was amusing enough. Some had such a penchant for leather that their pantaloons were covered with it from bottom to top; and it often occurred to me, while surveying the well-leathered trousers of those modern heroes, that, notwithstanding the great change in military tactics, since in the olden time the 'town was threatened with a siege,' they still clung to the forcible opinion delivered by the currier on that very memorable occasion.

"Quantities of hair, a regular 'Brutus,' a pair of *moustachios*, and screw-brass spurs, were essential to a first-rate 'Count,' for so were our dandies designated. The 'cut-down' hat, exactly a span in height, was another rage; this burlesque on a *chapeau* was usually out-topped by some extraordinary-looking feather; while again, others wore their hats without any feather at all: and indeed this was the most rational thing they did. In the paroxysm of a wish to be singularly singular, a friend of mine shaved all the hair off the crown of his head, and he was decidedly the most *outré*-looking man amongst us, and consequently the happiest."

Speaking of one of the army chaplains, another officer tells us this, by way of exemplifying the curious craze for bizarre or gay attire:

> None perhaps carried this so far as a 'minister of peace' attached to the army, who is distinguished by the title of the 'Fighting Parson,' and it is supposed, less in honour of his special calling than of his war-like *cognomen*, always wears a red hussar jacket!

For the army chaplains during the Peninsular War there is, indeed, from all accounts, not much to be said. Mr. Briscall, the chaplain at headquarters, was, we are told, "a man of refined manners and a good presence." He was favourably reported on in Wellington's dispatches, "especially on the ground that he kept down Methodism in the army." He performed Divine service every Sunday when in winter-quarters, "though I and many more," says Gleig of the 85th (who himself after the war took Orders and eventually became Chaplain-General of the

Army), "never saw him but once, and then could not hear a word he said." "A constitutional shrinking from any encounter with pain and sickness kept the reverend gentleman," we are also told, "from visiting the hospitals."[1]

It is added by the same writer that "reading the Burial Service over the dead during the wars of the French Revolution was a thing unheard of. Into huge pits dug to receive them the slain in battle were cast, and the victims of fever and privation were in somewhat similar fashion disposed of. Even the officers, though interred apart, had no prayers read beside their graves."

Reverting to the tastes of the officers in the matter of attire, we are told this by Mr. Larpent:

"At headquarters," says the judge advocate-general in his diary, "the dress is a cap made of velvet, cloth, and fur, with a peak over the eyes (that is, a foraging-cap). The handsomest are all of fur—dark or grey fur, the former the best—with a broad gold band and tassel on top. With this is worn a dress great-coat or plain one with military buttons, and grey pantaloons: this is the costume for dinners. Morning dress: overalls, boots, and white, or more generally fancy, waistcoats; in winter, blue and black velvet, with fancy buttons of gold and narrow stripes of gold as an edging."

"General Picton," we are also told, "during the Battle of Vittoria wore, while directing his division, instead of a cocked, a round and very old hat." On the march, to shade his eyes from the weakness at which at all times he suffered greatly, Picton invariably carried, as he rode on horseback at the head of his Staff, "a huge white umbrella lined with green."

Speaking of the army in the spring of 1813, when the campaign of Vittoria was about to open, one of the officers also tells us this:

> I suppose no army ever had less baggage. Besides two *calashes*, one belonging to Lord Wellington and another to the officer commanding the corps of Guards, a wagon containing the printing-press for the publication of general orders and circulars, and our common ammunition-wagons and forges, there is not another carriage in the army. We have much less baggage than the French, although we carry three tents to each company of infantry.

Next we may take a brief glance at how officers and men passed

---

1. *The Subaltern* by George Robert Gleig, (also published by Leonaur).

their time in winter-quarters, when active hostilities were not going on. Many curious glimpses are to be got of the life they led. They found, as it would appear, plenty to amuse themselves with. At the same time, of course, no slackness was permitted in matters of service and duty.

Field-days twice a week were the rule, and route-marches twice or three times a week took place regularly in all the camps. At the outposts the utmost vigilance was maintained continuously. There, with the divisions nearest the enemy, "all got under arms," we are told, "every morning before daybreak, and remained till it was light enough to distinguish a grey horse a mile off." After that, things being quiet to the front, and the routine duties of the camp performed, officers and men turned aside to throw themselves with a will into various diversions and recreations—hunting, shooting, fishing, or athletic sports.

Lord Wellington, so we are told by one officer, writing in the spring of 1813, "had, the last two winters he passed on the Portuguese frontier, a good pack of hounds; and the Light Division turned a barn at Gallegos into a tolerable theatre; while racing, shooting, trout-fishing, cricket, smoking and whist (the last, by the by, a favourite game at headquarters) aided in driving away dull care."

Several packs of hounds and of various kinds were kept in the divisional camps. "We have three odd sorts of packs of hounds here," writes Mr. Larpent from the headquarter-camp at Frenada; "firstly Lord Wellington's, or, as it is called here, 'the Peer's'—these are foxhounds, about sixteen couples. The next set of hounds are greyhounds, run by the commissary-general, Sir R. Kennedy. Thirdly, the *Capitan Mor* here, who is the principal man of the place, keeps an old poacher in his establishment with a dozen terriers, mongrels, and ferrets, and he goes out with the officers to get rabbits."

General Hill, in another part of the country, had his own pack, and with his officers passed his spare time whenever opportunity offered by "going out a-coursing three times a week."

"We have excellent coursing," writes Sir Rowland, "and now and then a fox-hunt, and sometimes attack a wild boar and the deer."

One of the officers of the Fourth Division also speaks of "a grand wild boar and wolf hunt" got up by General Cole from his camp, "at which all the well-mounted officers of the division were present."

Fair shooting seems always to have been got in the neighbourhood of most of the camps during winter-quarters: "woodcock, hares, snipe and plover, and occasionally partridge; and in spring, trout-fishing in most of the mountain streams."

Race-meetings were held now and then at some of the camps, but there was little, as a rule, to show by way of sport, owing to the poor condition of the horses: "half starved beasts, after months of chopped straw and winter grass," as an officer of the 43rd remarks of one of the Light Division meetings, where, as he also tells, most of the horses "came down heels over head from sheer debility, and the rest floundered over them."

Camp sports were always popular, and, of course, easiest of all to arrange.

> We frequently got up foot-races (our horses being in poor trim for such feats), played matches at football, and rackets against the tower of the village church; had duck-hunting with the dogs in a piece of water; and sometimes turned a pig loose with his tail greased, when he was pursued by the soldiers, and became the lawful prize of the man who could catch and hold him, which was no easy matter.

In some regiments, again, "walking-clubs" were in favour as a regular thing in winter-quarters; parties of officers going off two or three times a week, sometimes for twenty-mile tramps across country between morning drill and dinner-time.

In the evenings, relates one of the Light Division officers, "we got the village *belles* together and frequently danced through half the long winter nights; nor were our fair partners at all averse to hot punch between the *boleros* and *fandangos*. Our nights were spent in the utmost conviviality and harmony in an old barn where we messed."

Another form of recreation for the long evenings in winter-quarters, which found great favour, was theatricals, which, indeed, got to be quite the rage, particularly with the Light Division. They were first started by the 95th Rifles, who, to begin with, "converted an old house near the camp at Gallegos into quite a presentable theatre."

On the occasion of their opening performance, we are told, "the blankets and great-coats of the soldiers made capital side-scenes, and had not too much wine and grog found their way behind the scenes, no doubt the piece would have gone off with much *éclat*; but, as the truth must be told, they all forgot their parts."

The fame of the Gallegos theatricals spread in due course all over the army, and on one occasion "Wellington and his Staff rode over from headquarters one dark night to witness a performance."

A copy is in existence, as it happens, of the programme of the play given by the Light Division at Gallegos on that night. It is neatly and plainly printed with, by way of ornamentation on top, a representation of the Royal Arms, taken from some official document.

Light Division Theatre, Gallegos
On Thursday, February 4, 1813,
Will Be Performed the Comedy of

THE RIVALS

Men

Sir Anthony Absolute	Lieutenant Paterson, 43rd Regiment
Captain Absolute	Captain Beckwith, 95th Regiment
Faulkland	Lieutenant Pemberton, 95th Regiment
Sir Lucius O'Trigger	Lieutenant Cox, 95th Regiment
Acres	Captain Cator, Royal Artillery
David	Lieutenant Hennel, 43rd Regiment
Fag	Lieutenant Havelock, 43rd Regiment
Coachman	Lieutenant Hamilton, 95th Regiment

Women

Mrs. Malaprop	Captain Hobkirk, 43rd Regiment
Lydia Languish	Lieutenant Hon. C. Gore, 43rd Regiment
Julia	Lieutenant Lord C. Spencer, 95th Regiment
Lucy	Lieutenant Freer, 43rd Regiment

After Which a Variety of Comic Songs
VIVAT WELLINGTON!
[Printed at Frenada,]

Colonel Leach of the 95th, who was behind the scenes during the performance, adds this little touch:

> It is impossible to imagine anything more truly ludicrous than to see *Lydia Languish* and *Julia* (which characters were performed by two young and good-looking men, dressed uncommonly well, and looking very feminine on the stage), drinking punch and smoking cigars behind the scenes at a furious rate between the act!

In other respects, further, life at the front when fighting was not going on had its alleviations. In most of the camps, for one thing, they got the London newspapers with fair regularity, ten days or a fortnight old as a rule, it is true, but still sufficiently regularly to keep them in touch with the doings of people at home. Our Light Dragoon friend tells us about that, speaking specially of his own regiment in the period when, between 1812 and 1813, the army was on the Portuguese frontier.

"These papers," he says, "arrive in series of a week or ten days at a time, and their contents are speedily devoured. We do not generally follow the example of an officer of the Guards, who, to deceive himself into being near St. James's, husbands his papers, and has a fresh one damped, as though it was just from the press, and laid every morning on the table at his breakfast! Their contents furnish us with conversation, and the *critiques* of the editors in commenting on our operations and movements afford a fund of amusement."

Among other news from home that reached Wellington's army through the papers was the unpleasant intelligence of the persistent naval disasters of the earlier part of the American War of 1812. Referring in particular to what was said on the subject among the staff-officers at the headquarter-camp, Mr. Larpent makes this comment in his diary:

> People here are all very sore about the Americans and our taken frigates. I think we deserve it a little. Our contempt for our old descendants has always rather disgusted me, and with some English is carried so far as not to be bearable. These reverses may set things right. The Americans have faults enough; we should allow them their merits! Our sailors all thought the Americans would not dare look them in the face. I think the Army rather rejoice at all this falling on the Navy, as they bullied them so much before.

The English papers received in camp at the end of 1812 brought also the first news that reached Spain of the Moscow disasters and the annihilation of Napoleon's Grand Army, in the Foreign Office dispatches from St. Petersburg, reprinted from the *London Gazette*. By way of spreading discouragement among the enemy the papers containing the dispatches, after being read in camp, were collected and sent to the outposts, to be got, if possible, surreptitiously into the hands of the French troops.

"We are trying," says Mr. Larpent, the judge advocate-general, in his diary under date January 5, 1813, "to send the *Gazettes* of the Russian business to the French armies, to give some of them a better notions of affairs in that quarter, as it seems the armies hear little or nothing from France, and very seldom."

Certain officers on the Staff were also sent round to distribute the newspapers and spread the intelligence in various parts of Spain: a risky business for some of those concerned. One officer who was caught in the act had, as he describes, a narrow escape of being shot as a spy by the French general before whom he was promptly brought. Another detail of army social life under Wellington in Spain, as recorded by one of the officers, is this:

> Little change is afforded to our society beyond our corps of officers in the brigade. We have not lately had any idle aspiring cavaliers come to witness our prowess. During the retreat to the lines covering Lisbon in 1810, and during the time we occupied them, several joined headquarters; and one, a noble *marquess*, was so taken with our *métier* that he enlisted, and has since become one of Lord Wellington's most active *aides-de-camp*. The only description of amateurs we have at present are what the provost calls 'Gentlemen who come to fight for their commissions'; being volunteers, often the friends of officers of the regiment to which they are posted. They act as privates, though associating with the officers, till, an Ensign being killed, gives an opportunity for their being recommended to fill the vacancy.

Some officers, it would appear, tried to learn the language of the country; but most of them did not take kindly to "either the sonorous high-sounding Spanish or the less attractive nasal Portuguese." Nearly everybody, however, we are told, managed to acquire a smattering of both languages, if few troubled about grammar: "a language of the camp, a sort of *Lingua Franca*, was established and became current between us and the country people and followers." "A horrible jargon" is what one officer calls it.

As to how the men, the rank and file, managed the matter of the language: "You cannot, with the most lively imagination," says an officer of the 11th Light Dragoons, "conceive a more absurd failure than the attempts of our soldiers as linguists. I doubt if many of them ever thought, before their arrival at Lisbon, that there was any other language than English; and I can easily believe the joke, however stale, of the astonishment of some of them on finding that even the smallest and youngest children spoke Portuguese! Though they make but little progress beyond the names of the few necessaries of life, they are highly enraged at the peasantry if they do not understand a whole sentence of English, in which a single word of Spanish or Portuguese is introduced; and in such cases damn them roundly for 'not knowing their own language!' I leave you to judge of the correctness of the pronunciation when they use '*hogwar*' for '*aqua*,' '*palka*', for '*paga*' (pronounced '*pakha*—i.e., payment), 'akefent' for '*aqua-ardiente*,' '*pebble*' for '*pueblo*' (small town or village), '*fogo*' for '*fuego*,' and so on."

Remarking also on the many and varied callings represented in the ranks, one officer mentions incidentally that Wellington's soldiers included among them even naval dockyardsmen. "A regiment in the Fourth Division," he tells us, "produced one day, when there was a call for men who could lend a hand in making a portable field-telegraph, fifteen sail-makers and eighteen riggers," who had been all duly enlisted among the ordinary linesmen.

These casual glimpses of everyday affairs among Wellington's officers and men in the Peninsula may be concluded with two incidental details.

It was in the midst of the Peninsular War that the first regimental dinner of officers of the British Army ever held took place; an interesting fact on its own account in these days when regimental dinners have long since become part of military social life and an annual festivity and treasured institution. Indeed, as to that,—1912—marked the centenary of the origin of these social gatherings. The dinner was given, as it happened, to commemorate Albuhera—while the regiment concerned was in the field before the enemy, on the way to a battle.

On May 16, 1812, the two days' halt at Galisto, on the south side of the Tagus, three days before the surprise of Almaraz, while on the march with Hill's Division to carry out that exploit, the 28th so celebrated the first anniversary of the battle in which they "spoiled the Frenchmen's dancing." They determined to signalize the event, we are told by an officer, "by giving a dinner to Sir Rowland and the Staff of the Second Division."

"But," proceeds the narrative, "they had neither tables nor chairs. This did not deter them from their purpose, and ingenuity, never wanting where there is inclination, soon invented a mode of giving a *banquet alfresco*. Lieutenant Irwin selected the softest and most even piece of turf he could find, on which he marked out the due length and breadth of a table for no less than 100 guests. The turf was carefully pared off, and a trench was dug round it large enough for all the company. The table was formed in the centre of the sods and moulds, duly levelled and excavated to give ample room for the legs; and then the green turf was once more gently laid on and supplied the place of a table-cloth. Each officer invited was desired to bring his own knife, fork, and plate, and not be particular about having them changed. The cookery was of the substantial order, the heavy artillery of field *cuisine*. There were ponderous joints roasted and ponderous joints boiled; there was soup in abundance, in which the shreds of meat gave assurance that it was, at least, unsparingly concocted; there were pies baked in camp-kettles turned upside down, of dimensions and quality Friar Tuck would not have disdained!"

As another interesting fact, the second regimental dinner on record was also held in the field before the enemy fourteen months later, by the Rifle Brigade, the then 95th Rifles of the Light Division. That took place a few days before the storming of San Sebastian. The three original battalions of the regiment happened to be serving together at the moment, and it was resolved to commemorate the anniversary of the formation of the regiment.

Following the method adopted at the Albuhera dinner, about which all the army had talked, "a trench was dug round a parallelogram of turf, which served as a table, and the diners sat with their feet in the trench. Healths were drunk and honoured enthusiastically. The dinner over, news came that an immediate attack by the French was expected, and the diners stood to arms for a great part of the night. It was a dramatic occasion, and worthy of remembrance," remarks the chronicler of the event, "for it is seldom that three battalions of one regiment meet; also so interesting an occasion in the surroundings must indeed be hard to equal."

17

Foemen Worthy of Each Other's Steel! How the Brave on Both Sides Met as Friends Between Their Battles

The bond of *camaraderie* that came into being between the fighting-men on both sides was one of the most curious and interesting features of the Peninsular War. It stands, indeed, by itself. Nothing like it is on record of any other war. Nothing so instances and typifies the spirit of soldierly chivalry—

The brotherhood
That binds the brave of all the earth—

as do the tales of the friendly personal dealings with one another of Wellington's men and Napoleon's on so many occasions in the intervals between their combats.

They surely, if any soldiers did, understood what it meant

To honour while you strike him down
The foe that comes with fearless eyes.

That, of course, was apart from and distinct from the meetings that took place from time to time on business under flags of truce. The courtesies that passed in such cases were quite different; they followed normal conditions under the ordinary laws of war. On such occasions the procedure was strictly regulated.

This, for instance, was the way in which these parleys took place, as a dragoon officer at the front relates, "according to the more legitimate mode of a flag of truce."

"Taking a trumpeter," he says, "you approach the nearest of the enemy's posts, and when close upon the *vedettes* or sentries, he sounds, and you halt until the officer in command of the picket is called up. Although your message or letter," proceeds the officer, "is soon delivered, both parties wish to prolong the interview—from curiosity and a desire to suck each other's brains, and perhaps deceive their adversary—while the two trumpeters are bound, like the squires of old, to drink to each other's welfare." These official *rencontres*, though, had sometimes pleasant sequels. In addition to often meeting interesting people in this way, the same officers sometimes met over and over again, and occasionally exchanged mementoes. Remarks an officer:

> I received as a souvenir from one Lieutenant Bourssard, of the 10th Chasseurs, a sheet of the last new fashionable ladies' bonnets from Paris.

On occasion, also, Wellington himself, as has been said, entertained prisoners of rank at his table, and other courtesies in that connection at all times passed between the two armies. "Baggage and money," we are told, "have always been received on both sides for officers who have had the misfortune to be made prisoners."

How chivalrously Marshal Victor treated his wounded prisoners of the 23rd Light Dragoons after Talavera has been told. This, in addition, is on record of the fine courtesy on the same occasion of "Marshal Beau Soleil," as his soldiers nicknamed their leader, because of his very round and red face. It was a few days later when Wellington had begun to fall back towards the South.

> When he entered Talavera, Victor found some of the wounded, French and English alike, lying on the ground in the *Plaza*. After complimenting the English, and observing that they understood the laws and courtesies of war, he told them there was one thing they did not understand, and that was how to deal with the Spaniards. He then sent soldiers to every house, with orders to the inhabitants immediately to receive and accommodate the wounded of the two nations, who were lodged together, one Englishman and one Frenchman, and expressly directed that the Englishman should always be served first!

"One very fine young officer," we are told, "who had lost a leg, seemed particularly to attract Victor's sympathy. The marshal supplied him with money for his drafts and other conveniences, and, when he was well enough, released him on *parole*, and gave him leave to return home through Paris, where he was present at the *fêtes* for the marriage of Napoleon to Maria Louisa of Austria."

Marshal Ney, the "Bravest of the Brave," before that had shown himself a man of no less chivalrous a stamp towards his opponents. The incident took place sometime after Corunna, where Captain Charles Napier had been taken prisoner. Napier's pluck under fire in the battle, had, as it would seem, quite taken the fancy of the enemy. To encourage his men, he had jumped on a wall in full sight of the French waving his hat and sword. Yet no fire was opened on him. As he himself afterwards related, the French captain in charge at the point had himself stopped his men from firing at him. "Instead of firing at him," said the French captain, "I longed to run forward and embrace the brave officer!"

Some months after Corunna, when Wellington had taken the field, nothing having been heard of Napier in the meantime, "a flag of truce was sent to the French headquarters with inquiries, and this message was taken to Marshal Ney by Baron Clouet. 'Let him see his friends,' said the marshal; 'he can tell them that he is well, and well treated.' Clouet made no move, but continued looking earnestly at Ney, who at last, with a smile, asked, 'What more do you want?' 'He has an old mother, a widow and blind,' replied the gallant and tenderhearted Clouet. 'Has he?' answered Ney, with that chivalry that played so prominent a part throughout his brilliant career, 'let him go, then, and tell her himself that he is alive!'"

It did not take long apparently for a spirit of mutual confidence and forbearance to come into being among the rank and file on both sides, before civilities began to be exchanged. That, however, was after Wellington had taken the field. At the outset of all, during the Corunna campaign things had been different: the earlier spirit of national animosity was too strong, and had not had time to become tempered. Persistent "sniping "at the outposts on all occasions was one form that it took.

"At Corunna," remarks an officer of the 11th Hussars, "when we were very young soldiers, we could not be satisfied without making riflemen creep along the banks and hedges and shoot the helpless single cavalry-*vedettes* of the enemy. At the time I thought this very fine and praiseworthy, but since, being more grown, I have considered an officer approving of such acts as little better than giving countenance to assassination."

It was at Talavera that the soldiers of the opposing armies first really made each others' acquaintance on friendly terms (of a kind): during that strange lull on the second day of the battle, in the middle of the action. The British and French soldiers, who were facing each other on either side of a narrow valley, broke their ranks, and hundreds of them wandered down to drink at a brook—the Portina, it was called—which ran between the two positions.

Frenchmen and Englishmen mingled in frank good fellowship, without fear or suspicion, seeking shelter together under the mulberry-trees from the burning heat.

The stream was muddy; in places it was bloody; at one place it formed a small stagnant pool. But that did not matter. The soldiers on both sides were hot, and parched with thirst. They laid aside their muskets and mixed together; stooped down and drank side by side, helping one another here and there, lending one another tin cups and *pannikins* and exchanging flasks. "*À votre santé, Anglais!*" said some. "Here's to you, Crappo!" was the reply. A number, we are also told, were able to talk to one another, after a fashion, in a camp *patois* or *lingua franca* used in both armies in dealing with the natives, about what had happened, or would probably happen. For over two hours the men mingled, until, suddenly, the French bugles sounded the order to stand to arms, and the British bugles the recall. With mutual farewells and handshakes in not a few instances, we are told, the men on both sides turned away and ran back hastily, to re-form ranks and be ere long again shooting and stabbing at one another, in the midst of another furious combat at close quarters.

A non-commissioned officer of the Gordons, for one, Sergeant Nicol[1] of the 92nd Highlanders, describes how they all mingled together beside the brook:

> About eleven o'clock the enemy, being baffled in all his attacks, withdrew his troops a little. As we did not move to follow them, they deliberately piled arms and set about kindling fires and cooking their victuals. A brook ran through the plain, and to it both armies went for water as if a truce was between us; looking at each other, drinking, and wiping the sweat from our brows, laughing and nodding to each other, all thoughts of

---

1. *Sergeant Nicol* by Daniel Nicol, (also published by Leonaur).

fighting being for the time forgotten.

"Many officers came down later," we are also told, "and after a short colloquy agreed that either party might take off its wounded without molestation. As hundreds of French were lying on the west bank of the Portina and many English on the other side, there was a complete mixture of uniforms as the bearers passed and repassed each other at the bottom of the ravine; but no difficulties arose, and for more than two hours the two sides intermingled."

After the Battle of Busaco, parties of both British and French soldiers "became fairly mingled" on the field as they went wandering about searching among the wounded and the dead, until at length Wellington had to order the French back. "Some of their soldiery," says a British officer, "had strolled up—I spoke to several of them—to the very summit of the hill, even beyond where their advance had penetrated in the previous attack."

This is another incident after Busaco, as the army was falling back into the lines of Torres Vedras: "As we neared that position, in front of the lines, there were several sharp skirmishes. In one the French made a dashing attempt to storm a British field-work, held by men of the 71st, and got into the work; but were driven out at the point of the bayonet. The whole skirmish and the repulse were speedily over, and when all firing had ceased they called for permission to carry off their killed and wounded men, who were strewed over the little field in front. To this we assented, and they sent a party, accompanied by an officer, who commenced the removal. Whilst they were so employed the officer came up to Reynell (the colonel of the 71st), and with some flippancy, mingled with mortification, said: '*Après l'affaire nous sommes des bons amis!*'"

"Some of the French," we are told by one of the officers in the Second Division, "actually shook hands with the English soldiers as they slaked their common thirst from a narrow rivulet that ran at the bottom of the hill."

A sort of *entente cordiale*, indeed, would appear to have come into being during the lull in active operations while Wellington's army stood at bay in the lines of Torres Vedras. The outposts on both sides often held friendly intercourse, officers and men exchanging courtesies and fraternizing across the narrow stream which at places divided the sentries, only a few yards apart.

"One day," according to a subaltern in the Light Division of one of these meetings, "some of their officers saluted us from the opposite bank. '*Bon jour, messieurs,*' they began, and then they asked after Lord Wellington and praised his conduct of the campaign, saying that he had done wonders with the Portuguese. They also asked after King George, asking if it was true he was dead."

George III. at that time had just been stricken by the final attack of the mental malady from which he never recovered.

We quizzed each other; they asked us how we liked *bacalao* and *azete* for dinner instead of English roast beef, and we replied by asking what they did in Santarem without the *cafés* and *salles de spectacle* of Paris. They answered, laughing, that they had a theatre, and asked us to come and see the play of that evening: '*L'Entrée des Français dans Lisbon!*' One of our party quickly answered that he recommended to them the repetition of a newer piece—*La fuite des Français!*' They burst into a loud, long, general laugh, the joke was too good, too home! Their general then pulled off his hat and wishing us 'Good-day' with perfect good humour, they went up the hill.

On another day at another point along the outpost line, where the 92nd Highlanders were posted, some of the French troops were about to kill a bullock. "The outposts were so near that we could see the French soldiers cleaning their arms and lying about. The bullock broke loose and scampered towards the 92nd, one of whom shot it, whereupon the 92nd proceeded to cut up the prize, in full view of their hungry and disappointed foes. Two French soldiers on that, waving white handkerchiefs by way of flag of truce, came over with a message from their officer that he was sure the Scottish soldiers were too generous to deprive his men of their only provisions, on which half the beef, with some bread and a bottle of rum, was sent back."

"Again," records a sergeant of the 40th (the 2nd Somersetshire as it was then), whose regiment was also quartered on the outpost line, "we were so near the enemy that we very often wandered into the same vineyards and exchanged compliments by shaking hands."

"If we wanted wood for the construction of huts," says an officer of the Connaught Rangers, "our men were allowed to pass without molestation to the French side of the intervening river to cut it. Each day the soldiers of both armies used to bathe in the same stream, and an exchange of rations such as biscuits and rum between the French and our men was not uncommon."

"It happened on more than one occasion," according to another officer, "that the French officers at the outposts would ask of ours to obtain for them some little luxury from Lisbon—a box of cigars, coffee, stationery, or other objects, which requests were always readily complied with."

This incident took place during Masséna's retreat from Portugal. It was on the evening of July 5, 1811. The French pickets and sentries at the time occupied the right bank of the Dos Casas stream, our own Light Division being posted along the left bank.

"I am glad to see you here," called out a French field-officer, as he posted his picket, to a captain of the 52nd on the other bank. "We shall now understand each other. When you want water, and our sentries challenge, call out *agua*, and you shall have it. Have the goodness to give your boys (*vos enfants*) similar orders."

Many other incidents to the same effect took place during the spring campaign of 1810, when Wellington and Masséna were closely watching each other in Eastern Portugal.

"It was customary for our cavalry pickets," describes a dragoon officer, "to patrol every morning before daybreak, to ascertain if any change or movement had taken place in the French chain of cavalry posts. One morning, in a thick fog, a small patrol of ours found themselves close to a superior force of French cavalry. They instantly retired, but, in the hurry, one of our dragoons dropped his cloak. Our patrol had ridden but a short distance to the rear when it was called to by the French, one of whom, riding up to within a short distance, dropped the captured cloak on the ground and rode away, making signals to the English dragoon who had lost it to pick it up. This," adds the officer, "was carrying on the war as it should be; it is but justice to add that we rarely found them deficient on this point."

Colonel Leach of the 95th, in describing how, in the spring of 1810, the officers of the Light Division at the outposts when off duty used to go out with guns, pointers, and often got good bags of quails and snipe and golden plover, tells us this:

> In these pastimes the French cavalry pickets, posted in the marshes, never interfered with us or interrupted our sport, although we frequently coursed hares and shot quails within half-range of their carbines. On the contrary, their conduct was courteous and, if I may use the expression, 'gentlemanly' to a degree.

"A very friendly intercourse," relates one of the Rifle Brigade on duty at the outposts (Edward Costello),[2] "was carried on between the French and ourselves. We frequently met them bathing in the Rio Mayor, and would often have swimming and even jumping matches. In these games, however, we mostly beat them, but that was attributed to their half-starved, distressed condition. This, our stolen intercourse, soon made us awake to, until, at length, touched with pity, our men went so far as to share with them the ration biscuits which we were regularly supplied with from England. Indeed, we buried all national hostility in our anxiety to assist and relieve them. Tobacco was in great request: we used to carry some of ours to them, while they, in return, would bring us a little brandy."

"One day on picket in 1810, on the Agueda, opposite Gallegos," says Sir George Napier, a Captain in the Light Division, "some of the French soldiers" (of a picket opposite) "asked my leave to come across and get some tobacco from our men, as they had none and could not get any. I allowed two of them to come, who immediately stripped off their clothes and swam across—I would not let them try the ford. They got the tobacco, told us all the news from France, and returned quite happy."

This is another story from the outposts of the Light Division: "After dusk one evening a French soldier, a sergeant, was captured within the British lines, and brought as a prisoner before Captain Love of the 52nd, He explained that he had come into the village to bid *adieu* to his Spanish sweetheart.

"'*C'est l'amour qui m'a fait votre prisonnier, mon capitaine,*' explained the sergeant.

"'*Eh bien,*' was Captain Love's reply, '*pour cette fois-ci nous ne serons pas trop exigeants. Retournez chez votre capitaine, et dites-lui que si l'amour vous a joué un mauvais tour, l'amour vous dédommagé. Je m'appelle Love; vous ne m'oublierez de sitôt.*'

"The sergeant went back to his comrades vowing eternal gratitude."

"I used to be very much amused," writes Kincaid,[3] of the Rifle Brigade, referring to life at the outposts while the main army lay within the lines of Torres Vedras, "at seeing our naval officers come up from Lisbon riding on mules, with huge ships' spyglasses, like 6-pounders, strapped across the backs of their saddles. Their first question invari-

---

2. *Rifleman Costello* by Edward Costello, (also published by Leonaur).
3. *The Complete Kincaid of the Rifles* by John Kincaid, (also published by Leonaur).

ably was: 'Who is that fellow there?' pointing to the enemy's sentry, close to us, and on being told that he was a Frenchman, the answer invariably was: 'Then why the devil don't you shoot him?'"

Repeated acts of civility passed between the French and us during this tacit suspension of hostilities. "The greyhounds of an officer followed a hare on one occasion into their lines, and they very politely returned them." That piece of courtesy Kincaid records.

Another was this:

> I was one night on picket at the end of the bridge when a ball came from a French sentry and struck the burning billet of wood round which we were sitting. They sent a flag of truce next morning to apologize for the accident, and to say that it had been done by a stupid fellow of a sentry, who imagined people were advancing upon him. We admitted the apology, though we knew well enough that it had been done by a malicious rather than a stupid fellow from the situation we occupied.

This also is one of Kincaid's stories:

> General Junot, one day reconnoitring, was severely wounded by a sentry. Lord Wellington, knowing that they were at that time destitute of everything in the shape of comfort, sent to request his acceptance of anything that Lisbon afforded that could be of any service to him; but the French General was too much of a politician to admit the want of anything.

At that time all in the French camps were on the verge of destitution, their convoys and foraging parties being harassed incessantly by the Portuguese irregulars.

> Subsisting entirely on plunder, the invaders soon exhausted the resources of their neighbourhood, and had to send farther and ever farther afield for their subsistence. 'Heaven forgive me,' wrote a Portuguese spy to Wellington from Santarem, 'if I wrong them in believing they have eaten my cat!'

Here is another instance of the friendly terms existing between the outposts at this time. Says an officer, writing in November, 1810:

> We are here without any idea of attacking or being attacked, with our *vedettes* close to each other, and pickets whose sentries are relieved by the same road. The French have double sentries,

and when you approach near them they strike the butts of their firelocks, as if to say, 'We are here, and there is no use for both of us.' This has only taken place lately. At first our sentries and the French used to drink together. Our men, of course, got drunk. One of the Buffs left his firelock, which was brought after him by one of the Frenchmen. General Hall has very wisely put a stop to this, and we are now perfectly polite, and not so disgustingly familiar. I was at our outposts yesterday. The French *vedette* saluted us, not with a shot, but by kissing his hand. Is not this civilized warfare?

Occasionally, as might be expected, the familiarity of intercourse led to incidents which might have had unpleasant consequences. This adventure, for instance, befell one of the men of the 52nd, an Irish private named Tobin. It was while Masséna, after his withdrawal from before Torres Vedras, was halting in winter-quarters at Santarem, the outposts of both armies, as before, being in close touch.

Opposite where the 52nd were, in advance of all, was a wine-house, we are told, between the English and French outposts, where the patrols of both used to meet secretly and have grog. Tobin drank too much there once, and fell asleep. He was picked up by a French picket, unaware of the arrangement, and carried off, being later brought before Masséna himself by an Irish *aide-de-camp* of the marshal's, who wanted to help a countryman in trouble. He accompanied the prisoner as interpreter.

Tobin answered the questions put to him by the marshal fairly well, until asked the strength of the Light Division. Here the poor fellow was at fault; but, not willing that his division should be poorly thought of, he replied in an off-hand Irish way: "Tin thousand!" That was too much for Masséna. The marshal got irritated. "Here, take away the lying rascal!" he ejaculated.

Taken aback at the marshal's angry outburst, Tobin turned to the *aide-de-camp*, and, with much *naïveté* of manner, exclaimed: "Why, what's the matter with the Gin'ral?" The *aide-de-camp* replied: "He says you are telling him lies; he knows the Light Division was very little above four thousand when it advanced, and, as it has been engaged about four times since, it must have lost at least four or five hundred men."

"Och, thin, the Gin'ral don't belave me!" was Tobin's response. "Till him to attack us the next time he meets us with tin thousand men; and if we don't lick him, I'm d——d!"

The *aide-de-camp* explained this *verbatim* to Masséna, who was so tickled at it that he offered to make Tobin a sergeant in the Irish Legion (a regiment of refugee Irish rebels from the rising of '98, enlisted in Napoleon's service), if he would go over. Tobin cunningly asked for twenty-four hours to consider, and, having made friends with a cook, filled his haversack and escaped back to his own regiment that same night.

After the first day's fighting at Fuentes de Onoro, there was a truce to pick up the wounded. "During the truce," relates Colonel Leach of the 95th,[4] "several French officers came down to the little bridge over the Duas Casas at the foot of the village, on which happened to be posted a file of my own company, whilst two French grenadiers were on sentry at the other end of it. On the centre of the bridge three French officers met and conversed a considerable time with the officers of my company, and were politeness itself. After offering us a pinch of snuff by way of prelude, the events which had taken place during the day were discussed. They passed many compliments on the gallant conduct of our army, and declared that tomorrow would be a great and decisive day and full of glory for one of the two armies."

According to another story of Fuentes de Onoro, after the close of the first day's fight, "the village was between the two armies. Men from each were scattered over it, somewhat mixed, in search of chairs, or kitchen utensils, or conveniences, to take out to their respective bivouacs. To prevent confusion, or perhaps quarrels, they drew a line of demarcation along the street which neither was to pass, and this amicable arrangement was respected by both."

One of our Light Dragoon officers had this experience in following up the enemy at the close of the same battle:

> On the day the French retired from Fuentes de Onoro, the last troops they withdrew from our front were some squadrons of cavalry. Accompanied by a friend of mine, we quietly followed their retrograde movement, and, secure in the speed of our horses on the open plain, gradually neared the rearguard. When we came within a few yards an officer rode out and begged that we should not encroach so much, or otherwise he should be obliged, but with much regret, '*à faire charger les tirailleurs!*' It is needless to tell you that we did not farther obtrude on his good

---

4. *Captain of the 95th Rifles* by Jonathan Leach, (also published by Leonaur).

nature or civility.

This incident took place a very short time after Fuentes de Onoro, the two armies being again in presence. Edward Costello of the Rifle Brigade is the recorder of the story.

At one point the opposing lines of sentries were very close to each other, the French being divided from us only by a narrow plank thrown across the mill-dam, which was occupied on one side by our company, who were now on picket. A blacksmith of ours, of the name of Tidy, who had erected his forge in the old mill, was at work close by shoeing the officers' horses. The French sentry had crossed the plank to light his pipe, and was standing carelessly chatting with me, when who should I see approaching but General Craufurd, inquiring if Tidy had shod his horse. The Frenchman's red wings soon attracted the general's notice, and he suddenly, with his well-known stern glance, inquired 'Who the d―――'s that you're talking with, rifleman?' I informed him it was the French sentry who had come over for a light for his pipe. 'Indeed,' replied Craufurd, 'then let him go about his business; he has no right here—nor we either,' said he in a low whisper to his *aide-de-camp*, and away he walked.

The story is told elsewhere of how, on the occasion of Hill's surprise of the enemy at Arroyo dos Molinos, the officers of the French 34th, on surrendering to the British 34th, their captors of the pursuit, fraternized with them, claiming kinship through the common bond of the regimental number. "*Ah, messieurs!*" one of the French exclaimed, "*nous sommes des frères; nous sommes du 34me Régiment tous deux!*"

Here is another interesting anecdote, in spirit much of the same kind:

"In the fighting with the French troops attempting to relieve San Sebastian," says an officer of the 51st, "after one action, the ground originally occupied by our advanced skirmishers was in possession of the French, and some of our wounded who had been left behind were most kindly treated by them. We had been engaged with the French 51st Regiment. Pointing to the number on their caps, they said that 'all belonged to the same regiment, and our men should fare as their comrades.' They fed them, they dressed their wounds—nay, they did not even plunder their packs, and in the morning we found these soldiers whom the French, owing to their wounds, could not take away with them in their retreat, all speaking in the highest terms of the treatment they had received. This," adds the officer, "is the chivalry of modern warfare, and robs it of half its horrors."

As an instance, too, of how chivalrous the French could be in fight, there is the noble story of Captain Felton Harvey's adventure. It was in the cavalry affair at Aldeaponte, at the time of the El Bodon action, near Ciudad Rodrigo. Captain Felton Harvey had lost his right arm, while leading his squadron, as has been told, in the brilliant charge of the 14th Light Dragoons at the close of the battle at Oporto. As he now charged into the enemy well ahead of his men, a French dragoon came at him with his sabre raised on high to strike. The two met, and instinctively, to ward off the coming blow, Hervey raised the stump of his right arm. The noble-hearted Frenchman saw the action and the maimed limb. Holding back his blow with a hasty effort, he lowered his sword to the salute and passed on.

Captain Brotherton, of the same regiment, the 14th Light Dragoons, tells this story of a hand-to-hand encounter that he had on one occasion on the battlefield with a young French officer, "between the two lines of skirmishers, French and English, who stood still to witness it." The British captain killed his antagonist; but "I shall never forget," he says, "his good-humoured, fine countenance, during the whole time we were engaged in this combat, talking cheerfully and politely to me as if we were exchanging courtesies instead of sabre-cuts."

It was on the morning of the Battle of Fuentes de Onoro again that this occurred. Costello, of the Rifle Brigade, witnessed the affair and describes it:

> On the left of the enemy, in front, a regiment of cavalry were conspicuously formed, a troop of which soon came trotting leisurely towards us to reconnoitre our position. This movement induced a corresponding one on the part of some of our dragoons, when both parties threw out their *vedettes* and remained halted, with some 400 yards of ground between them. One of their *vedettes*, after being posted facing an English dragoon (one of the 14th or 16th) displayed an instance of individual gallantry in which the French, to do them justice, were seldom wanting. Waving his long straight sword, the Frenchman rode within sixty yards of our dragoon and challenged him to single combat.
>
> We immediately expected to see our cavalryman engage his opponent sword in hand. Instead of this, however, he unslung

his carbine and fired at the Frenchman, who, not a whit dismayed, shouted out so that everyone could hear him: '*Venez avec le sabre; je suis prêt pour Napoléon et La Belle France!*' After having vainly endeavoured to induce the Englishman to a personal conflict, and after having endured two or three shots from the carbine, the Frenchman rode proudly back to his ground, cheered even by our own men, while we hissed our dragoon, who, it was afterwards stated, for the credit of the gallant regiment he belonged to, was a recruit.

This incident, from Captain Brotherton's diary, took place at Busaco:

> Several of the French soldiers who had fallen wounded within a few yards of our line lay gasping in agony and thirst, calling out for water to drink; but such was the galling fire kept up by the enemy on this point that it appeared almost certain death for anyone to show himself for an instant beyond the shelter which some rocks afforded. I observed, however, a noble young fellow, an Hanoverian belonging to the German Legion, walk coolly and deliberately from behind a rock, and going to the nearest wounded French soldier who was calling out for drink, but lay in a most contorted and painful position (one of his legs, which was broken by a musket-shot, being bent under him), applied his canteen to the poor fellow's mouth, after having, without the least degree of hurry or trepidation (though the fire continued most heavy), settled his head on his knapsack, and otherwise made his position less painful. The fine young fellow did this successfully to several wounded Frenchmen, and then returned to his regiment. When first this young officer stepped out, the enemy, fancying he might be leading an attack, redoubled their fire; but when they perceived what he was doing, the firing immediately ceased, and was succeeded by vociferous cheering at his conduct.

"A day or two after San Sebastian was taken," says someone else, "the garrison having retired to the castle, and everything being still in confusion, one of our officers pressed on to the buildings at the foot of the steep hill, to ascertain and fix the limits occupied by the French. He walked into the open doors of a church which was backed against a hill, and was going cautiously up the centre aisle, when he heard a voice from the arched ceiling calling out, '*Retirez vous, retirez vous!*' Looking up, he could see nothing, but became at once aware that the enemy had access to the ceiling from the hill, while they had abandoned the floor. There was probably a musket or two directed on to the floor from some holes, from whence of course, he might have been shot but for the enemy's courteous conduct. He, of course, took the hint, made a low bow, and retired."

"At Badajoz," according to an officer of the 51st, "French and English soldiers, on the night of the storm, were seen arm-in-arm together, plundering and carousing, and the best of friends in the world, while, not an hour previously, they had been engaged in the most sanguinary conflict at the fatal breach!"

This occurred before the Battle of Salamanca, at the time of the dramatic marching of the two armies side by side, so strikingly narrated by Napier, towards the point at which the battle was fought. "Hostile columns of infantry, only half a musket-shot from each other, were marching impetuously towards a common goal, the officers on each side pointing forwards with their swords, or touching their caps and waving their hands in courtesy."

It was at Salamanca that this gallant little act was performed. At the outset of the fighting there was a sharp skirmish between a detachment of the French and the light company of the 88th Connaught Rangers, under Captain Robert Nickle. The French "came on in gallant style, headed by their brave commanding officer, who was most conspicuous, being several paces in front of his men." But the "Rangers of Connaught," as Picton always addressed the ever-daring regiment, were too formidable in fight for their antagonists. The enemy gave way and ran back, leaving among others on the field their brave commander, mortally wounded. Thereupon this took place.

> Captain Robert Nickle ran up to his bleeding opponent, and rendered him every assistance in his power. He then advanced alone, with his handkerchief tied on the point of his sword, which he held up as a token of amity; and, thus reassured, some of the French soldiers returned without their arms, and carried away their officer with them. They were delighted with the considerate conduct of Captain Nickle, and embraced our men on parting.

"In the advance, after Salamanca, towards Burgos," relates a cavalry officer, "our *vedettes* were close to the enemy, and we had a good deal of conversation with them during the day. At dark two officers from the 22nd Chasseurs rode up to us. Since Salamanca their tone is a good deal altered; they talk of nothing but joining the Grand Army in the north, and say the Emperor is at St. Petersburg."

One of the most distinguished of the French commanders in the Peninsular War, the celebrated General Foy, it is related, often used to avail himself of the amicable relations existing between the outposts on both sides for his private purposes. He had all his fortune invested in British securities, and would constantly ride out to the picket-lines in order to try and get the loan of a London newspaper, through the courtesy of one or the other of the British officers on duty on posts facing his own men, in order to learn the market quotations of his stock.

It was especially in the last two or three years of the war that the dealings between the men of the two armies became so curiously cordial and friendly in the intervals of their fighting. In particular was this the case in the last campaign of all, after Vittoria; during the series of battles in the Pyrenees and when Wellington and Soult were facing each other along the French frontier.

"I never knew an advanced sentry of either army to be wantonly shot at the outposts," remarks an officer of the Light Division in a letter home at this period. "I have often myself, strolling too far in advance of my own picket, been waved back by the French, but in no one instance was I fired upon."

"The French and English soldier," writes another officer, "had no feeling of animosity towards each other. They fought bravely in the field, but on picket they have been known for days to be within musket shot, the sentries, perhaps, separated only by a ditch, yet not a shot was fired except at the proper time. They knew it was useless to harass each other for nothing, and, though they both did their duty in the most vigilant manner, confidence was never abused, and we frequently conversed familiarly with the French officers at the advanced posts with as much feeling of security as in our own tents."

"One instance I may relate," adds the same officer, "not much to the credit of the individual concerned, but to show the bearing and generous conduct of our gallant foes. A British officer commanding a picket supped one night with the French officer in charge of the one opposite his post, and to his own eternal disgrace actually got drunk. He was brought back about midnight to his own men on the backs of four unarmed French soldiers, laughing and enjoying the joke most heartily. Well was it for this drunken sot that his regiment was unacquainted with this feat; nor was it known to them till long years after he had been obliged to leave his corps. It is, however, an undoubted fact."

Our own 11th Hussars and the French 21st Chasseurs, while facing one another on outpost duty in the campaign after Vittoria, "from being all the winter opposite one another, became quite intimate. One of our subalterns," relates a captain of the 11th in a letter, "who speaks French and German fluently, knows several of their officers, and on my visiting a distant picket which he commanded under my orders, some days since, on inquiring for him, I was told that he was 'over at the enemy's picket!'"

"While Hasparen (a small town near the Nive) was the headquarters of the Fifth Division," says Grattan[5] of the Connaught Rangers, "the pickets of both armies avoided every appearance of hostility. Each occupied a hill, with sentries about 200 yards apart. The French, on one occasion, pushed forward their *vedettes*, and seemed as if they designed to trespass on the neutral ground. The Captain of the English picket reported this encroachment, and received orders not to allow it. On the following morning he observed that the French *vedette* had been advanced about fifty yards, and he thought it advisable to demand an interview with the French captain of *Chasseurs*. A peasant was dispatched, and returned with the message that the captain would wait upon the British officer immediately, and in a few minutes the parties met on the neutral ground.

"The Briton stated the orders he had received, and explained that, to avoid so *lâche* a proceeding as to fire upon a *vedette*, he had solicited a meeting with the brave *chasseur*. The Frenchman expressed himself in the most flattering terms, and begged that the hussar might point out a situation which would be agreeable to him. A thorn-bush, about 100 yards behind the spot the French *vedette* was posted upon, was mentioned as equally advantageous for the security of the French picket, while it would be such as the hussar was permitted by his orders to allow. The *chasseur* gave orders accordingly; the *vedette* was placed on the very spot which was recommended, and the Frenchman, having expressed his satisfaction at the interview, produced a bottle of cognac. Two or three officers on each side now joined the party, a happy termination to the war was drunk, and the captain, whose name was, we think, Le Brun, said 'he trusted that it would not

---

5. *The Complete Adventures in the Connaught Rangers* by William Grattan, (also published by Leonaur).

be the fate of war to bring into collision the parties who had met in so amicable a manner.'"

This also was one of the incidents of the period of the Battles of the Pyrenees. "After one fight," says a British officer, (William Hamilton Maxwell), the author of *The Bivouac*, "we perceived, not twenty yards off, a wounded *voltigeur* extended on the ground and a young comrade supporting him. The Frenchman never attempted to retreat, but smiled when we came up, as if he had been expecting us. 'Goodmorning,' he said; 'I have been waiting for you, gentlemen. My poor friend's leg is broken by a shot, and I could not leave him until you arrived, lest some of these Portuguese brigands should murder him. Pierre,' he continued, as he addressed his companion, 'here are the brave English, and you will be taken care of. I will leave you a flask of water, and you will soon be succoured by our noble enemy. Gentlemen, will you honour me by emptying this canteen? You will find it excellent, for I took it from a portly friar two days ago.'

"There was no need to repeat the invitation," adds the narrator. "I set the example, the canteen passed from mouth to mouth, and the monk's brandy vanished. The conscript—for he had not joined above a month—replenished the flask with water from a spring just by. He placed it in his comrade's hand, bade him an affectionate farewell, bowed gracefully to us, threw his musket over his shoulder, and trotted off to join his regiment, which he pointed out upon a distant height. He seemed never for a moment to contemplate the possibility of our sending him in durance to the rear, and there was about him such kindness and confidence that, on our part, no one ever dreamed of detaining him."

These, again, are one or two jottings by one of the officers of the 95th Rifles:[6]

> At the time that the allied army were in front of St. Jean de Luz, and shortly before the Battle of Nivelle, it was very difficult—nay, almost impossible—to procure any good wine; and being one day on outpost duty at a post which we used to call the Chapel Hill Picket, it occurred to a German officer and myself that, being on good terms with the French, and in the habit of often chatting with their officers at the outposts, we might be able to get a case of claret by their means. On going to the front

---

6. *Captain of the 95th (Rifles)* by Jonathan Leach, *Lieutenant Simmons of the 95th (Rifles)* by George Simmons, *The Compleat Rifleman Harris* by Benjamin Harris are all published by Leonaur.

we were immediately joined by a French officer, who expressed every wish to oblige us; but he said he really could not afford to purchase the wine himself, with the chance of losing his money in case any movement should take place in either army, but that, if we chose to take the risk upon ourselves, and would entrust him with the price of it, his regiment would be again at the outpost in three days' time, and that we should then have our wine. He was true to his word: on the third day there was a case of the most excellent claret waiting for us, which he had been kind enough to bring upon a mule from St. Jean de Luz; and we parted, after exchanging names, and mutually expressing a wish that we might renew our acquaintance at some future period under happier auspices.

A second of the writer's stories is this:

At the Chapel Hill post there was a small open chestnut-grove between the French and English pickets, which was not occupied by either party during the day; but at night sentries were pushed forward close to each other amongst the trees. One fine moonlight night our advanced sentry called the attention of Colonel Alexander to the French sentry in his front, who was distinctly seen in the moonlight leaning against a tree, and fast asleep, with his musket by his side. Alexander went quietly up to him, and took possession of the musket, and then awoke him. The man at first was much frightened upon finding himself disarmed and in the hands of an English officer. Alexander gave him back his firelock, merely remarking that it was fortunate for him that he had found him asleep on his post, instead of one of his own officers. The poor fellow expressed the greatest gratitude; and, by way of excuse for such an unsoldierlike act, said that, his regiment having been removed from the extreme left of the French army, he had been marching for some hours through bad cross-roads, and having been immediately put upon outpost duty, he was overcome by fatigue.

Shortly after the Battle of Nive, (to add another story by the same officer), Colonel Alexander, in returning from the front on a very dark, stormy night, missed his way, and his horse falling over a bank, both horse and rider came clattering down heels over head into a lane, and close to a French sentry, who instantly challenged. Alexander hearing the *'Qui vive!'* and the click of the musket, thought that he was going to fire, and called out: '*C'est l'officier du poste Anglais—ne tirez pas!*'

'*Non, non, mon colonel,*' replied the sentry at once. '*J'espère que vous n'êtes pas blessé!*' The same corps was in our front at this time that had been opposed to us at Chapel Hill, where Alexander had awoke the sentry who was sleeping on his post; and if that story was known amongst the man's comrades, it may possibly have been the reason of the Frenchman's forbearance in the present instance.

It was at the same post, (adds our friend of the Rifles), that, one day, seeing a French officer coming towards us, another officer and myself went out to meet him. He said that he was aware that Prince R—— belonged to that part of our army, and inquired whether the prince happened to be then on outpost. We answered that he was so, and was, moreover, field-officer of the day, and that we would punctually deliver any message that he might have for him. He replied: 'Well, then, I have most important news for him: there has been a great battle fought in the north of Europe, in which his elder brother has been killed, and the prince serving in your army is now the head of his family.' A few days after this occurrence I was informed that Prince R—— had obtained leave to return to Germany for the purpose of looking after his affairs.

Napier tells this story of the good feeling and generous trust established between the Light Division—to which, as has been said, he belonged—and the French soldiers. It was immediately after the Battles of the Pyrenees, when Wellington was across the French frontier:

> On December 9 the 43rd were assembled within twenty yards of a French out-sentry, yet he continued his beat for an hour without concern, relying so confidently on the customary system as to place his knapsack on the ground. When the order to advance was given, one of the British soldiers told him to go away, and helped him to replace his pack before the firing commenced. Next morning the French in like manner warned a 43rd sentry to retire.
>
> At another time, Lord Wellington, desirous to gain the top of a hill occupied by the enemy near Bayonne, ordered his escort of riflemen to drive the French away, and, seeing the soldiers stealing up too close as he thought, called out to fire; but with

a loud voice one of those veterans replied, 'No firing!' Holdng up the butt of his rifle towards the French, he tapped it in a peculiar way, and at the private signal, which meant, 'we must have the hill for a short time,' the French, who could not maintain it, yet would not have relinquished it without a fight if they had been fired upon, quietly retired; yet this signal would never have been made if the post had been one capable of a permanent defence, so well did those veterans understand war and its proprieties.

Other stories are related by officers of incidents on the French frontier, during the temporary cessation of active operations owing to the severity of the stormy weather.

"During this period of mutual repose," says one, "the French officers and ours soon became intimate. We used to meet at a narrow part of the river (the Adour) and talk over the campaign. They would never believe (or pretended not to believe) the reverses of Napoleon in Germany; and when we received the news of the Orange Boven affair in Holland, they said it was impossible to convince them. One of our officers took the *Star* newspaper, rolled a stone up in it, and attempted to throw it across the river; unfortunately, the stone went through, and the paper fell into the water. The French officer very quietly said, in tolerably good English:'Your good news is very soon damped!"

This is another story of a similar type:

During the campaign we had often experienced the most gentleman-like conduct from the French officers. Once, when we were upon our alarm-post at break of day, a fine hare was seen playing in a cornfield between the outposts. A brace of greyhounds were very soon unslipped, when, after an excellent course, poor puss was killed within the French lines. The officer to whom the dogs belonged, bowing to the French officer, called off the dogs, but the Frenchman politely sent the hare, with a message and his compliments, saying that we required it more than they did!

A very amusing story of the interval of temporary quietude is told by an officer of the 28th—the "Slashers"—Colonel Cadell:[7]

A daring fellow, an Irishman named Tom Patten, performed a singlular feat. At the barrier there was a rivulet, along which

---

7. *The Slashers* by Tom Cadell, (also published by Leonaur.)

our lines of sentries were posted. To the right was a thick low wood, and during the cessation of hostilities our officers had again become intimate with those of the French, and the soldiers had actually established a traffic in tobacco and brandy in the following ingenious manner: A large stone was placed in that part of the rivulet, screened by the wood opposite to the French sentry, on which our people used to put a canteen with a quarter-dollar, for which it was very soon filled with brandy. One afternoon, about dusk, Patten had put down his canteen with the usual money in it and retired, but, though he returned several times, no canteen was there. He waited till the moon rose, but still he found nothing on the stone. When it was near morning Tom thought he saw the same sentry who was there when he put his canteen down; so he sprang across the stream, seized the unfortunate Frenchman, wrested his firelock from him, and, actually shaking him out of his accoutrements, re-crossed, vowing he would keep them until he got his canteen of brandy, and brought them to the picket-house.

Two or three hours afterwards, just as we were about to fall in, an hour before daybreak, the sergeant came to say that a flag of truce was at the barrier. I instantly went down, when I found the officer of the French picket in a state of great alarm, saying that a most extraordinary circumstance had occurred (relating the adventure), and saying that if the sentry's arms and accoutrements were not given back, his own commission would be forfeited, as well as the life of the poor sentry.

A sergeant was instantly sent to see if they were in the picket-house, when Patten came up scratching his head, saying: 'He had them in pawn for a canteen of brandy and a quarter-dollar.' He told us the story in his way, whereupon the things were immediately given over to the French Captain, who, stepping behind, put two five-*franc* pieces into Patten's hand. Tom, however, was not to be bribed by an enemy, but generously handed the money to his officer, requesting that he would insist on the French captain taking the money back.

The Frenchman was delighted to get the firelock and the accoutrements back, and the joy of the poor fellow who was stripped of them may be conceived, as, if it had been reported, he would certainly have been shot by sentence of court martial in less than forty-eight hours.

"To the very end," writes one of the men of the 95th, "we kept up an excellent private feeling on both sides at the outposts. As an instance, although I must remark a general order had been promulgated prohibiting all intercourse with the enemy on pain of death, our company was on picket near a dwelling called Garrett's House, when we clubbed half a dollar each, and sent a man into the French picket-house to purchase brandy. It was, I recollect, Christmas night. Grindle, the name of the man who was our messenger, staying longer than was usual, we became alarmed, and imagining that something must have happened, sent two other men in quest of him. These learnt from the nearest French sentry that Grindle was lying drunk in their picket-house. Fearful that the circumstance should come to the knowledge of Lieutenant Gardiner, the officer of our picket, they went and brought Grindle back with them, quite drunk. Just as they were emerging from the French lines who should ride down to the front but Sir James Kempt, who commanded our division at that time. He instantly ordered Grindle to be confined; but he was fortunate to escape with only a slight punishment."

This story may be added. The incident occurred after Wellington had crossed the Spanish frontier into France, while the troops were facing each other, awaiting orders for their last battle. Wellington had just before issued instructions that the amenities between the outposts were to be put a stop to; but they had gone almost as far as was possible already.

"Before this order was issued," says an officer, "the most unbounded confidence subsisted between us, and which it was a pity to put a stop to, except for such weighty reasons. They used to get such things as we wanted from Bayonne, particularly brandy, which was cheap and plentiful; and we, in return, gave them occasionally a little tea, of which some of them had learned to be very fond. Some of them, also, who had been prisoners of war in England, sent letters through our army-post to their sweethearts in England, our people receiving the letters and forwarding them.

"The next day, there being no firing between us and those in our front, three French officers, seemingly anxious to prove how far politeness and good breeding could be carried between the two nations when war did not compel them to be unfriendly, took a table and some chairs out of a house which was immediately in our front, and one which we had lately occupied as barrack, and bringing them down into the middle of the field which separated the advance of the two armies, sat down within 100 yards of our picket, and drank wine, holding up their glasses, as much as to say 'Your health' every time they drank. Of course we did not molest them, but allowed them to have their frolic out. During the day, also, we saw soldiers of the three nations—*viz.*, English, Portuguese, and French—all plundering at the same time in one unfortunate house, where our pie, our pig, and wine had been left. It stood about 150 or 200 yards below the church, on a sort of neutral ground between the two armies; hence the assemblage at the same moment of such a group of these motley marauders. They plundered in perfect harmony, no one disturbing the other on account of his nation or colour!"

It was during the final operations of the campaign on the French frontier that this very remarkable occurrence took place, related by one of our officers who was looking on:

> During the operations in the Pyrenees Soult was observed one day to be moving in front of our right centre. Wellington took the move for a reconnaissance. As soon as the French marshal saw us making preparations to receive him, he sent a flag of truce to demand cessation of hostilities, saying he wanted to shoot an officer and several men for atrocities committed on the farmers and peasants of the country. The execution took place in view of both armies, and a terrible lesson it was!

Last of all we have these two pictures of the way our soldiers were received in Southern France, among the people of the enemy's land.

One is from an officer of the 52nd, in the Light Division, Lieutenant George Gawler:

> We were cantoned in a town in Gascony, called Castel Sarrasin, beautifully situated near the junction of the Tarn and Garonne. It was principally inhabited by respectable, well-informed people, always ready to show hospitality to strangers, and particularly attached to the Bourbon family. From our soldiers having behaved remarkably well from our first arrival in the country we were, of course, received with open arms. We had scarcely been in the town a week when we were completely domesticated; the soldiers, surprised at a reception so different to what

they were accustomed to in Spain, took every method of showing their gratitude. On market-days they assisted their hosts in carrying the goods to the Place Publique, and in their leisure hours nursed the children with all the affection of brothers. The officers were equally comfortable.

Each family took it in turn to have its little party, and once a week the whole neighbourhood assembled to a grand ball, which (thanks to the spirits of the French ladies) seldom finished before morning. The beauty of the season often allowed us to have *fêtes champêtres* on the verdant banks of the Garonne. There was nothing but pleasure; care never dared to make his appearance. Even the charms of our native country were forgotten in this terrestrial paradise.

The second is an amusing description of his experiences by a sergeant of the 40th, William Lawrence:[8]

We were generally billeted on the inhabitants during our halts—they could not have behaved better to us if they had been our own countrymen, and I well remember how at the last stage where we put up before coming to Bordeaux, two of us, myself and a private of the same company, were billeted at quite a gentleman's house, the owners of which were unusually kind to us.

We found we had completely jumped into clover, and fortunately it happened to be Saturday night, so that our halt was till Monday morning—not that Sunday in those times had been used to make much difference to us, for two of our bloodiest conflicts had happened on that day; but in this case, our haste not being urgent, it gave us a kind of sweet repose.

As soon as we arrived at our house we were shown into our room, which was a very nice one and beautifully furnished; and when we had taken off our accoutrements, we went downstairs to a sort of bathroom, where we had a good wash in tubs of water that were placed in readiness for us. Then the gentleman had some clean stockings brought up to us, and when we had made ourselves comfortable, he sent up to our room a loaf of bread and a large bottle of wine, holding about three pints, which we found most acceptable, and, it not being long before the family's dinner was ready, our hostess would insist on our dining

---

8. *Sergeant Lawrence* by William Lawrence, (also published by Leonaur).

with them. For my own part, not being used to such pomp and never having before even seen it, I would sooner have crept out of the invitation; but, being pressed, we consented, and having been shown into the dining-room, we sat down to an excellent repast, with nobody else but the lady and gentleman.

The table was laid out most gorgeously with glittering silver, which came very awkward to our clumsy hands, as we had been more accustomed to using our fingers for some years, to set off which gorgeousness our waiter wore an out-of-the-way fine and ugly dress, with his hair plastered up with white powder, of which I had such an aversion during the first part of my stay in the army. A most palatable dinner was served, of which I freely partook, though I had very little idea of what it consisted; and some good wine was likewise often handed round, with which our glasses were constantly kept filled.

After dinner was over the white-headed gentleman entered with coffee, a fashion which then surprised us very much; but, nevertheless, more out of compliment than because we needed it, we took a cup each, with some sugar-candy, which was also handed round to sweeten it. When that was finished, just to keep us still going, the gentleman asked us if we smoked, and on our saying we both did, the bell was rung, and the footman entered with tobacco. We then took a pipe with the gentleman, the lady having previously retired into the drawing-room. Then, getting more used to the distinguished style, and the wine no doubt having made us more chatty, we for a time thoroughly enjoyed ourselves with our pipes, and began to feel new men with all our grandeur.

We were next invited to partake of tea in the drawing-room, but, being very tired, we begged to be excused; and this being granted, the bed-candles being rung for, and having wished him goodnight, we went to our room, and there had a hearty laugh over the evening's business, though we had not been able to understand half what the gentleman said, not being used to the French as well as the Spanish language. We retired to rest in a fine feather-bed, which, being a luxury we had not seen for years, was consequently too soft for our hard bones, and we found we could not sleep, owing to the change. My comrade soon jumped out of bed, saying: 'I'll be bothered, sergeant, I can't sleep here!'

'No,' said I, 'no more can I.' So we prepared our usual bed by wrapping ourselves into a blanket, and then, with a knapsack as a pillow, we lay on the floor, and soon sank into a profound slumber.

18

Triumphant Vittoria and the Royal Spoil

Vittoria, Wellington's crowning triumph of the war, the battle that decided the fate of Spain and hurled the crown from the head of Joseph Bonaparte, presented the British Army with, in addition to amazing spoil, as fine trophies as were won on a battlefield—King Joseph's Sword of State and the *bâton* of the French Marshal in command. Both these trophies are at the present time in the possession of His Majesty the King at Windsor Castle.

Only one other *bâton* of a Marshal of Napoleon ever found its way into an enemy's hands. The Russians possess that—the *bâton* of Marshal Davout, found by a Cossack plunderer in the Marshal's travelling carriage amid the snows of the Moscow retreat.

A yet bigger prize still, though, all but came to Wellington at Vittoria—King Joseph himself. The "King of Spain and the Indies" evaded capture by just a hair's breadth, so to speak. His personal agility and a fast horse was all that saved King Joseph from going to London in the same ship with his State Sword and Marshal Jourdan's *bâton*. The 10th Prince of Wales Own Hussars it was who so nearly had the honour of making the capture.

That all but successful *coup* was the culminating incident, indeed, of the day's events at Vittoria, of a day of combat brimful of dramatic happenings. The great battle-drama of Vittoria was nearing the close of its last act when Sir Colquhoun Grant, a Major-General then, and the leader at Vittoria of Wellington's Hussar Brigade, received the order to advance.

These are some of the glimpses through the battle-smoke, as it were, that one gets during the hours of hard fighting on that longest day of the year, exactly 100 years ago, (as at time of first publication),—that Sunday, June 21, 1813. It was in the early forenoon that the first gun was fired.

Take first of all, at the outset of the day, a glance round at the scene across the field before the battle, as some of our officers and men saw things.

The British troops stood to arms at all points before daybreak, and moved forward in the dark from their bivouacs. They had camped during the night at a short distance outside the valley of the Zadora River, near which the city of Vittoria stands, and where the French army was in occupation.

"A magnificent panorama of the pomp and circumstance of glorious war," is how one officer speaks of the marshalling by torchlight and moving off of the columns as they started for the battlefield, while martial sounds filled the air all round: "the neighing of the cavalry horses, the roll of the tumbrils and gun-arriages, the distant yet distinct words of command, the mingling music of many bands, the trumpets of the Horse, the bugles of the Rifles, the hoarse wailing of the war-pipes of the Highland regiments ever and anon swelling on the breeze, pealing among the heights of Puebla and dying away among the vales of Zadora."

"There was a little light rain about daybreak, followed by some mist and fog, but that did not last, and then it became fine and clear." "The morning was extremely brilliant: a clearer or more beautiful atmosphere never favoured the progress of a gigantic conflict." So two other officers who were there describe.

Sir Rowland Hill's corps of 20,000 men, in round numbers, with twenty guns, moved forward on the right. Their orders were to advance by the Puebla pass and heights, a range of steep and rugged hills to the south of the valley, and attack the French left wing. Hill was to hold the enemy fast while General Graham, with another 20,000 men and twenty guns, marched round at the back of the mountain-range to the north of the valley to outflank and drive in the French right wing and seize the Bayonne road, barring thus the enemy's only line of retreat towards the Pyrenees and France. Wellington himself commanded in the centre, having there the Light Division, and the Third, Fourth, and Seventh Divisions, and all the cavalry—some 30,000 men. The personnel of the three corps was made up, with additions of Portuguese and Spanish regulars and light troops, to a grand total of 90,000 of all arms.

On the French side King Joseph and Marshal Jourdan had from 60,000 to 70,000 men on the field, and 152 guns. Wellington had the advantage of numbers in men, but the French were very considerably the superior in artillery.

The enemy had been in position since the day before. They "occupied a line of nearly eight miles, the extreme left placed upon the heights of La Puebla, and the right resting on an eminence above the villages of Abechuco and Gamorra Mayor. The centre was posted along a range of hills on the left bank of the river; while a strong corps, resting its right flank on the left centre, was formed on the bold high grounds which rise behind the village of Subijana. The Reserve was placed at the village of Gomecha, and the banks of the Zadora and a small wood between the centre and the right were thickly lined with *tirailleurs*. . . . That part of the position near the village of Gomecha, having been considered by Jourdan his most vulnerable point, was defended by numerous artillery. The bridges were fortified; the communications from one part of the position to the other were direct; a deep river ran in front, the great roads to Bayonne and Pampeluna in the rear."

In rear of the lines of French soldiers, in Vittoria itself and beyond, was massed a vast assemblage of convoys from all over Spain—hundreds of wagons laden with treasure and stores, and public and private plunder, the produce of the five years of the French occupation of Spain, together with vehicles conveying the whole Court of King Joseph, or packed with the wives, mistresses, and children of officers and civilian officials. All were intermingled with a huge horde—some mounted, some on foot—of commissaries and sutlers, camp-followers and traders, and other non-combatants, besides great droves of pack-horses and other beasts of burden, sheep, and cattle.

The French were evacuating Spain *en masse,* under pressure of Wellington's persistent advance—in a manner like the Israelites as they left Egypt on their march to the Red Sea with Pharaoh's army following in pursuit. They had been for days on the retreat as far as Vittoria, and were now all jammed together in confusion, crowded in the narrow streets and on the plain beyond the walls, while struggling to file off along the one road to the north, which was their only means of getting away to safety.

This was our first view of the enemy as Wellington's divisions in the centre took up their posts.

"The dark and formidable masses of the French were prepared at

An engraving of on the battlefield of Vittoria

all points to repel the meditated attack: the infantry in column with loaded arms or ambushed thickly in the low woods at the base of their position; the cavalry in line with drawn swords; the artillery frowning from the eminences with lighted matches. On our side," adds the narrator, in describing what he saw, "all was yet quietness and repose; the chiefs were making their observations and the men walking about in groups amidst the piled arms, chatting and laughing and gazing, and apparently not caring a pin for the fierce hostile array in front."

"We could see," so another observer notes, "a white standard on the right of the enemy's centre, where King Joseph had his headquarters. Generals and mounted officers were riding about, and now and then occasionally guns were fired at some of our reconnoitring patrols. Among us there was the hammering of flints and loosening of cartridges, the rattle of guns and tumbrils careering up to take position, and the galloping of *aides-de-camp*."

"Lord Wellington, meanwhile," as one of the staff-officers tells, "was on foot, on an eminence considerably elevated above the Zadora line, on its right bank, and nearly opposite the village of Arinez, busy watching Hill with his glass. He was dressed in a short grey great-coat, closely buttoned over his embroidered Spanish sash; a plumed hat alone denoted his rank." Wellington continued at that point during the opening stages of the battle, "observing the progress of the fight and directing the movements of the divisions as calmly as if he were inspecting the movements at a review."

This, by way of contrast for one moment, is something else that one of the officers close beside Wellington in the early morning, Sir Augustus Frazer, of the Horse Artillery, saw:

> We had a full view of both armies. Between both, and while closing to engage, an old woman and her two boys were gathering vegetables in a field with philosophical composure!

Towards noon came Wellington's appointed hour for the move forward of the British centre divisions, as the distant thunder of Graham's opening guns, and "a curling smoke faintly seen far up the Zadora on the enemy's extreme right," told that the all-important flanking movement was making progress.

"The men stood to their arms. 'With ball-cartridge prime and load!'" was the word then given. All levity and mirth passed away from their countenances, and an expression of grave determination took their place.

Picton's men led the main attack in the centre; storming the hill of Arinez, the key of the enemy's first position, and then advancing to fling the enemy roughly back from King Joseph's second line at Gomecha. They were brought into the battle without waiting for Wellington to give the word: not exactly as Wellington had designed. Picton broke away like a leashed hound tearing himself loose. He was in a characteristic mood that morning. "Old Picton came up," describes Kincaid of the 95th Rifles in the Light Division, who saw the "Fighting Third" reach their ground, "riding at the head of the Third Division, dressed in a blue coat and a round hat, swearing as roundly all the way as if he wore two cocked ones."

Picton had been made to wait for two other divisions to arrive, until his short patience could stand the delay no longer. The men were spoiling for fight, eager and boiling over, and Picton lost his temper. "D—n it!" he exclaimed furiously, "Lord Wellington must have forgotten us." The stick Picton always carried on horseback, and with which in battle he used, while watching the fighting, to keep time to the firing, "fell on the horse's mane often and savagely as he kept riding backwards and forwards, looking out for the arrival of an *aide-de-camp*."

One came galloping to the spot at length, and, reining up, asked Picton if he knew where Lord Dalhousie was with the Seventh Division—one of the divisions for which Picton had been directed to wait. Irritated by the question, Picton answered back sharply: "No, sir, I have not seen his lordship. Have you any orders for me, sir?"

"None, Sir Thomas!"

"Then, sir, what orders do you bring?"

"Why, that as soon as Lord Dalhousie with the Seventh Divison shall commence an attack on that bridge"—pointing to one on the left—"the Fourth and Sixth are to support him."

It was too much! That another division should attack in front of his "Fighting Third!" The idea was more than Picton could stand. He burst forth in a fierce passion: "You may tell Lord Wellington from me, sir, that the Third Division shall, in less than ten minutes, attack that bridge and carry it, and the Fourth and Sixth Divisions may support if they choose." On that Picton spurred off to head his "fighting villains"—one of his names for his men—into the battle.

The Third Division went forward with the Light Division, the Fourth, Sixth, and Seventh coming up in the nick of time to take part in the attack. Wellington, from not far off, marked the move forward.

With a cavalcade of staff-officers at his heels he came galloping across to give them a lead. To the 95th Rifles, who headed the charge on the conical hill and village of Arinez, across the river right in front, Wellington called, as he rode forward near them: "That's right, my lads, keep up a good fire!" Stopped at one point by a high brick wall, on one side of which the French clustered thickly, the Rifles had a desperate hand-to-hand fight to get across. "So close were the combatants," describes Kincaid, who was in the thick of it, "that any person who chose to put his head over from either side was sure of getting a sword or bayonet up his nostrils."

To the Rifles fell the first French gun taken at Vittoria. It was after the storming of Arinez and just beyond the village. A Lieutenant Fitzmaurice took the gun. He saw a French battery hurriedly retreating on a road nearby and raced off, with the men of his company close behind him, to intercept it. The men, however, who were in heavy marching order, could not keep up with their more lightly-equipped leader, and when Fitzmaurice got to the road only two privates were with him. Five guns of the French battery had galloped past. The young officer at once sprang daringly at the leading horses of the sixth gun and caught one by the head. The driver blazed off his pistol in Fitzmaurice's face, but, luckily, just missed him, the bullet going through the young officer's cap. Fitzmaurice held on pluckily, and the next moment his men fired and shot down one of the centre horses of the team, which brought the gun to a standstill. Immediately afterwards the rest of the company came rushing up, and the gun was seized and the gunners made prisoners.

On the right, meanwhile, Sir Rowland Hill, in a resistless onsweep, stormed the heights of Puebla. "The ascent," says an officer, looking on from a short way off, "was so steep that while moving up it they looked as if they were lying on their faces and crawling." The 71st had the lion's share of the fighting at first and nobly did their work. Their colonel, one of the finest officers who ever buckled on sword, the Hon. Henry Cadogan, fell in the fight, mortally wounded. "Carry me to where I can see how the battle goes," were his words to those who first ran to his aid. He was borne to some high ground near whence his dying eyes could watch the scene.

At the last, when vision failed him, on hearing some cheers, he asked what they meant. He was told that the enemy were giving way. "God bless my brave fellows!" he exclaimed, and the next moment all was over. "My grief for the loss of Cadogan," wrote Wellington, after the battle, "takes away all my satisfaction at our success." So deadly for the 71st was the contest at the storming of the Puebla heights that not one man in three escaped either death or wounds. In the words of one of them: "There were only 300 of us on the height able to do duty out of 1,000 who drew rations that morning."

The 28th,[1] while holding the village of Subijana de Alava, which they had had a share in capturing, had to shoot the French out of the trees of a wood nearby; bringing them down like pheasants knocked over while roosting in covert. "Directly in front of the village which we defended," says one of the "Slashers," "there was a thick olive wood. We had a number of men knocked down, but could not see where the fire came from, until at last a Frenchman was seen to fall out of one of the trees, which explained the mystery. We instantly opened a sharp fire into the thickest part of the wood, which brought them down in great numbers."

A similar experience, it may be mentioned by the way, is on record for another regiment earlier in the war—at Vimiero. There, the 43rd, discovering the French up the trees of a wood from some way off, charged forward and "carried the grove, before those 'sweet little cherubs that sat up aloft' could get down and join their retreating comrades, shooting them down like rooks, at least till they saw the game was up and called for quarter."

To get to the wood Hill's men had to push their way through cornfields with the grain standing breast-high. "A field of corn, standing just four or five feet high and just ready for the sickle, was between us and the wood," describes Captain L'Estrange of the 31st, "and as we advanced through it, besides the bullets from the wood, an occasional cannon-ball rolled along through, its course being easily seen by the lowering of the ears of corn as if reaped. As they rolled through it, I felt as if I could have stopped some of these balls with my foot, they appeared to roll so slowly. Fortunately for me, I did not try the experiment, as the loss of a leg would have ensued."

"Beyond the wood," as L'Estrange relates again, giving a personal experience, "when we emerged at the opposite side, we saw the dark line of the French army, still in their position, within point-blank distance. A perfect hailstorm of bullets was poured down upon us, which, if it had lasted, must have swept us all into eternity. But we pushed for-

---

1. *Private O'Neil*, by Charles O'Neil, the recollections of an Irish rogue of H. M. 28th Regt. the "Slashers", during the Peninsula & Waterloo Campaigns of the Napoleonic Wars, also published by Leonaur.

ward, and the French turned. I ran on frantically to the front, screaming at the top of my voice, 'Come on, 31st' which cry could not have reached the ears of the half of my company in consequence of the roar of the battle. But these brave fellows did not require to be called upon to advance; the only difficulty was to keep them back."

General Graham, with his flanking column on the left, after a furious give-and-take fight at the bridges of Ariaga and Gamorra Mayor during the afternoon, crossed the Zadora and successfully stood astride of the Bayonne road, barring the French retreat exactly as Wellington had planned.

His men on their side had severe fighting; in particular at a bridge where the high road to Bilbao crossed near Gamorra Mayor, which the French made furious and repeated efforts to regain. The village had been barricaded and entrenched, and was strongly held, but a brigade of the Fifth Division stormed it, regardless of the hot artillery and musketry fire which faced them, without firing a shot in reply. After being twice repulsed, they carried the bridge with the bayonet, taking three guns. "The regiments, exposed to a heavy fire of musketry and artillery, did not take a musket from the shoulder until they carried the village. The enemy brought forward his reserves and made many desperate efforts to retake the bridge, but could not succeed. This was repeated until the bridge became so heaped with dead and wounded that they were rolled over the parapet into the river below."

Nearby, Vandeleur's Brigade of the Light Division, which had been sent along the river to lend a hand, captured another fortified village on the French left, and also two batteries of artillery. The 52nd Oxfordshires led here, "deployed into line as if at Shorncliffe," with the Riflemen "five or six deep, keeping up a fire nothing could resist."

"After that," as one of the 52nd also records, "we rushed at the village, and though the ground was intersected by gardens and ditches, nothing ever checked us until we reached the rear of the village, where we halted to re-form—the twelve guns, tumbrils, horses, etc., standing in our possession." Not far off at the same time "in a wild *mêlée* the 87th carried the village of Hermanadad."

To the last the French resisted with stubborn endurance, holding out for more than five fierce hours. Some of the British batteries, indeed, in that time used up their shot and shell. "To add to the confusion of the enemy," says an officer, "towards the end the commandant of Artillery actually directed the nearest guns to keep up a fire of blank cartridge."

Wellington from first to last pressed his centre attack strenuously, advancing for over six miles across rough and difficult country: "over broken ground, forming lines, columns, or threading the windings of the difficult paths, according to the nature of the country or the opposition of the enemy." Steadily the British in that part of the field bore down the fierce efforts the enemy repeatedly made to force them back. The centre divisions, moving steadily forward, kept charging the French alternately. Their order all through was magnificent.

"The alignment was taken up," says a lieutenant of the 52nd, speaking of the steadiness of his regiment, which may be taken as typical of all, "with the same precision as on a field-day, and a beautiful line was formed; the enemy's balls knocking a file out at every discharge, the sergeants in rear calling out 'Who got that?' and entering their names on the list of casualties."

All through the day, continually in front, Wellington exposed himself freely, at times riding directly across the fire-swept zone under the incessant cannonading of the French artillery.

> Through this tremendous fire Lord Wellington had to pass as he galloped.... His route being nearly in a parallel line, he ran the gauntlet of about eighty pieces of cannon, and fortunately escaped untouched.

Vittoria, it may be added, was Copenhagen's first battle with Wellington on his back. Wellington had not long before bought his famous charger from Sir Charles Stewart.

The troops in the centre fought their way forward from Arinez across those fiercely contested six miles step by step. In places they were hard put to it at times, some of them, to hold the ground they had won against the enemy's repeated counter-attacks; but comrades were ever at hand to assist or reinforce, and the stubbornly resisting French were steadily pressed back. This, as one who was at Vittoria witnessed it, is how the battle in the centre took shape in the course of the afternoon:

> The Fourth Division pushed back the left centre of the French, and were fighting successfully and performing prodigies of valour among crags and broken ground. The Seventh Division came in contact with the enemy's right centre, which resisted so desperately, and galled them from a wood and windows of houses with such showers of bullets, that victory for a short time was doubtful. However, the Second Brigade of the Light

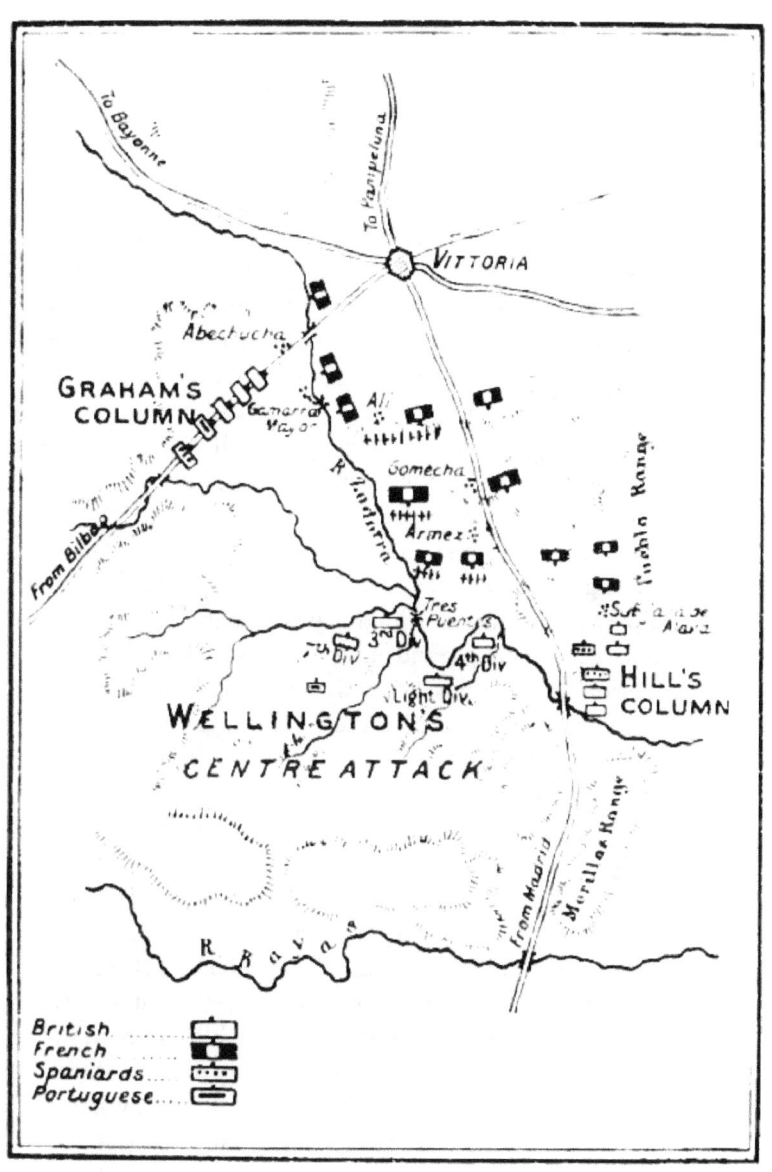

The Battle of Vittoria June 21, 1813

Division coming up, fresh and with closed ranks, assisted by the Sixth Division, broke through all opposition at a run and routed the enemy at the point of the bayonet. The four divisions of the centre continued to gain ground, shooting forward alternately, leaving the killed and wounded scattered over a great extent of country. At six o'clock in the evening, by a sort of running fight, with hard contests at certain points, the centre of the army had gained five miles in this amphitheatre.

At half-past six we were within one mile of Vittoria. The French army now drew up and showed such an imposing front that our left centre, facing Ali, was completely kept at bay, owing to the blazing of 100 pieces of cannon vomiting forth death and destruction to all who advanced against them. This roaring of artillery continued for more than an hour on both sides with unabated vigour The smoke rolled up in such clouds that we could no longer distinguish the white town of Vittoria,

During this momentous struggle the centre of the French covered a bare hill and continued for a considerable time immovable, pouring their musketry into the now thinned ranks of the Third Division, it was doubtful whether the latter would be able to keep their ground under such a deadly fire from very superior numbers, but they maintained this dangerous post with heroic firmness, having led the van throughout the battle. At this period of the action it was absolutely necessary to strain every nerve to win it before nightfall.

The Fourth Division on our right shot forward against a sugarloaf hill and broke a French division, who retired up it in a confused mass, firing over each other's heads, without danger to themselves, owing to the steepness of the ascent. I was laughing at this novel method of throwing bullets when one struck me on the sash and fell at my feet, thereby cooling my ardour for a short time. However, when a little recovered from my pain, I picked it up and put the precious piece of lead in my pocket.

The scene that now presented itself was magnificently grand: the valley resounded with confused sounds like those of a volcanic eruption, and was crowded with red bodies of infantry and the smoking artillery.

The enemy sacrificed all their cannon with the exception of eight pieces, while withdrawing the right of their army behind the left wing under cover of this tremendous cannonade, which was the only chance left them to quit the field in a compact body. The left wing retired by *échelon* of divisions and brigades from the right, while delivering then fire. Their last division quitted the field with nearly empty cartridge-boxes. They managed to drag their eight pieces of artillery across the fields for nearly a league, but coming to marshy ground they stuck fast, and three of them rolled into a ditch, with mules struggling to disentangle themselves from their harness.

Two pieces only the enemy carried out of action, owing to the roads being so blocked up with wagons. "To prevent their being immediately used," adds another British officer, "the French cannon were in many instances thrown into the ditches and narrow ravines, where, overturned and mixed with tumbrils and the bodies of dead and wounded soldiers, they presented unusually marked indications of defeat and evidence of the consequently secured victory already obtained."

Then came the British final advance.

"I heard a tremendous rush on our left," describes L'Estrange of the 31st, "the ground seemed actually to quake under me, and, looking in the direction of the sound, I saw the whole British host—artillery, cavalry, and infantry—throwing themselves on the line of the French army. Three or four regiments of cavalry were at the moment charging, and galloped up to the foot of the eminence on which the French line stood: it was too steep for the horses to ascend, and they were obliged to wheel. But the firm and uncompromising style in which the British army advanced was too much for the nerves of the French. They turned in retreat along their whole line, and the Battle of Vittoria was won."

The moment for the cavalry to do their work had arrived, and Wellington sent off an *aide-de-camp* at full gallop to summon up Sir Colquhoun Grant and his hussars.

> Reports were coming in of the guns taken, and that the French were hurrying through the town and giving way at all points. Long trains of wagons and beasts of burden were now seen issuing from Vittoria.

Wellington asked Leith Hay of his staff, who had been a prisoner in the hands of the French, and had been exchanged only that morning just before the firing opened, if the retreating carriages they saw were on the Irun road.

"On being told," records Leith Hay, "that it was the Pampeluna road they were on, and that Graham must have already cut off the retreat by the Bayonne road, Lord Wellington pressed the pursuit more animatedly still."

Sir Colquhoun Grant came up now at the head of the Hussar Brigade along the Camino Real at a rapid pace. He was told "to branch off to the left and charge the flying enemy."

The order was obeyed on the instant.

Making their way rapidly towards the left of the town, the 10th Hussars dashed forward, the foremost of the British light horse, and got to the city gate on that side close on the heels of the hindmost French infantry as they ran through. Many of the Frenchmen were overtaken and sabred before the gate was reached; some of them cut down as they ran, others after making a brave effort to sell their lives dearly.

"I saw," says an officer with the Horse Artillery, following closely after the cavalry rush, "more than one instance of desperate refusals to surrender. One poor fellow was at length cut down by three dragoons, who in vain required him to surrender."

The Prince's Hussars reached the gate before it could be shut, and rode through. King Joseph had passed that way not many minutes earlier. Getting into his travelling carriage, a roomy six-horsed *berline*, in front of the house where he had lodged on the night before, Joseph had hastily driven off, trampling a passage through the mob of fugitives in the streets, his mounted escort using their swords to clear the way. He was just passing the eastern gate of Vittoria, on the far side, as the 10th Hussars came clattering through the western gate.

Forward went the pursuing hussars at a rapid trot through the streets, hardly checked for a moment amid the confusion that was rampant on all sides, and being cheered by the Spanish townsfolk, frantically calling out to encourage them, and shouting down "*Vivas!*" from the windows of the houses. The hussars, making a turn to the right in the town, found their way quickly to the Pampeluna gate and out on to the main road beyond.

There they immediately came on an immense, jumbled together crowd of vehicles of all descriptions and sizes—carriages and carts, tumbrils and baggage-wagons, intermixed and jammed together in a hopeless block along the road, and for hundreds of yards to each side of it, as far as eye could reach, among a mob of transport animals and panic-stricken drivers, women, and followers, shouting and cursing and vociferating noisily as they thronged together in utter disorder and confusion.

The scene of chaos, indeed, almost beggared description. The ground "for nearly a square league" was "choked up with carriages filled with imploring ladies," as one of our officers saw it. "wagons with specie and ammunition, droves of cattle and sheep, goats and mules." Heavy *fourgons*, lettered "*Domaine Extérieure de S.M. l'Empereur,*" stopped the way in one place. At another stood a string of Spanish Court conveyances alongside of a huddled mass of commissariat-wagons and tumbrils, rows of powder and baggage wagons, carts laden with provisions and wine-casks, ox-carts heaped up with furniture or costly property, booty plundered by the French in all parts of Spain.

On every hand were carriages, carrying the wives and children of officers of rank and civil officials, or ladies who were not wives, the *femmes de campagne* of various people. Some of these poor things were wearing the garb of nuns, hapless young women torn by force from their convents, and doomed to attend the fortunes of their lovers amid the scenes of that awful evening. Not a few of the carriage occupants, some of them fashionably-dressed ladies, had abandoned their carriages in sheer fright at what was going on all around, and were to be seen, in a British officer's words, "scuttling about with tucked-up petticoats," and frantically entreating assistance, some of them holding shrieking children in their arms, others carrying lap-dogs, or parrots in cages, or monkeys.

Everywhere there was frantic terror. The guns of the pursuing army were thundering with shot and crashing shells on the retreating French battalions, and every minute the din of the firing was coming closer. "As the English shot," describes an eye-witness, "went booming overhead, the vast crowd of people started and swerved with a convulsive movement, while a dull and horrid sound of distress arose."

Already their chance of escape had gone. The enormous convoy trains, almost as they began to move, had had to halt. The road had got blocked some way ahead by an overturned wagon, bringing everything in rear to a standstill. It was a fearful moment for that surging, swarming mass of terrified non-combatants penned together there, and powerless either to go forward or to get back. The transport-men over yonder were labouring their hardest, and tugging with every muscle to drag the clumsy upset vehicle off the road, but time was against them. Unless, though, they were able to clear the heavily packed *fourgon* out of the way, it was impossible for a single wagon in real to get by. King Joseph, fortunately for him, so far, had passed the spot just before the great baggage-wagon went over.

In the midst of this scene it was that the British hussars suddenly appeared.

As the leading squadron of the 10th, headed by Captain Henry Wyndham and the Marques of Worcester, emerged clear of the city gate and moved forward for as far as they could get alongside the road, a body of French soldiers from nearby, part of the rearmost baggage guard, made at them to keep them off. The Frenchmen were charged and ridden down and dispersed on the spot, and several taken prisoners. The next moment, as the hussars were re-forming and securing the prisoners. The French dragoon regiment came unexpectedly on the scene in their rear. The copper helmets came out of the city through the same gate by which the 10th had come.

Apparently, the dragoons had been blocked in another street in Vittoria as the 10th Hussars passed through, and so now came out behind them. They began to form in rear of the hussars, as though about to attack them, when more of the enemy, a French column of infantry from somewhere else, also appeared, coming on in that direction. One of the battalions fired a hasty volley at the hussars and emptied a number of saddles, killing or wounding men and horses, but the troopers of the 10th did not flinch, it was impossible to charge owing to the ditches and broken ground. Then, the next moment, their assailants suddenly turned their backs and went off at a run alter the rest of the retreating army. The other squadrons of the 10th were close at hand by now, whereupon Captain Wyndham, with his own men, the leading squadron of the regiment, promptly again took up the pursuit, leaving the others to collect prisoners and follow.

Wyndham and his men were jostling their way forward near the high road, when, at a little distance ahead at one point, they caught sight of a huge vehicle on the road before them, galloping hurriedly forward with a cavalry escort. It was King Joseph, who was inside the big travelling-coach as it went jolting and swaying and rocking forward at a high speed, escaping in his *berline*, but that of course the British could hardly have guessed. They had not much time in the rush, although as they neared the coach the sight of the Royal Arms of Spain, with an *escutcheon* of pretence displaying the Napoleonic Eagle gaudily painted on the panels, might have told the tale.

Captain Wyndham, ahead of the troopers by a few yards, got up to the carriage first. The royal escort were mostly ahead at the moment, clearing a passage, it would seem. Wyndham had a pistol in his hand, and, racing up abreast of the door, he fired into the carriage through the near window. The next instant the opposite door flew open, and King Joseph bounded out into the road. Running in among his escort before any of the British could reach him, he was hastily helped up on to a spare horse and was off and away, with his guard closing in round him. The outriders bolted at the same time, and the carriage was stopped and made a prize of. A minute or two later the rest of the 10th Hussars came dashing up to the spot. After that all went forward again to take their part in the general pursuit, which was kept up until the coming on of night compelled a halt.

King Joseph's Sword of State was found by a Spanish officer in another of the royal carriages—there were three taken at Vittoria altogether—blocked on the road behind. In them and in the royal *berline* were also found, rolled up for transit, as they had been cut from their frames when Joseph left Madrid, the priceless art treasures now at Apsley House, among them some of the finest of the pictures of Velasquez, Coreggio, Murillo, and Titian. Wellington, at the close of the war, desired to hand them all over to the restored King of Spain, but Ferdinand, with magnificent courtesy, requested him as a personal favour to retain the entire collection.

"His Majesty, touched by your delicacy," wrote the Spanish Ambassador to Wellington in reply, "does not wish to deprive you of what has come into your possession by means as just as they were honourable." Wellington was formally requested to "let the matter rest where it stands and not refer to it further."

A clean sweep, indeed, was made of the royal belongings, State insignia and wardrobe; richly-embroidered velvet and satin garments, silken underwear, cut-glass scent bottles, a luxurious silver travelling-service and Sevres china plates and dishes. "King Joseph," in the words of one of Wellington's Staff, "that night had neither a knife or fork nor a clean shirt with him."

Paddy Shannon of the 87th, or a private of the same regiment, which of the two is not quite clear, got hold of Marshal Jourdan's *bâton* in ransacking the marshal's campaigning coach which was captured among the jammed together conglomeration of vehicles which fell into our hands on the Pampeluna road. The marshal got away just in time, going off wrapped up in a blanket. He was suffering from a severe attack of ague, and had had, indeed, to keep in his carriage on the battlefield all day, being too unwell to mount a horse. Jourdan had, though, to get into the saddle at the last moment to make his escape in the general stampede.

The finder of the *bâton* wrenched off the gold bands that tipped it at either end before handing it over to Colonel Gough of Barrosa fame, who commanded the 87th at Vittoria. It was handed round among Wellington's Staff next day, and Sir Augustus Frazer, who also saw it, describes it in a letter. "I have just seen Jourdan's *bâton* or staff of marshal: it is covered with blue velvet, is a foot or more long, and has thirty-two embroidered eagles on it. It is enclosed in a red Morocco case with silver clasps and eagles. At each end is printed in gold characters: '*Le Maréchal Jean-Baptiste Jourdan.*'"

"There is also," adds Sir A. Frazer, "a colour belonging to the '100me Régiment du Ligne, 4me Bataillon': the colour is a yard and a half square."

The *bâton*, together with the captured flag, was sent by Wellington to the Prince Regent, who, in return, conferred on the victor of Vittoria the rank of a British Field-Marshal and presented him with the "*Bâton* of England," a gold-plated staff, some twenty- four inches long, bearing the arms of Great Britain on it, and decorated with laurel and oak bands, plaited to form a series of diamond-shaped patterns with lions in the centre, the upper end being surmounted with a figure of St. George and the Dragon, and the lower end bearing the inscription: "From His Royal Highness George Augustus Frederic, Regent of the United Kingdom of Great Britain and Ireland, to Arthur, Marques of Wellington, K.G., Field-Marshal of England, 1813."

"Your glorious conduct," began the letter which accompanied the *bâton*, "is beyond all human praise, and far above my reward. I know no language the world affords worthy to express it. I feel I have nothing left to say, but most devoutly to offer up my prayers to Providence that it has, in its omnipotent bounty, blessed my country and myself with such a general."

Marshal Jourdan's *bâton* and the flag of the 100th of the Line were displayed in London at the Grand Banquet and Festival held at Vauxhall Gardens on July 20, at which the Princess of Wales and five Royal Princes, the Dukes of York, Clarence, Sussex, Cambridge, and Gloucester, attended, as well as the members of the Ministry and all the foreign Ambassadors in London. A bust of Wellington formed the centre of the elaborate scheme of decoration, draped in national flags, with Jourdan's *bâton* conspicuously placed beneath the bust. Close by, between two State trumpeters, stood a grenadier of the First Guards

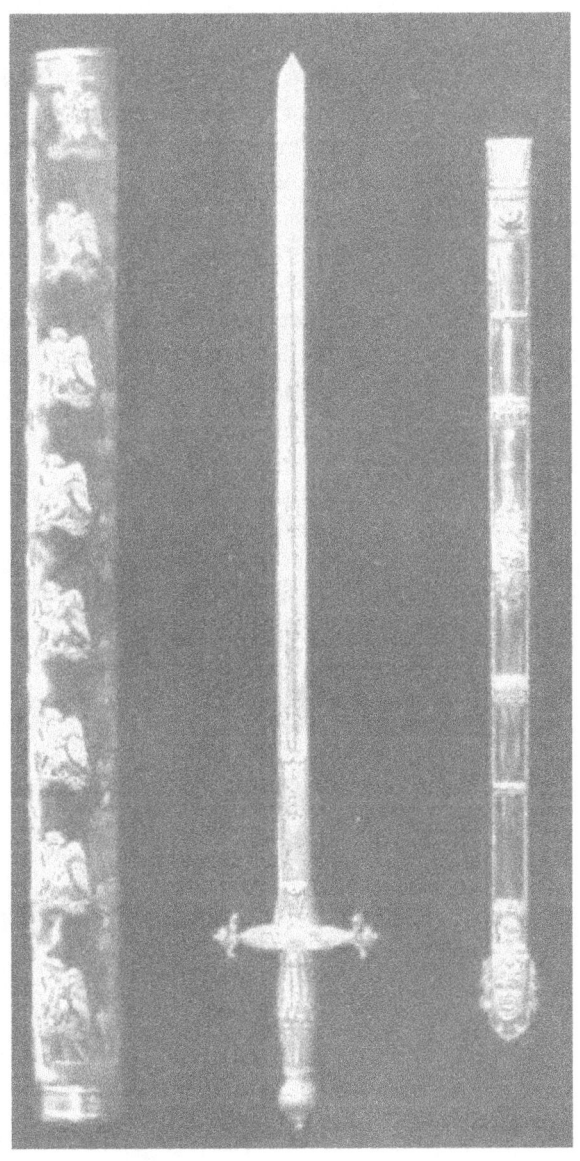

THE VITTORIA TROPHIES AT WINDSOR CASTLE
Marshal Jourdan's *bâton* (enlarged for detail)
and Joseph Baonaparte's sword.

holding the captured colour of the 100th of the Line.

Such is the story of Wellington's trophies from the crowning triumph of Vittoria now in the custodianship of His Majesty the King at Windsor Castle.

"Never before in modern times," says the historian Allison, "had such a prodigious accumulation of military stores and private wealth fallen to the lot of a victorious army. Marshal Jourdan's *bâton*, Joseph's private carriages and Sword of State, 151 brass guns, 415 caissons of ammunition, 1,300,000 ball-cartridges, 14,000 rounds of ammunition, and 40,000 pounds of gunpowder, constituted the military trophies of a victory, where 6,000 also were killed and wounded, and 1,000 prisoners taken. It at one blow destroyed the war-like efficiency of the French army, swept them like a whirlwind from the Spanish plains, and made Joseph's crown fall from his head. No estimate can be formed of the amount of private plunder which was taken on the field, but it exceeded anything in modern war; for it was not the produce of the sack of a city, or the devastation of a province, but the accumulated plunder of a kingdom during five years, joined to the arrears of pay of the invader's host for two, which was now at one fell swoop reft from the spoiler. Independent of private booty, no less than five millions and a half of dollars in the military chest of the army were taken; and of private wealth the amount was so prodigious, that for miles together the pursuers may be almost said to have marched upon gold and silver, without stooping to pick it up!"

19

Where Wellington's Trophies Are Now

(As at time of first publication-1912)

How many guns did Wellington's soldiers take from the enemy? Wellington himself did not know.

"Returning with him one day from the hunting- field,"" says Lord Ellesmere in his *Recollections*, "I asked him if he could form any calculation of the number of guns he had taken in the course of his career. 'No,' he said, 'not with any accuracy; somewhere about 3,000 I should guess. At Oporto, after the passage of the Douro, I took the entire siege-train of the enemy; at Vittoria and Waterloo I took every gun they had in the field. What, however, is more extraordinary, I don't think I ever lost a gun in my life. After the battle of Salamanca,' Wellington went on to explain, 'three of my guns attached to some Portuguese cavalry were captured in a trifling affair near Madrid, but they were recovered next day. In the Pyrenees Lord Hill found himself obliged to throw eight or nine guns over a precipice, but those also were recovered, and never fell into the enemy's hands at all.'"

How many of Wellington's 3,000 trophy cannon are in existence now? A dozen? Hardly as many. There are four French field-guns from Vittoria and Waterloo displayed as trophies in the grounds of Chelsea. There is one kept as a curiosity at the Rotunda on Woolwich Common. Apparently, the only other artillery trophy existing is the great Cadiz mortar on the parade by the Horse Guards—the "Prince Regent's bomb," it used to be called. Marshal Soult during his long siege of Cadiz, between 1809 and 1812, had the mortar specially cast at Seville in order to be able to shell the Spanish lines from the Trocadero batteries, two and a half miles off. So great was the concussion every time the monster piece was fired that on each occasion it shattered its solid timber-mounting to pieces, and had finally to be slung in chains when in action. Soult abandoned it when he had to raise the siege of Cadiz as one result of the Battle of Salamanca, and the Cadiz Regency thereupon presented the mortar to the British government as a trophy and thank-offering for the invaluable services rendered in the defence of the city by the British soldiers in garrison, and the naval squadron on duty off Cadiz in support.

Two guns, one from Vittoria, one from Waterloo—"two fine brass field-pieces," as they are described—used to be kept at the Tower in the great "Military Trophy" in the Armoury; but both were destroyed in the disastrous Tower fire of 1841, which deprived the nation of so many other priceless relics won by the heroism of our soldiers and sailors all over the world.

A number of Peninsular War and Waterloo trophy cannon, it was originally projected, were to have had a place round the Wellington monument on Black Down, near the little town of Wellington, on the Devon and Somerset border. They were sent round by sea from Woolwich to Exeter by order of the War Office, but through some blundering, and general public indifference in the West Country, they were left lying for years on the quay at Exeter, where they were finally sold—so at least it is said—as "old metal." At any rate, the trophies have long since disappeared.

Many of the French cannon taken in the Peninsular War were made over by Wellington on capture to the Spaniards, and went to form batteries for their armies. Most of those brought as trophies to England were melted down at Woolwich Arsenal in 1820, to be re-founded as British field-guns for the Royal Artillery—an inexpensive and practical way of saving money for the Treasury. Of those that were left, some of the Peninsular War trophy guns were granted for the Achilles statue in Hyde Park, erected to Wellington in 1822; some were given to be recast in the shape of lamp-posts on the rebuilt London Bridge of 1831; some were utilized for the metal frame of Wellington's funeral car.

Several of the regiments of our modern army, of course, possess trophies won in action in the Peninsular War. The Arroyo drums of the Border Regiment, the Drum-Major's staff of the South Lancashire's, and that captured by the Royal Inniskilling Fusiliers; the "Drummer's Colour": of the Northumberland Fusiliers; the "Jingling Johnny" of the Connaught Rangers, are among the best known of them.

Wellington sent home to England from the battlefields of Spain in all seven Eagles and thirteen French flags and colours. All the flags—or practically all, as far as they can be traced—are still in existence, hung as trophies, most of them, round the walls of the chapel and hall of the Chelsea veterans. Five of the Peninsular Eagles only, however, exist, all now at Chelsea Hospital. The two that have disappeared were the one stolen, the other lent—unofficially, while the trophy was at Whitehall—to an artist who, according to the explanation offered, "forgot" to return it.

Barrosa's trophy— the "Eagle with the Golden Wreath," as it was commonly spoken of at the time—was the first of Wellington's spoils of victory to reach London, sent home to King George, "to be laid at His Majesty's feet." It was stolen from the Chapel of Chelsea Hospital, in April, 1852, during the pensioners' dinner-time at noon, by a cool thief, attracted by the fact that the wreath was of pure—if rather thin—gold. Using a ladder that some workmen, then doing repairs to the roof of the chapel, had left in position, the scoundrel got on to the roof, and through a trap-door into the organ-loft, in front of which the wreathed Eagle hung, its staff projecting into the nave. He broke the Eagle from its staff and hid it under his coat, and got away with it undetected. Nor was anything ever heard of it afterwards.

A gilded imitation eagle represents the Barrosa trophy at Chelsea now, as is frankly stated on a brass tablet fixed underneath the memorial emblem now there, set up among the twelve genuine Napoleonic Eagles which we possess. A careful drawing of the Barrosa trophy had, fortunately, been made not long before by one of the Captains of the Royal Hospital, reproducing the "Eagle with the Golden Wreath" exactly to scale, and from it, and also by taking a mould of one of the other Eagles, the existing effigy was made.

The two Eagles taken at Salamanca, those of Napoleon's 22nd and 62nd of the Line, were the next to arrive in England, in a condition that told vividly what they had gone through on the field of battle. "They were," describes somebody who saw them on their reaching London, "dreadfully mutilated and destroyed in the conflict." One of them, the writer adds, "has lost its head, part of its neck, one leg, and the thunderbolt." Each Eagle was perched on a thunderbolt, which was fixed on to a square brass tablet, bearing the regimental number in raised figures. Underneath the tablet was a screw by which it was fastened to the pole carrying the silken tricolour of the regimental standard.

The fourth Eagle seen in England was that of the French 29th of the Line. That arrived a few weeks later, together with two others, making the fifth and sixth of the series. It was fished up by some Portuguese peasants out of the River Coa, where it had been dropped when its bearer was shot in a night-battle during Masséna's retreat from in front of the lines of Torres Vedras, in which the French rearguard was driven in rout across the river. A reward was offered by Wellington for its recovery, and the peasants searched for it for weeks.

The other two, the Eagles of the French 13th and 51st Regiments, were found in the Buen Retiro, the French arsenal at Madrid, the garrison of which surrendered on summons when Wellington's victorious troops marched into the Spanish capital after Salamanca. They had been deposited in the arsenal for security while their regiments were on detached service among the mountains, fighting guerilla bands of Spanish peasants.

Our seventh trophy Eagle from the Peninsular War was taken in one of the Battles of the Pyrenees, in the combat at the Pass of Maya. It was the Eagle of the French 28th Regiment, and, as it chanced by the fortune of war, the British regiment into whose hands it fell was our own 28th, the celebrated "Slashers," the present-day 1st Battalion of the Gloucestershires. This Eagle reached England in 1814, and, as there was peace with France at the time, Napoleon having abdicated and been sent into banishment at Elba, no public display and official military ceremonial attended its reception, as had been the case with the other Eagle trophies. Hung in the Chapel Royal, Whitehall, some years later (a "high personage," according to one story, an official of the War Office, according to another), privately lent the Eagle to an artist friend to make a drawing of it for a picture he had in hand. It went to the artist's studio, and was never seen again. For obvious reasons after that the whole business was hushed up and kept quiet.

Thus the tale is made up of Wellington's seven Eagle-trophies from the Peninsular War.

One other that was taken, the Eagle of the 52nd, captured at Pampeluna, Wellington sent as a gift to the Spanish Regency. It has since disappeared as have most of the Peninsular War trophies that fell into Spanish hands. The only Eagle now in Spain is that of a French man-of-war, taken at Vigo dockyard in May, 1808.

That other Eagles besides these were captured but never reached England is quite possible.

On other battlefields British soldiers more than once or twice picked up Eagle-poles stripped of their flags, and with the Eagles that had topped them gone. After Talavera, for instance, where Wellington made a halt for the night on the field of battle, a British officer found some of his men "round a bivouac fire, using part of what had plainly been a French Eagle-pole for a poker while cooking their rations." Broken lengths of other Eagle-poles were picked up on that evening. "We took several silk standards, but the poles were much broken and the silk torn," writes another officer.

The 27th (now the Worcestershire Regiment) captured in the battle two French standards without their Eagles, but having "on the top of each pole a plate with screw-holes, showing they had had an Eagle each." There are several cases on record of the detaching of Eagles from their poles by their bearers to prevent capture and enable them to be hidden and got away with. The metal plates with screw-holes, mentioned by the officer of the 29th, were of course really put there for convenience, so that the Eagles might be easily detached for cleaning and polishing, and an Eagle-bearer would naturally take advantage of the screw- fixing in a moment of distress for the saving of the Eagle.

This also happened after Talavera. A party of soldiers of King George's former Hanoverian army who fought under Wellington in Spain as the "King's German Legion" found, first some pieces of a broken staff, and then, after a careful hunt all round, organized by a sharp young officer, came upon the Eagle itself, which had been at the head of the staff. It was found concealed beneath the dead body of the gallant French officer who had borne the standard in the battle. He had evidently broken the Eagle from its pole, hoping to be able to make off with it hidden under his uniform, but had been killed in the attempt. That French Eagle is now at Berlin among the Napoleonic trophies displayed in the Old Garrison Church there, having been removed from Hanover on the absorption of the State by Prussia after the war of 1866.

Certain of the silk standards we took at Talavera may have either belonged to Eagles, or have been the colours of "provisional regiments," of which the French had many in Spain: scratch battalions made up of detachments from corps serving elsewhere; amalgamated for the campaign and allowed silken tricolour standards, but without Eagles on top.

At Salamanca, when the fight was over, four French Eagle-poles were found on the field, from which the Eagles had been removed.

A very strange statement is made in this connection by Southey, in his *History of the Peninsular War*. "More than ten were captured, but there were men base enough to conceal them and sell them to persons in Salamanca who deemed it good policy as well as a profitable speculation to purchase them for the French." Where he got the story from Southey does not say. It is an ugly statement indeed to make, but it need not reflect on any of the British soldiers who won the battle—camp-followers, prowling over the field afterwards, would be just the rogues to do that sort of thing.

The two Salamanca Eagles sent to England by Wellington were taken openly, as has been said, by two officers in personal encounters; but several French regiments were all but annihilated on the field—practically a whole division at one point, the battalions ridden down and crushed by the terrific onslaught of the British Heavy Cavalry Brigade. As has been told, the British troopers swept over them *en masse* at full gallop, bursting through the French ranks, charging on without delaying to make prisoners or take trophies. In their track were left only dead and dying, and a horde of scattered fugitives whom the advancing British infantry in rear accounted for. There were undoubtedly Eagle-standards lying there, with their dead bearers beside them; for, up to the moment of the charge bursting on the enemy, the French array had been intact, and advancing to, as it looked just then from their side, certain victory.

None of the additional French Eagles were accounted for, as far as our British officers knew. No reckoning was possible after the battle of the immense quantity of loot which fell into the hands of the Spanish and Portuguese camp-followers and peasant-marauders, who, as usual, swooped down like vultures when the firing ceased and prowled all over the field during the night after the battle and on the following days, to strip and to spoil the dead and wounded and carry off everything they could lay hands on. They had the field to themselves, for Wellington and most of his army were miles distant by next morning. The battlefield harpies would know what to do and where to go with any French Eagles they picked up; how they might readily turn their finds into ill-gotten cash. They would guess instinctively that French army agents would pay handsomely to recover the treasured emblems of Napoleon's army and prevent them becoming trophies among the victors.

One reason, too, why, of the seven Peninsular War Eagles now at Chelsea Hospital, only three were actually captured in hand-to-hand fight on the battlefield in the five years of the Peninsular War—the Eagle taken at Barrosa and the two taken at Salamanca—is this: Napoleon's Eagles on a battlefield were always few in proportion to the combatants; only one to a regiment of from 3,000 to 4,000 men.

"If the French," says one of Wellington's officers, referring to the few Eagles that fell into British hands, "carried one quarter of the number of Eagles with their regiments that we have of colours, a much bigger proportion would find their way to Whitehall. A weak battalion of British infantry always carries two large colours—very heavy and inconvenient—whilst every French Eagle—about the size of a blackbird, and easily screwed off its staff and put in a pocket on emergency—means a regiment composed of three, four, or five battalions.

For convenience in the field, at the same time, not a few French regiments removed the flags altogether from their Eagle-poles and displayed as their standards the Eagle only. Particularly was this practice common with the French in Spain. Asked one day after the war about the inscription and "battle-honours" borne on the flag of his regiment, an infantry commanding officer, or *chef de bataillon*, of one of Napoleon's regiments who had served in Spain for five years on end, from 1808 to 1813, frankly confessed that he had "never set eyes on it." The silken flag, he explained, had been removed from the regimental Eagle-pole before he first joined as a lieutenant, and had always, as he understood, been kept at the depot of the corps in France, rolled up and locked away in the regimental chest. The Eagle on its bare pole was all that he had ever seen.

And there is this further reason why there are not more Peninsular War trophy Eagles now at Chelsea. Napoleon gave his marshals in Spain permission to grant colonels of regiments, in certain conditions, discretionary powers as to the disposal of their Eagles. Colonels were authorized, whenever their regiments were proceeding on what might be termed "exceptionally hazardous service," or on operations against irregulars or bands of guerillas in difficult country, to keep the Eagles back and leave them in camp or in a fortress, stowed away in the regimental chest. That is how Wellington in 1812 came, as has been said, to find the Eagles of the French 13th and 51st of the Line at Madrid.

Yet another reason, indeed, may be added. Early in 1813, after the disaster in Russia, a special order was issued by Napoleon to the army in Spain, requiring the Eagles of most of the infantry regiments to be sent back to France. Napoleon at that moment was in Paris, engaged in getting together a new Grand Army to replace that destroyed in Russia. The regiments in Spain, wrote Napoleon, would be so weakened by the intended withdrawal of the battalions which he was recalling in order to reinforce his new army collecting in Germany, that the Eagles in charge of the remaining battalions would be exposed to too much risk. "In future," wrote Napoleon, "there must in Spain be only one Eagle to each brigade of three regiments, that of the senior regiment of the brigade." Napoleon after that sent off this order to his cavalry generals: "No regiment of cavalry of the army in Spain is to retain its Eagle. Those who have not done so are immediately to send theirs to the depot in France."

There were two or three other Eagles, besides those spoken of, which might well in the course of the war have found their way to Chelsea.

On July 28, 1813, after a sharp running fight in the Pyrenees, the 40th (now the First Battalion of the South Lancashire Regiment) intercepted and made prisoners the First Battalion of the French 23rd, isolating it in a ravine and charging down on it with the bayonet. During the earlier fighting, while the French were falling back in confusion, they were seen to cast away their Eagle in a deep pool in the bed of a raging mountain-torrent, but, high up the mountain-side as our men were at the time, it was impossible to prevent the sacrifice, and all attempts later to fish the Eagle up were unsuccessful. Another Eagle, that of the 31st Light Infantry, narrowly escaped capture in a charge of the British 14th and 20th Light Dragoons during Wellington's advance to the Douro before the Battle of Oporto, and the two Eagles of the French 34th and 40th of the Line only just managed to get away in the flight at Arroyo dos Molinos.

Five of Napoleon's Eagles, it may be added, were on view in London in 1815, at the so-called "Waterloo Museum," a popular show of relics from various battlefields—not all genuine it would appear. The five Eagles had been purchased after the final disbandment of the Napoleonic army after Waterloo by curio-hunters in France. One was the Eagle of Napoleon's "Elba Guard." It is now at Madame Tussaud's. Two were Eagles of the National Guard, which had never been under fire. The last two purported to be the Eagles of the 5th of the Line and of the Seamen of the Guard, presented by Napoleon at the Champ de Mai, three weeks before Waterloo, but neither of these, again, had ever been in battle.

Anyone can tell at a glance our captured Eagle-flags of the Peninsular War period from those taken at Waterloo. The Eagles themselves are on the same model, each bird perched on its thunderbolt, beneath which is a small tablet inscribed "*Empire Français*"; but the silken flags of the two periods differ entirely in pattern. The older flags have each a white, diamond- shaped centre, bordered with laurel, and having the corners of the flag alternately red and blue, each corner bearing on it an embroidered wreath, enclosing the number of the regiment.

On the white diamond-shaped centre is inscribed the legend: "*L'Empereur des Français au —— Régiment du Ligne*," according to the number of the corps; and, of course, the style is altered according to the various arms of the Service. The standards of 1813 were in design simply tricolour flags of silk, fringed with gold, bearing, lettered on the white central portion of the flag, an Imperial dedication similar to that just quoted, with the names of the principal battles in which the corps had taken part.

The storming of Badajoz sent four trophy flags to England. No Eagles were taken there: "The French battalions in the garrison had no Eagles," explained Wellington in his dispatch. But the garrison flag of the fortress was a trophy as good as any Eagle. No British trophy was ever better won. "It is like a sieve, and part of it quite red with human blood," writes one who saw it on its arrival in London. The second Badajoz flag, which is spoken of as being "in good condition," was the flag of the Picurina Fort, taken at the brilliant assault and capture of that important outwork one night shortly after the opening of the siege, a fortnight before the storming of the main fortress. The two other flags were taken on the ramparts at the storming: they were the colours of a Hessian Regiment in Napoleon's service. A private of the 4th King's Own, George Hatfield (or Hatton) apparently took both, bayoneting the officers who were carrying them. "He had the honour next day of presenting them, in the presence of the officers of his brigade, to Lord Wellington, who gave him some money, and desired that he should be promoted." All four of the Badajoz flags are at Chelsea Hospital.

Two other German flags (now also at Chelsea) were among the spoils sent home, the colours of the two battalions of a Prussian regiment in Napoleon's service—unfortunate soldiers levied compulsorily from the remnants of the Prussian army during the French occupation of their country after the Jena campaign, and tramped off to Spain, whether they liked it or not, to meet their fate under British bullets. Each flag—an ordinary French tricolour—bore the legend, "*L'Empereur dus Français au Régiment Prussien*" on one side, and on the other the words, "*Valeur et Discipline.*" Each was mounted on a staff, with a plain pike-head of steel in place of an eagle.

Six French second and third battalion colours were sent to England from Salamanca as trophies, in addition to the two Eagles. "They are of very coarse red and blue cloth, and must be of regimental make," describes one of Wellington's officers. "The *vivandières* of the regiments should have made better flags. Even the ironwork is inferior and not worth preserving." The flags belonged to the ill-fated 22nd and 62nd Regiments, so mercilessly handled by Le Marchant's Heavy Dragoons.

The remaining French flags from the Peninsular War bear no record as to how they came into our hands. One was the tricolour of a battalion of the 5th of the Line, one a colour of a "provisional" regiment, one is a "fort standard," but where they were taken is now unknown.

The colour of Napoleon's "*Corps Étranger*" was taken on May 19, 1811, by the 50th (now the First Battalion of the Queen's Own Royal West Kent Regiment) at the storming of Fort Napoleon at Almaraz. Two French flags were taken near Almeida by a British officer (Lieutenant Maguire), who, single-handed, met and cut down their bearers. He distinguished himself brilliantly at Vittoria, where, at one of the bridges over the Zadora, his company was twice repulsed. To encourage them he took the regimental colour from the ensign who carried it, and again rushing out to the front, attempted to set it up on the parapet of the bridge. So furious was the French musketry at that moment that the flag was shot to tatters before the daring young officer was successful in fixing the staff firmly. At Salamanca, and again at the storming of San Sebastian, French standards were taken by the Devonshires. The colour of the Fourth Battalion of Napoleon's 100th of the Line was taken at Vittoria and sent to London, where, as told elsewhere, it figured prominently at the great Vauxhall banquet in honour of that crowning triumph.

Elaborate and pompous State ceremonial, with gorgeous military display, attended the official reception in London of Wellington's trophies from the Peninsular War on two occasions. Both took place before members of the Royal Family, Ministers, and high officials in the service of the Crown, on the Horse Guards' Parade; after which, on each occasion, the trophies were carried in procession with triumphal music across Whitehall to the Chapel Royal, to be received at a special service, deposited on the Altar, and publicly affixed on the walls of the chancel.

The first parade, in May, 1811, was attended by three royal princes, the Dukes of York, Cambridge, and Gloucester, together with the Spanish and Portuguese Ambassadors, the Prime Minister and War Secretary, Headquarters Staff of the Army, the Speaker and Lady Wellington, besides, as a newspaper of the time puts it, "a large assemblage of titled and other personages of quality and a number of beautiful and elegant ladies of distinction."

At the second display, held at the same place on September 30, 1812, Queen Charlotte herself, with two of the princesses, and the Prince Regent "mounted on a cream-white charger," attended in addition, and on both occasions huge crowds of ordinary spectators— "all London" we are told—were massed outside the cordon of soldiers who kept the ground round the wide open space which forms the Horse Guards' Parade.

Detachments of the Guards and Life Guards, with their colours, paraded on three sides of a vast hollow square, round which a procession of sergeants bearing the trophies, escorted by grenadiers with fixed bayonets, marched to the sound of triumphal music. At a slow step the procession with the trophies marched round the square, passing close in front of the colour-parties of each of the Guards' battalions, the band playing as before. Opposite each British colour-party, the Eagle and other trophies were in turn dipped to the ground, amid bursts of cheering from the crowd, although some of those there could not help expressing aloud a sense of sorrow at so unnecessary a humiliation of the emblems of an honourable foe. Finally, the trophies recrossed the square, and formed in line in front of the royal party and their *entourage*, where, again, all were lowered to the dust as a salute, while the massed bands played "God save the King."

This over, the Eagle and trophy colours were lifted on high and borne, headed by the music of the bands, under the Horse Guards' archway, across Whitehall, through a lane of cheering people to the Chapel Royal, arriving there, as arranged, just as the special service was about to commence. While the organ pealed inside the chapel, the sergeants entered, and, pacing up the steps before the Holy Table, formed in a line across the chancel. After that, on a given signal, one by one the trophies were handed to the Sub-Dean, who laid first the Eagles and then the flags on the Holy Table. The *Te Deum* and Litany, then the Communion Service, and a sermon followed. As the grand *finale*, "God save the King" was played on the organ, and the trophies were hung up in the chancel, in fixed sockets prepared for them.

Such was the ceremony that marked the State reception in London of Wellington's trophies won in Spain, and at that point the curtain may conveniently ring down on the general story.

In St. Paul's Cathedral there are monuments to Wellington, of course, and to Picton, who met his death, as all the world knows, at Waterloo, and lies in the burying-ground of St. George's, Hanover Square; to Mackenzie and Langwerth, who fell at Talavera; to Houghton and Myers, who fell at Albuhera; to Le Marchant, killed at Salamanca; to the heroic Colonel of the 71st at Vittoria, the Hon. Henry Cadogan; and to the noble-hearted and chivalrous Sir Edward Pakenham, the leader of the "Fighting Third" at Salamanca, who died like the hero that he was at New Orleans in the American War.

www.ingramcontent.com/pod-product-compliance
Lightning Source LLC
Chambersburg PA
CBHW031619160426
43196CB00006B/195